THE ONENESS *of* BEING

BIRTHING THE NEW HUMAN

Marilyn Gewacke, Ph.D.

Luminous Moon Press, Boulder, Colorado

Published by Luminous Moon Press, Boulder, CO

Cover and interior layout and design by Carolyn Oakley,
Luminous Moon Design.

First Edition
First Printing: September 2015

Publication Data
Marilyn Gewacke
The Oneness of Being: Birthing the New Human

ISBN-13: 978-0-9968600-1-7
New Consciousness – Spirituality – Psychology

Printed and bound in the United States of America

Acknowledgments

This book would not have been possible without the support, love and encouragement from the beautiful people in my life. I would like to especially thank my wife and life partner, Diane Saunders. She never wavered from the knowledge that this book would be written, completed and published. Her understanding of consciousness and the human journey was invaluable in helping me stay steadfast and authentic in the book's evolution. My mother-in-law, Florence Saunders, who at 89, was one of the first readers of the book and upon finishing it exclaimed, "This should be a bible in everyone's home!" Her support and understanding of its significance is a gift I will always cherish. To my spiritual mentor, Marcia Dale Lopez, who saw the published book 25 years ago. And of course, my most faithful teachers, who were my mother and father. They always saw my light and taught me that I could be or do anything. They gave me the inspiration to be my authentic self, pursue my own dreams, expand my horizons and most of all, always be kind, thoughtful and loving to all others in my life. They prepared me to be a parent and mentor to my stepchildren, Mat and Ariel. As I watch these two become young beautiful adults, I continuously learn about the contemporary world, but mostly I keep learning about love.

Of course, it takes a village to design, lay out and edit a book and so I especially thank Jennifer Westacott who volunteered to steadfastly read and reread each draft, searching for corrections and edits, all the while stating that she was motivated by the calling within the book itself. Her steady vision of the final copy no doubt kept the process moving. I want to thank my professional editor Michelle Auerbach who gave me incredible support for its content and organization while she poured over the specifics of word choice, grammar and sentences. Her encouragement and insight were irreplaceable. And finally I have deep gratitude to my publisher, graphic designer, layout specialist, and coeditor, Carolyn Oakley. Working with her has been such an incredible process as she understood the content as well as the purpose of the book and created beautiful illustrations that flowed with the material. I have made a friend for life. What a wonderful thing.

Of course, so importantly, I want to thank my clients who, over the years, have taught me so much. Through them I have witnessed the arduous process of coming alive, healing the self and becoming important changemakers in the world. I have also learned the true curative value of humility and vulnerability…mostly my own. The overwhelming desire to grow, evolve and create the New Human paradigm lies within all of us.

Last but not least, I want to thank the Northeast CE-5 community. They continue to inspire me and give me hope that we indeed can be a New Human community, courageously moving our planet toward harmonic relations with the Cosmos.

It is difficult to come to this stage of completion, as I will miss the amazing loving soul comradery that developed around the birthing of this book. You are all in the pages of this book and forever in my heart.

Marilyn Gewacke, Ph.D.
September 26, 2015
Albany, New York

Table of Contents

Prelude to a Soul Symphony		i
Introduction		iii
1	The Flow	1
2	Wellness Revisited	13
3	The Rings Around Us & The Core Within	29
4	The Original Blueprint: Maps from Eternity	49
5	Presence As Path	67
6	Self-Love – The Only Way Out is In	91
7	The Quadrants of Experience	119
8	The Emerging New Human	149
9	I/Thou: Relations Beyond Self	187
10	Manifestation Mysteries: The Art of Dreaming Reality	227
11	Mission on Earth: As Above, So Below	265
Bibliography		293

Prelude to a Soul Symphony

Every human being houses a unique expression of Divinity. It's as if each individual human being is a fingerprint from the infinite hands of God. Through the actualization of this sole (soul) expression, we unify ourselves in sacred holiness. The voice of the Divine can be found in this inimitable unfolding process. In that irreplaceable manifestation of selfhood, we celebrate our connection to, and non-separation from, universal sacred truths. Thus forms one of the most awe-inspiring paradoxes in the land of the Divine mysteries: unique expression manifests universal divinity. In other words, being in and manifesting the extraordinary truth of who we are individually, fuels our journey towards oneness.

The most amazing transformational shift is happening on our planet Earth. We have the extraordinary opportunity to discover ourselves anew and take the next step in our evolutional journey towards conscious enlightenment. In order to awaken the cosmic spirit within, we first must learn how to tread softly in our inner domain so that we might learn to love ourselves with humility and grace. Until the "one" within is healed and loved, the external world will be void of the human species surviving and thriving. As we learn to truly love the self, we will be able to leave the old paradigms that have been harming, negative and dense and transition to a new age of loving and holding one another with compassion and grace.

Our planet is undergoing a "renaissance of consciousness," which will give rise to the birthing of the New Human. As we embark on this journey of soul awakening, we will feel the oneness of all life and understand unequivocally our responsibility to heal and nurture this beautiful planet and all of her inhabitants. We will never again feel threatened by someone's unique expression of selfhood, for each unique expression holds a holographic imprint of Divine cosmic truth. As the New Human chorus grows, we will create a soul symphony never heard before and the rippling effects will be felt throughout the universe. The journey is within, the path awaits you. Join me and take a ride of a lifetime.

Introduction

"We are always getting ready to live,
but never living."
–Ralph W. Emerson

"What lies behind us and what lies before us are tiny matters
compared to what lies within us..."
–Oliver W. Holmes

Welcome to your world. Hearing your voice within, actualizing the truths of this voice and manifesting your own divinely made dreams are the most important things you could possible do on Earth at this time. There is nothing I can write that you do not already know. We hold the entire universe within us. That, of course, includes the sacred Source from which we came and all the Divine intelligence that surrounds us. Unfortunately, over time, our Earth experience closes us off from that which is beyond and within. In fact, most of us in this lifetime alone, have gathered many veils of thickly stitched fabric that we steadfastly use to cover ourselves. We cannot see nor feel our connectedness to All That Is and therefore have forgotten our part in what I call the "oneness" that surrounds us. Yet, most of our living activities are desperate attempts at reconnecting and remembering our most precious truths. What a paradox. There is nothing more beautiful than the joyful tears of remembering the one within. It's in that moment that we also know the vastness of God beyond.

Within these pages lies a blueprint, a map of sorts, to inspire you to make your living journey more wakeful, lighthearted and soul connected. This book is an act of permission, permission to come home to the sacred meaning and ultimate mission of your life. The words on these pages aren't only written to stir the mind's mechanisms of contemplation, but to excite the ancient memories of recognition.

The very act of reading will transform how you think and who you think you are. This is not because of some magic formula written into the pages, but because you will begin your walk in that long forgotten corridor within. This walk will lead you to all that you are, have been and can be. This book is a cuing system, a beacon, by which you may find yourself. Your richest asset is your world within. From there, everything else can be found.

The words on these pages come from a deep inner knowing place that I have finally accepted as truth. I spent much of my lifetime ignoring, denying and dismissing this deep intuitive place. I chose instead to follow 'recipes for being' that were given to me by various outside sources. Many of these sources gave these prescriptions with caring and loving intentions, while some did not have such virtuous motives. Even though I've always felt this deep prodding within, it seemed that the vast libraries of knowledge outside of myself were evidence of the relative smallness of my own inner truths. Most of us have abandoned our inner wealth of information long ago. Hopefully, your experience in reading this book will mirror mine in discovering the importance of taking that walk inside yourself. This book is about the truths I have come to know that live within me. It is not so much that I expect or want you to believe in these exact same truths. These are my truths, and don't have to be yours. I am simply presenting a framework through which you can find your own. It's my belief that the world's problems, that we feel surrounding us, have much to do with our refusal to see the solutions that lie within us.

In these fast changing times, it's a critical age for all of us, including the Earth we live on, to regain momentum from the "inside out." This process of turning "inside out" is hard, painful, emotional, crazy and conceivably the most exhilarating and healing journey you could possible choose. In the depths of most change, growth and crises, you have no choice but to feel this; and therein lies one meaning of chaos and crisis. It's my hope, however, that we are coming to a new era, when our wish to thrive surpasses our need to survive, and ignites us to live in the rhythm of "inside out."

Life is meant to be a holy experience. It's only in our inability to live wholly that we lose sight of its sacredness. Although we have learned how to survive many of life's pitfalls, they still keep us separate because we build walls against further struggle. We haven't learned how to use our trials and tribulations to sew jeweled garments that can be worn to unite us instead of separate us. Whatever your struggle, whatever your triumph, know that you hold the holy. In that holding, you come home once again to the sacred in us all. In that moment you can feel the oneness of simply being.

1

The Flow

"The universe was born restless
has never since been still."
–Timothy Ferris

"Because we can change like quicksilver, the flowing quality of life is natural to us.
The material body is a river of atoms, the mind is a river of thought,
and what holds them together is a river of intelligence."
–Deepak Chopra

There is a flow throughout all life, a current of energy that is present in everything. This energy is always in motion, always evolving. In fact, physicists tell us that not only does the universe itself seem to be expanding, but even in the smallest world of subatomic particles there is undetectable movement traveling at unimaginable speeds. Furthermore, energy never vanishes it just changes its properties. Motion and fluidity seem to be a basic characteristic of life itself.

We do not have to be physicists to know and feel this flow of energetic motion. We can reach the top of a mountain after an exhilarating but exhausting climb and still in our heavy breathing and tired body become awestruck by the majestic view before us. Somehow in those moments we seem deeply aware of the life flow that is pumping through our veins, connecting our internal awareness of self to All That Is beyond. To be in love but once gives one the breathtaking experience of feeling the powerful energetic flow that two people in the throngs of love can generate. Just being a passenger in this life journey causes one to realize, painstakingly at times, that nothing stays exactly the same. Yet, there are perceivable rhythms and repeating variables throughout all our lives. There is an ebb and flow to all things that is manifested in the smaller matters that come and go and the larger cycles of birth and death. Life is a changing fluid process with a constant energetic flow moving through it all.

Understanding our own vital rhythms and flowing properties is crucial if we are to embrace the journey of life with vibrancy and resiliency. There are three realms of energetic systems: eternal, internal and external, that are most influential in the development of the human experience. (**see illustration 1**) The eternal energy system contains All That Is beyond us and yet still includes that Divine spark that lies within us. This realm is more invisible, transparent and effervescent, yet it is where permanency lies, infinite possibilities reside and ceaseless motion rests. This is where spirit lives and soul rejoices in its freedom to be. While the eternal realm holds all of the mysteries of the universe, it gently prods us to cherish what we know and to pursue with vigor what we do not know. Some might even say that the Divine being some call God, and others call the Goddess, commune in this place called the eternal.

The internal is that which lies within us. It has been called the self, individual essence, and personality. Because the soul lives within, the internal is always connected with the eternal. It is only our denial, our cloaking of this soul place that keeps us from knowing this connection with All That Is eternal. This internal energy system is more acutely felt, yet puzzling; more finite, yet always changing. This internal system has been the main study matter of psychology and is heatedly debated in philosophical classrooms. This is the place where frameworks are built for becoming astute observers in scientific endeavors and sensual connoisseurs on life's playing fields. The internal world is the synthesizer providing the bridge between what we know of the eternal and what we experience in the external. The internal world is where we live.

The external energy system includes All That Is outside of us in the three dimensional world. We spend most of our time attending to the maddening pace of this energy system; and so we often mistake this dynamism as a reflection of the internal self. While it might appear that this external realm is the most visible and tangible, it holds the paradox of being the most finite, yet least permanent and the most malleable of the three realms. The external realm is often where we look first for guidelines, rules and expectations about who and what to be. Standards for living most often reside in the external world, left over from historical texts of the past, ever changing customs of the present and future prospects for dreams and realities yet to come. The external world is where others live.

THE FLOW

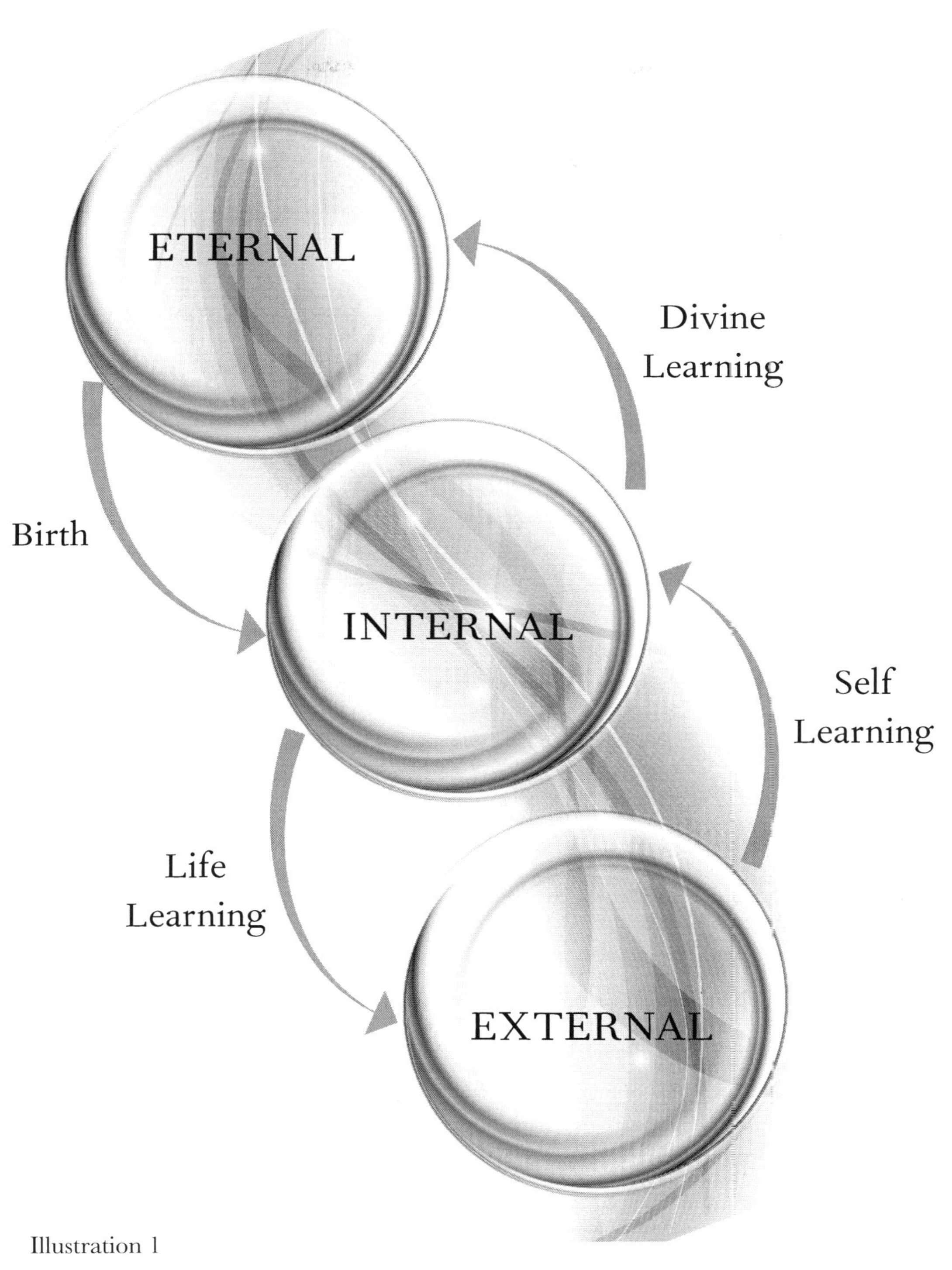

Illustration 1

Developmentally speaking, there is an initial outpouring of eternal energy that flows into the womb some time after conception. You might liken this to the human soul birthing process. This outward to inward current of energy lights up the prenatal world and a soul celebrates its arrival in the world of human beings. Several energy systems including physical, emotional and mental processes begin to churn into enormous activity during this gestation period within the womb. At the nine-month mark, the infant meets the often austere three-dimensional external world.

At first, the infant does not have the capacity to distinguish inside from outside otherness and, in fact, feels part of all that surrounds her. She has few boundaries of any kind in the beginning while she is adjusting to life within the body. Much as the soul understands its connectedness and non-separation from the Divine Source, so too the infant has little sense of its separation from mother. Perhaps, this is when we still have not forgotten the experience of oneness with the Divine Source. In psychological terms, this is called the symbiotic phase of development. Although there may be the pain from hunger and fatigue, the infant has not yet experienced the distress of separation. Therefore, when pain is experienced the whole world is part of this pain, which actually gives the infant the comfort of company and congruent reflection. Something many of us only wish for as adults!

Actually, our initial experience of real separation comes when our soul first realizes its physical embodiment. It is in this denser physical body experience that we begin to acknowledge that we are no longer one with the infinite source of All. This physical Earth body provides defined boundaries of matter that can be felt and weighed. It must be at this time, when the soul recognizes the heaviness of this new home, that we feel our first sense of abandonment from the wonder, wisdom and love of the Divine.

As we come into the first year of life, we become more familiar and adapted to our bodies. This marks the beginning of the extraordinary process of individuation and separation. We start to have the realization that we are contained in our bodies and we begin to experience our physical beings. The infant becomes more physically mobile, thereby, noting her physically distancing capabilities from the parents. As the infant moves to and fro in her world, she begins to realize her capacity to have free will and conscious directedness. In this process she begins to have clues that she is a physically separate entity from her parents and begins the arduous task of psychological separation. During this process, there is both joyful glee and painful anxiety about freedom and separation. For most of us, this paradoxical issue continues to be a prime conflict throughout the rest of our lives!

After we realize *that* we are, we commence with the exploration process of *who* we are. With this recognition of individuation, comes the realization that the external world is a separate reality that can seem chaotic, whimsical and out of control. The child learns quickly, however, to take cues from the outer world as to how she should behave, respond, act and be. This process of internalization occurs when the child tries on outer world notions of who he could or should be and makes them his own. The external world soon becomes the backdrop by which everything is compared. Attention shifts from the internal "my world" which has been everything, to the rich and sometimes haunting outer world.

As life progresses, we continue to define ourselves more by the outer trappings of life than by our inner needs, feelings and meanings. We soon learn that to belong and find a place in the world, we must be concerned about these external rules and guidelines for being, behaving and producing. We race to become more in tune and more in shape with these outside prescriptions of "fitting in", because our deepest wish is to be loved and united with the external and eternal realms. We may even begin to feel that our most important truths within should not be shown, and we begin to develop artificial parts to our self-presentation. As this inner world becomes dimmed so too the channels towards the transcendent world become clouded and invisible. We continue this search for meaning in the externalized three-dimensional world often mistaking safety and stability for meaning and mission. Paradoxically, the seductive pull of the external world keeps us scanning this outside place for meaning that only can be found in the 'within' realm of the soulful self.

Thus, our second point of true soul separation comes as the weight of this Earthly dimension pulls veils of opaqueness over our intuitive vision. We become blinded and cannot see the pathways back to our original source. We begin to forget the truth of this heritage and spend much of our lives anesthetized in soul amnesia. Because so much attention towards the outer world is required, we lose touch with those inner callings that echo the reverberations of our lost eternal world. Feeling the empty prodding of those unremembered hallways; we cash in so many resources in our lifetime attempting to find our way back home. While our focus has been sharpened for discerning safety and meaning in the ever-changing external world, it is not so surprising then, that in our search for soul, we look for outside answers ignoring the small portals produced by inside questions.

Nevertheless, the energetic flow changes directions several times throughout our lifetime. In the beginning the initial flow *from out to in* comes from the mysterious eternal realm into the internal world of human embodiment.

This initial phase in human form then begins its rhythmic journey beating from the inside out joining with all there is, feeling non separate yet internally whole. Early in the process of human development, the psychological self is birthed and the shifting tides of motion change as the external world begins its slow steady motion inward shaping and forming this new young being. While the child holds the sense of soulful self within, the external world begins to become the screen by which the child views and accepts reality.

The flowing motion of much of childhood and early adolescence is the *outward-in flow* that becomes the definition and shape of who we become. For much of this time we search outside ourselves for what will save us, redeem us and soothe us. And for many, the quality of life both psychological and physical depends on how well we internalize these outside definitions. In adolescence, it is our peers who prescribe who we ought to be, how to look, act and be with each other and ourselves. In fact, it is at this time that we first grapple with basic relationship issues, like acceptance, rejection and intimacy themes. The agitated times of later adolescence can often be seen as two powerful tides meeting; the outward-in external tide and the beginnings of the strong but unsure inner self moving back out into the world. This collision often continues for a lifetime, depending on how malleable and kind the external world is towards self-emergence.

Unfortunately, in much of western culture, there are many externalized pressures, prescriptions and panaceas for proper pathways to follow in life. We spend much of our time in young adult life trying to adopt the newest and most in vogue way to be. We wear different coats, fashioned by unknown designers, hoping to find that long last feeling of non-separation and connectedness we knew in the eternal and very early internal world of our life. We often dim our awareness of our internal guides about what we like or desire, in lieu of those more secure, acceptable outer models. Many of us begin to lose touch with who we are from the inside out, as we become convinced that safety and love exist in the external world only. While the external third dimensional world has many delectable things to offer, we often sacrifice our own inner growth for these outside attachments. We become masterful at being external world detectives looking for clues of meaning and love in all the wrong places.

We lose touch with our own sole (soul) talents and gifts especially if we have few people in our lives that are truly interested in seeing our uniqueness. So many of us have not had enough attention, witnessing, and validation regarding our unique "true" selves and sometimes have been told very directly that our internal desires, wants, skills, attributes, etc. are bad, ugly and not to be seen. Fear then drives us out of this internal realm and places us back out into the world to find replacements for these wounded parts. We abandon our inner-outer flow for the safer, observable currents of externalized information. The outer world forms our frame like a potter's hand shapes the clay.

As we move on through adulthood, more often the search for fulfillment, enrichment and meaning comes up short. And frequently, it is not the external world that is held culpable but the small internal world of the self. Often when we first pay attention to the internal world of self, we decide that we are not good enough, bright enough, attractive enough, strong enough, etc. to have enough and be loved enough. This debasing inner experience not surprisingly propels us back towards outer attachments and sensuous addictions. We then continue to define ourselves by outside means, all the while feeling divested of meaning and purpose.

Meanwhile for many of us, in our dim awareness of the dormant inner sleeping world, we begin to stir and twist and turn until we begin to awake. For there is inherent in all of us a deep inner sense of who we are and the uniqueness of our position in the world. This is where our inner vision lies; this is where our mission is most understood. Developmentally speaking, it is this internal search for meaning that eventually takes charge in middle age adulthood. All of us hold this awareness, however, faint it might be, that we must don our explorer's caps and return to the domain of our rich inner world. Therein, lies a treasure chest of internal resources that not only will guide us towards our own life's mission, but also will offer transcendent keys that will open an infinite number of portals to new and old worlds alike. We begin to once again shift tides so that we flow from inside out, rediscovering the wondrous world within and bravely sharing it with those around us.

Finally, it is in the final stages of life, that our attention turns once again to more eternal questings. Due to our reluctant acceptance of physical life's finiteness, we begin to ask questions about the immortality of the soul. As the body fades in its ability to be resilient and our ability to pay attention to the outer world dims, we interestingly enough become more absorbed in the invisible and the less tangible realms. So the cycle is complete, and we once again travel back to the eternal through the gateways of internal introspection. Our real home lies within and from there we finally become aware of our true inheritance of eternal sacredness and Divine love.

More and more of us have become disillusioned by the lure of outside solutions and have already begun this soulful quest for life's meaning in the internal and eternal energy realms. Many are realizing that their outside accomplishments, attachments and addictions have not yet extinguished the pain of abandonment experienced long ago. Our first felt soul/self abandonment catapulted us into a barren desert that we have been seeking refuge from ever since. The metaphoric playing field of the three dimensional reality continues to be very alluring, seducing us into the belief that the abandonment wounds originate "out there". We only need to experience one love loss to bolster this notion. As we continue to encounter losses in our lives, we re-ignite the original abandonment wounds from our Divine Source. We misperceive the tearing, painful motion of this as proof that the outside world is indeed both the bestower of possible panaceas and the bringer of torrential storms.

More and more people are seeking therapeutic assistance to help heal these original abandonment wounds. Although typically, the wounds are consciously felt in the form of more human losses and traumas, they originate from both the Divine separation felt initially when the soul was first embodied and the slow almost imperceptible shrouding of our soul's very existence throughout our lives. We, therefore, have lost both the experience of Oneness with the Divine Source and the experience of the Divine spark within ourselves. In other words, we have lost our souls.

Many of the things we have used as life giving remedies in the past are no longer enough. Questions of meaning, purpose and mission are being asked more frequently and more genuinely. We only have to look at the best-seller book list to see how attracted people are towards soul awakening and spiritual questing. This is a wonderful time of expansion and exploration. However, the awakening process is neither easy nor always very pretty.

I recently saw a highly successful professional woman who appeared as if she had it all. Her life story included many career accomplishments, a beautiful home, a marriage, successful children, plenty of stock market assets and financial security. As if these things didn't keep her busy enough, she also managed to have a five-year secret affair and a stockpile of recreational drugs for weekend fun. The pace at which she was living was killing her. Medical tests showed that there was evidence that she had already had a heart attack, but she couldn't quite place when. At night she couldn't sleep and when she did she had nightmares that she was alone in a desert without food or water. These dreams only seemed to thrust her into more accumulative and hedonistic endeavors in desperate attempts to avoid her worst fear: aloneness. She kept running from her inside world, until finally everything came crashing down. Her husband found out about the affair and left her. She began making unsound financial decisions and lost a good deal of money. The man she was having the affair with panicked at the thought that she was truly available and started seeing someone else. She ended up living alone in a small apartment to finally face her self. As the crisis was at hand, her soul began to speak to her through the chaos. Though in much pain and severe grief, she began sitting with the abandoned self and started to hear this tiny wise voice within. She barely recognized herself at first, for she felt tattered and bruised and ugly throughout. But as she held steadfast to the process of "sitting within" she began to take form and saw herself anew. So much had been buried; so much had been lost, yet she knew she was at the most important juncture of her life. As she began rethinking her position on relationships and love, she continued working hard on loving herself. As she has been in this process of reacquainting herself with her self, she has been quite amazed at rediscovering her love for the piano, sculpting wood and walking in the woods. She feels more alive now than she has ever felt in her life. As she described it, "I feel like I am surging from the inside out, no longer being dictated by outside definitions of who I am, but inside currents of what I must be. Delightfully, I think I am much more pleasant to those around me." Her spirit awakened; her goals for life changed

As her therapist, I simply was a witness to this process, a permission giver if you will. I gently held the space for her to encounter her darkness, while keeping the faith that this would give way to self-emergence and soul-awakening. She lives inside herself now, yet she contributes more to her outside world than she ever has been capable of before. She is a success story...she found her soul and shares this meaning with the world.

By definition we hold the imprint of the Divine within us. Luckily for us, no matter what strongholds we find in the outer world, our hunger for home will not be satiated. Some of us are being stripped of outer manifestations of safety, while others are quickly accumulating stashes of outside attachments. In either case, the tides are rapidly turning. Perhaps out of no choice, the deprivational model, or because of enormous choice, the abundance model, we are beginning to turn the tides of motion and are shifting to the inner realms for exploration and healing. This shift is causing great disruption both in the inner psyche and in the outer culture. As we move our focus from out to in, we will eventually begin the rhythmic movement of in to out. This movement is gathering steam and it is our very life struggles that are fueling the change.

We are finally moving into a time where we are beginning to understand the true meaning of self-actualization and soul-emergence. The significance of this does not just lie in new-found selfhood, but in the self's ability to offer service and healing to the very external place where it has spent so much time. Perhaps as we are all looking for new answers, we can begin this internal process proactively.

Unfortunately, raising children with these themes in mind is more foreign than practiced. As a result, most of us in adulthood seem to need the prodding that pain, struggle and suffering bring to us. Chaos and crises become changemakers. Life experience holds the library of knowledge. So it would then follow that being here…right now…is the only key we need to open these doors. We then become the path makers towards finding our way home again, to our original heritage. And in this journey we are never alone.

Soul Remedies

#1 – The Inner Flow

This may be the most important exercise you do in all of your life.

Take one moment…right now…find a place where you can sit comfortably…with yourself…without distractions.

Now be with yourself and do nothing else.
Go within and listen.
Notice what makes you alive right now…
The movement of your breath
The rhythmic beat of your heart
The ideas floating across your mind
The feelings rising to the surface
These things are all in motion…flowing inside of you.

As you become more conscious of these life currents within
You will know everything you need to know.

Stay with yourself…don't go away.
When you stray…simply come back.
You never have to lose this place again.
From here you can see everything.

Soon you will feel the movement of "inside out"
Then you will be in the world…while in yourself.

The first step towards oneness is staying with the self.
This will be the hardest and grandest thing you do…

See what you find and celebrate whatever it is. *Start now…*

2

Wellness Revisited

"Life becomes not a problem to be solved, but a reality to be experienced."
—Kierkegaard

"The art of living lies less in eliminating troubles than in growing with them."
—Bernard Baruch

"The Soul would have no rainbow, had the eyes no tears."
—John Vance Cheney

It's time to revolutionize our ideas about wellness.

Our models of physical and mental health are, at the least, outdated if not antiquated. In both medical and mental health fields, wellness has been defined as freedom from ailments, afflictions and dis-ease. The goal of treatment typically is to reduce and eliminate symptoms, problems and pathological states. Pain, struggle and suffering are marked and diagnosed for future extermination. We hold the notion that the less painful the treatment, the more sophisticated the method. We are much more apt, for instance, to medicate rather than illuminate. If we've not become comatose to our suffering and pain before it's duly noted and recorded, we surely will be after it's been treated.

The human being has an amazing ability to experience both searing pain and exalting pleasure over and over in one life. We can feel the extraordinary expansiveness of love and the unbearable constriction of loss. We can experience the despair of depression and feel removed from life and then, we can feel the jubilance of joy and be life itself. It seems then, that we've the remarkable ability to feel the full spectrum of life's offerings and experiences. Shouldn't we then find ways to celebrate, embrace and fully be in these places in order to truly be a full, well human being? Being holy surely has to include living whole-ly. Cutting ourselves off from certain experiences simply because they don't feel good makes us unhealthy. Perhaps wellness should instead be the ability to have the entire continuum of life experiences while staying alert, awake and aligned. Wellness models up till now have suggested that health can only be found on one half of the continuum. How can we feel truly alive when we access only half of who we are? (**see illustrations 2 & 3**)

Questions:

Without hopelessness where do we find faith?

Without tears how do we know joy?

How do we know what feels right if we don't have a backdrop of what feels wrong?

How do we see the beauty of a sunrise without the darkness of the night?

Pain and suffering have sometimes traveled far to reach us, can we listen to them?

When we feel the sinking movement of going down, could we simply be gathering momentum to go further up?

Isn't experiencing vulnerability part of wellness?

By trying to dampen these flames, do we not risk putting out the fire within?

Before commencing on the inner journey, it's important to examine what keeps us out. We've spent so much time attending to the rigors of the external world that we've become less and less familiar with our internal sense of self. And, even when we do venture in, we've been given so many notions of what this internal self should be like that it's never what we expect. We've become masters at disguising the truth within. We've learned to fit our form into shapes that are not quite right, yet this discomfort is barely felt. It's often more uncomfortable to feel some deeply hidden truth than to bend our frame into some small-unfitted space. We live under the illusion that many of the things within are wrong, unimportant and unworthy of attention. As a result, we've hidden many desires, wants, fears and worries in the deep chambers of our inner world. It's not so surprising then that the trip within is fraught with misperceived dangers, narrowly defined maps and an ill equipped knowledge base.

CURRENT WELLNESS MODEL

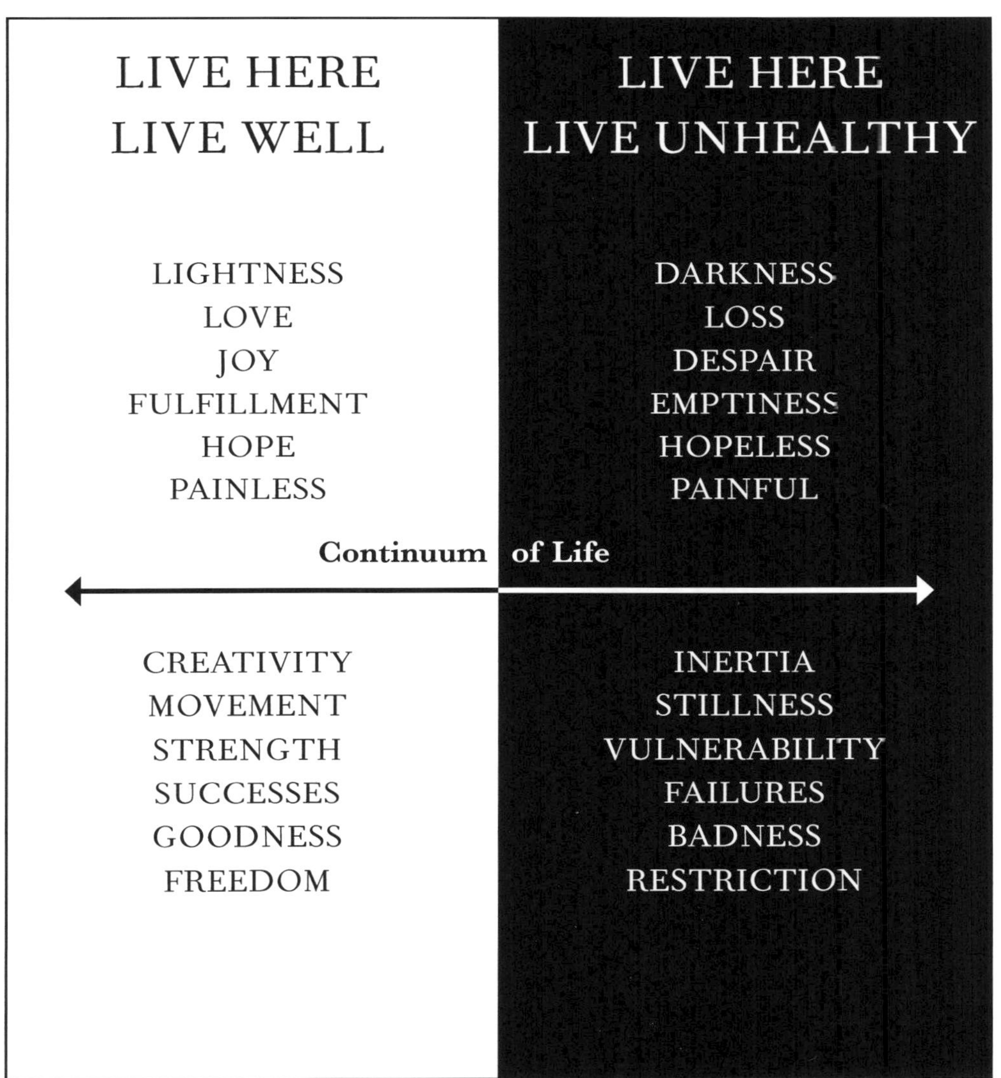

Illustration 2

NEW WELLNESS MODEL

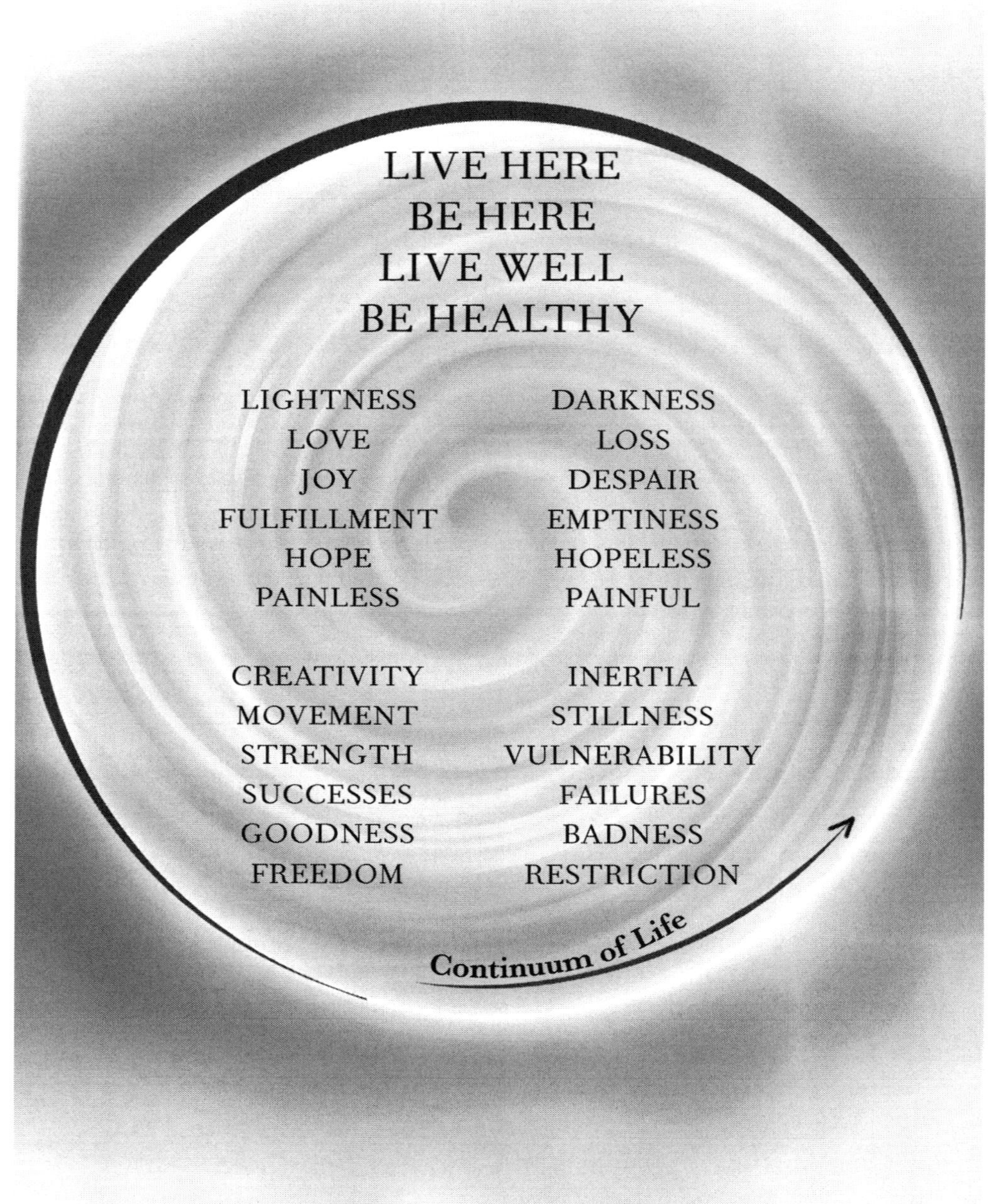

Illustration 3

Perhaps if we were not so ashamed by our painful reactions to life's dilemmas we would be more capable of getting through them. We have more methods for escaping pain and discomfort in our culture than we have ways of simply walking through them. The message is strong: feel good, be good and you will have good. Feel bad and you have a problem. Thomas Moore states in his book *Care of the Soul* that therapy has operated according to the model 'if it is broken fix it'. Instead of observing what is revealed in suffering, psychology wants to alleviate it. In his mind, hiding the dark places within is like hiding the soul, for some of the best work of the soul takes place in these dark places. He contends that caring for the soul isn't about removing problems and symptoms but rather attending to the small details of life.

Life becomes shapeless without the details. *For in the momentary conscious experience of daily minutiae, we find the finer points of extraordinary living.* Yet, in our search for wellness, it's these details we choose to ignore. We must change our definition of what a fully functioning human being means. I see so many people come through the doors of my therapy practice, desperate to get rid of their woes and their ailments, so they might have less ordinary lives. They anxiously look outside of themselves for some painless panacea that will quell the uncomfortable prodding of their inside aliveness. When we first sit together, it's very hard for most people to listen, hear and know the inner voices of struggle and strife. Yet, when deep suffering surfaces, they are looking for clues that it's safe and they are sound. Respecting and witnessing the 'dark side' is one of the most valuable healing tools that we have. Sadly enough, often the dark side is simply composed of unseen and unfelt feelings. I find that most people are relieved when they understand that I'm not there to resurface their landscape or redesign their homes within. I'm simply there to be a quiet guest, who can honor, see and embrace all that lies within. I'm always amazed how quickly people, when simply given permission, find the wisdom inherent in the dark and use this to guide them to some lighter, restful place.

We must not be so afraid to live on the entire continuum of life experience, so we can become more vibrant and dynamic human beings. The energy that is housed in depression, for instance, is neither more nor less than the energy housed in joy. It's all emotional energy. Holding back because an emotion is on the wrong side of the track can only diminish our health not improve it. However, bringing together and holding the entire spectrum is difficult because it challenges our dualistic ways of thinking and often feels chaotic. You can only be right or wrong, republican or democrat, for or against, good or evil, etc. We've polarized positions on just about everything. Staying polarized helps make things safe and predictable.

Learning to hold and integrate the multiplicity of experience by definition causes much discomfort. Yet, it's my contention that this simplistic way of living in a polarized style causes more ill health than wellness. As humans, we are actually entirely capable of holding more complexities and it's in this venture that we will actualize the extraordinary beings we are. Exploring and accepting this rich internal world will actually help us learn more discernment in living with more compassionate and loving actions. If we can learn to embrace those things we previously judged, condemned and separated out, we will begin to see the true picture of this fabric of living. Constructing this more holistic view, we may see things in the horizon of our future that we cannot even conceptualize now. It's in the holding of our true nature that we can birth some new, more natural way of being. In this opening to all, we come back to the oneness of being.

We've all been taught to strive for the brighter, more vibrant things in life. We often think that despair and depression are ugly, dark and stagnate. This isn't the case. Despair is simply what you get when you turn joy inside out. Imagine that you own a beautiful sweater woven with the most colorful textures of wool. You wear this sweater over and over and people always seem to notice and comment on how beautiful you look. You've forgotten, in your admiration of the sweater's outside appearance, that the inside has kept you quite warm and cozy. However, you have worn this sweater so much, it's gotten soiled and worn, and the colors of the fabric have run together on the inside where it's rested against your skin. One day, in a rush, you take it off inside out and toss it on your bed. Later that night you notice this crumbled up, dingy, dirty looking piece of fabric on your bed. For a moment, you can't even imagine what it could be. From the inside out, this clump on your bed seems far from looking like your beautiful sweater. In fact, you think about throwing this soiled strangely textured fabric away. But in reality the beautiful sweater and the clump on the bed are two versions of the same thing. Ridding ourselves of the inside would only destroy the fabric of the sweater. Joy and despair are two versions of the same thing. We cannot have one without the other. Trying to do away with one actually dissolves the integrity of the other.

Many of us think life's task is to have little struggle and much ease. We don't realize the richness of life's strife. Contests, conflicts and confusion never cease to flow in the rapid rivers of life. Yet, we constantly look for resting grounds and shortcuts. We often spend most of our lives on the grassy banks, feeling stuck yet strangely safe. More time is spent in avoidance of life's ills than in simply being in life's twists and turns. Yet, it's the curve of the river that takes us to unseen landscapes. Learning acceptance, while diminishing avoidance makes us well and whole.

It's interesting that the desire for calmness, safety and peace is what actually drives avoidance. However, it's the act of avoidance that causes the least peace. In acceptance, a struggle changes shape and becomes more digestible. In that digestion, life stays fluid and creates a current where peace and experience coexist.

The energy of resistance is heavier than anything you might encounter on the road towards wellness. Walking through the resistance leads you to the entire experience of the moment. When you decrease resistance, you increase the fluidity with which you approach anything. Resistance dims the experience of life, loads it with denseness and keeps you from the richness and fuel of the experience itself. Every life encounter has the potential to shape new pieces to life's puzzle. There is certain information, for instance, that can only be obtained through pain and struggle. We often don't realize how much we love someone until we feel the pain of losing that person. In addition, pain is the biggest motivator for change. Pain and suffering tell an important story that can catapult us to move to some new unknown territory. Pain opens portals that we must go down in order to know that nothing is to be avoided.

In acceptance, we free all the energy used in resistance. The very act of feeling something actually changes what you thought it was. It's only in our resistance to it that we hold the feeling in a frozen state. So if we resist some depression, or despair or grieving, we actually keep these things encased in ice, heavy and cold. Then, we feel the heavy burden of the frozen ice and think it's the sadness or despair. Actually, the experience of sadness and despair is quite warm and flowing.

At the very moment we invite these dark night guests in, something new and alive begins to stir within. Someone comes to my doorstep and I peer out the window to see who's there. If it's some windswept unkempt visitor, I may pretend I'm not home or worse, spend hours boarding up the windows and doors, and begin to identify and associate this struggle of guarding against the visiting intruder with the very characteristics of the visitor himself. This continues the vicious cycle of peering out and keeping in. In keeping torrential winds out, to keep my house well and safe, I have begun to live in a house without rejuvenating air. Finally, in desperate attempts to breathe, I take the boards down, open the windows and feel the cool breeze fill my lungs with fresh life.

I begin to let these very patient visitors into my house, and I discover that I have much to learn from them, if I dare to listen. They begin to change faces and shapes as I give up my resistance. I realize that my reaction to the struggle is often worse than the struggle itself. I accept that there's always wisdom in the winds that whip through my windows. Stagnation comes with keeping out, not letting in.

Imagine a windmill where each spoke on the windmill represents a continuum for one particular life experience. Each particular continuum is inclusive of both the darkest and lightest parts of that experience. All potential spokes initially lie horizontally and as we walk across these experiences we begin to energize the spoke and bring it into three-dimensional form. (**see illustration 4**) However, before each spoke can become an alive and viable part of the windmill energy system, it must achieve some degree of balance. For instance, if we spend too much time at one end of the spoke, that end will begin to hold most of our energy and the spoke will become lopsided. If the energy is concentrated at the darker end of the spectrum, it becomes heavier and denser. Eventually the spoke breaks in two, and dangles at the bottom of the windmill. Without its lighter, sister half it cannot begin the energetic windmill motion that I call the "sacred spin." On the other hand, if most of one's time and energy is spent at the lighter end of that particular life energy or experience then the whole spoke again is neglected and the lighter half breaks off and spins up and stays in this upward position. It remains trapped in this upright, vertical position because it has little to move it towards the 360-degree windmill motion.

It's only when we are willing to develop and experience the entire spoke that we allow the energetic building necessary to obtain a viable, live spoke. This spoke can then start a slow steady spin by the energy created by its very formation. The more balanced the spoke, the steadier and smoother is path. Of course, the ideal motion of the windmill is when all spokes are moving synchronously, creating the energy of never-ending movement. The dance of life that results from this has yet to be witnessed.

Most of us have been encouraged to stay at one end or another. For instance, the mental health field has suggested that wellness can be found when we live more permanently on the lighter side of the continuum, i.e. living in the absence of "darker symptomatology." Others have suggested that a person can only be trusted to be real when much of their living experiences have been on the darker side. While we must take up residence on different sides at different times in order to feel and become the experiences, it's crucial to be open to the continual currents that can carry us to the far end of the spectrum and everywhere in between. Human beings are capable of all these life encounters. Our ability to walk in all places creates a three-dimensional

SACRED SPIN

Living on one side of spoke makes it bottom heavy.

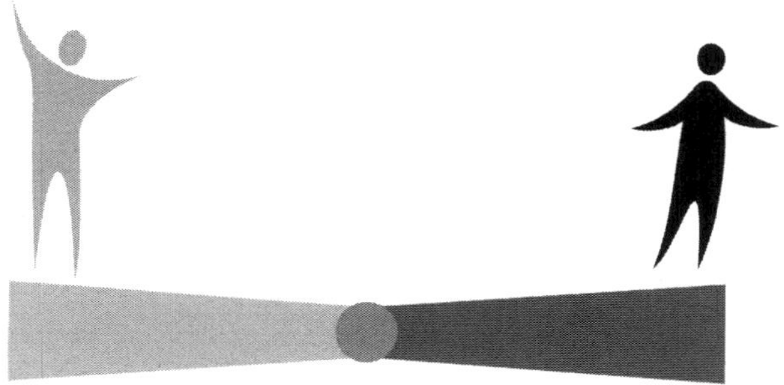

Balance created when living on both ends.

Walking an entire spoke creates movement which creates Sacred Spin.

Illustration 4

schema of vast energies being created by small spokes whirling into motion by their own completeness. Each person becomes a reservoir of creative energies. We become more than the sum of spokes, we become the energy created from the movement of all of our experiences. As we create this vision that includes all of our capabilities, we bring into motion an entirely new system of energy that can support itself in ceaseless, tireless motion. What can be birthed from this is wonderful beyond our imagination.

When we are unwilling to hold and acknowledge the entire spectrum of human potential, some members in our society will hold on steadfastly to one side of the continuum and others to the other side just to keep the balance. For instance, some people may act evil and bad because they are holding the energy of the dark side for those of us who are in complete denial of this part of the human experience. I'm amazed at the lengths people will go to deny their own shadowy shortcomings. Most of the time it's because we think we won't be accepted or loved so we give to someone else that which we don't like in ourselves. Many people in this kind of denial eventually end up exploding, hurting and exploiting the world around them. On the other hand, it shouldn't be so surprising that over time when hate is projected onto another human being, eventually the hate energy quotient builds up enough to cause that person to burst forth with hateful actions. Our world seems more violent and chaotic not because we've been too lenient in tolerating the dark side, but because we've not been tolerant enough. If we really want a nonviolent culture, we must spend more time acknowledging, accepting and healing our own inadequacies rather than asking others to do this for us. We must learn to first accept who we are, before we can become more discerning about what we do.

Yet, there are other folks who seem so apt at being wonderful deed doers and seem almost saintly. They appear to hold the light so that the rest of us will not forget the importance of goodness and kindness in the world. But, if each of us takes responsibility for our own truths along the whole continuum, then no one is solely responsible for exemplifying one place. For most of us, it's simply too difficult to live on one side alone. How many idols, heroes and gurus have fallen from their place of grace because their darker sides were finally discovered? A history of even a minor episode of depression can ruin a politician's career. A minister who divorces to be with another often loses his place of sacred calling because of his willingness to be all too human. Often we have very little compassion and acceptance for these idolized individuals when they fall from heightened platforms of perceived perfection. It does appear that more and more leaders from many walks of life seem to be falling from grace. We secretly love these gossip torn stories, because they give us permission to be just a bit more human. Rather than continue our search for the perfect human being (which none of us can be) we should begin to search for paths that help us handle the imperfect human journey with more compassion, grace and humility. *Forgiveness isn't only a gesture of healing, but an act of embracing the truth of the entire spectrum of human possibilities.*

It's very difficult for us to acknowledge that we are a blend of so many potentialities. When murderers and other such criminals find God in prison, we again are judging skeptics. We can't allow ourselves to believe that once imprisoned in darkness, anyone can find the light. When we're able to walk more consciously and gracefully through all the experiences we are given in life, we can begin to glean from them the energy that will catapult us into the next evolutionary step. The real issue isn't whether we are capable of living in the sultry shadows of life's landscapes because we can and do. The real issue is how we take responsibility for it and learn from it. When we are able to do this we transmute one experience into the next and the next and the next. Permission to be and live on the entire continuum turns stagnation into metamorphic action, as dualistic thinking is replaced by holistic living.

We have the potential to become a spinning vital, alive energy system. We can become more fully actualized spiritual beings. Let me introduce the idea of overriding spiritual arcs. When we're able to walk the full continuum of a life experience or feeling, we begin to energize ourselves to live in the field of the overriding spiritual arc. For instance, there is the spoke that contains the polarized positions of joy and despair. When we are able to know both the experience of human felt joy and despair, we can begin to live in the field of spiritual rejoicing, which knows both. (**see illustration 5**) An overriding arc combines all experiences in the human field, to create some new synthesized spiritual experience. It's not unlike the Buddha, who is seen bending over, crying for all the suffering in the world. Yet, he maintains enough detachment to continue feeling joy and amazement for the human journey as he accepts that suffering is simply part of life. Living in the overriding spiritual arc of anything helps us live with less attachment and ambivalence, while living with more acceptance and freedom. It's as if the two opposing experiences of joy and despair combine to create some new third reality, which is a synthesis of the lessons and energy of both, causing us to know and behold spiritual rejoicing.

SACRED ARCS

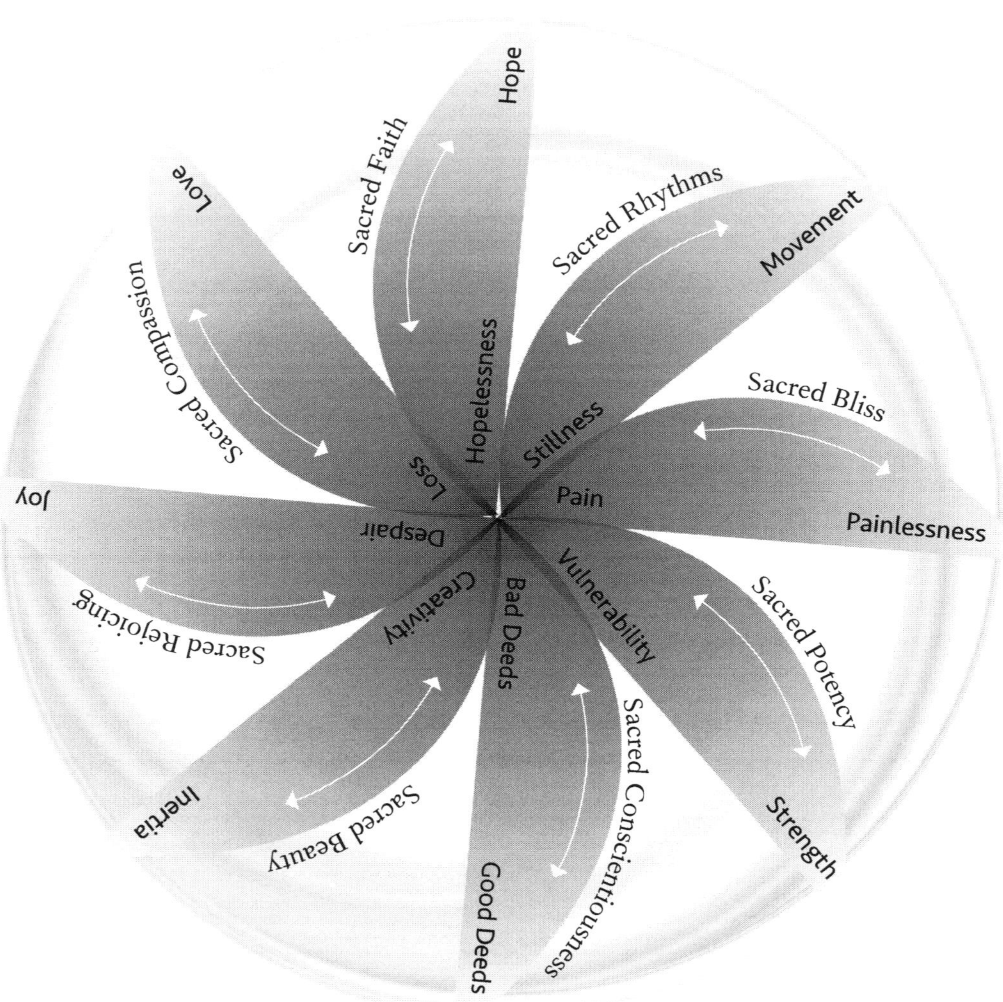

Illustration 5

While there are an infinite number of potential overriding spiritual arcs, identifying some may be helpful here.

JOY + DESPAIR = SPIRITUAL REJOICING
Through the windows of joy we see delight and are caught in the rapture of beauty and laughter. In despair we are filled with grief and anguish, knowing the agony of life's defeats. Spiritual rejoicing is the celebration of knowing life exists in both.

STRENGTH + VULNERABILITY = SPIRITUAL POTENCY
Knowing strength and how to use it is no more important than understanding that humility and dignity come from vulnerabilities. Physical strength without the knowledge of the body's vulnerabilities could be deadly. Emotional vulnerability lets in crucial ingredients for building fortitude. Spiritual potency must then by definition include the ability to be strong enough to experience the world of vulnerabilities.

LOVE + LOSS = SPIRITUAL COMPASSION
Love opens our hearts; loss solidifies the hugeness of this. It's both our ability to open our hearts and our ability to be mindful of the heart's importance that bring us to the gentle position of spiritual compassion.

HOPE + HOPELESSNESS = SPIRITUAL FAITH
In hope, we create a vision and an intuitive knowing, while hopelessness creates a blank screen with unknown proportions. Both are necessary for the creation of Faith.

CREATIVITY + INERTIA = SPIRITUAL BEAUTY
Both the flow of creative juices and the quiet times of digestion help us move towards the creative power of spirit. Human creations gather unseen spiritual beauty in the quiet still moments in between.

PHYSICAL MOVEMENT + PHYSICAL STILLNESS = SPIRITUAL RHYTHMS
It's our ability to experience both the serenity of stillness and the vibrancy of movement that we begin to be stirred by the rhythmic flow of spirit.

GOOD DEEDS + BAD DEEDS = SPIRITUAL CONSCIENTIOUSNESS
Only by experiencing the felt energy of both doing good and bad do we become more conscientious deed doers.

FREEDOM + RESTRICTION = SPIRITUAL LIBERTY
The desire and drive for freedom actually comes from the experience of being restricted and constrained. The experience of freedom naturally motivates expansiveness. Spiritual liberty can be attained when we are mindful about our intentions towards expansiveness.

PAINLESSNESS + PAINFULNESS = SPIRITUAL BLISS
The doorway to painlessness is often found in the room where pain is most present. Accepting and embracing the truth of pain actually teaches us the lessons of detachment. Through the process of letting in and letting go we begin to walk on the path of blissful awareness.

It's the practice of spinning light threads from these overriding arcs throughout our entire being that will help us journey on the sacred path. We are on the eve of a new evolutionary step, weaving the deeply textured, beautifully colored fabric that we were meant to be. In that fabric we will move into a new era. Our mission will not be so much fighting to control human nature, but utilizing human nature to elevate us to some new spirit nature. In this way, we can come to know that being in our true human nature is far more than we've come to believe. Wellness is about the process of lifting the veils and stretching out towards our true nature.

Soul Remedies

#2 – Be Well

Take one moment…right now…find a place where you can sit comfortably…with yourself…without distractions.
Go within and listen…

Know that everything within you is safe and sound. Everything you find in this inside place is meant to be. Accept and Hold what you discover with compassion and unconditional regard
and you will be on the path towards wellness.

First direct your awareness to a current difficult emotion.
Something that feels heavy and less illuminated in your mind.
Hold your attention on this with nonjudgmental consciousness
Just see it…hear it…feel it...name it…and be with it.
Know it serves some important purpose and let it be.

With your mind's eye place this energy in half of a circle
and let it rest.

Now concentrate on a delightful feeling,
a lighter perhaps more illuminating feeling.
Hold this feeling in your awareness again without judgment.
Now place this feeling in the other half of the circle
adjacent to the heavier feeling.

Now let the two begin to merge.

As the two energies join together and become one,
you begin to feel the birthing of an even larger energy
that is much more than either emotion alone.

Label this new circle of merged energies anyway you want.
You have the ability to transmute these two different feeling states
into some new third state. And this third state can be
whatever you design it to be.

You now have more energy for exactly what you desire. Take this energy with you for the rest of the day…the rest of your life. .
And *Be Well.*

3

The Rings Around Us & The Core Within

"Who looks outside dreams
Who looks inside wakes"
–Jung

"People are like stained-glass windows
they sparkle and shine when the sun is out,
but when the darkness sets in,
their true beauty is revealed only if there is light within."
–Elizabeth Kubler-Ross

It's time to take up the challenge and experience the vast territory of the internal realm. For it's here, in the world within, that all else can be found. Yet, the journey back to ourselves is surprisingly difficult – with sweet seductions luring us back out at every turn. We give much power to all other sources of knowledge and yet the wisest and surest knower of all is the "you" that lives inside. All the answers for living, loving and healing can be found in this soul habitat within. The passageway has simply been blocked.

Coming back home can feel very awkward, difficult and at times painful. It's a challenging process to trust our own home especially when others have failed to see the beauty in it. Returning to a place where there has been invasion and intrusion, and remnants of fear and pain, can be scary. However, we cannot heal this home and discover its wonders if we are not willing to be there. In order to get there, we need to develop more ways of cultivating safety while riding the tides of our inner turbulence. Once inside, we let the churning, whirling mayhem we first encounter be proof that we should be elsewhere on our search. In addition, it frequently feels that to do this internal work we must give up the very things in our external world that have made life easier. Interestingly enough, it's often those things outside of us that indeed make life harder. Owning this strange and mysterious inner world (which is the only world we can own) is far better than owning nothing.

Every time we run outside of ourselves we ignore the home within. *Paradoxically, it's the very feeling of aloneness that usually drives most of us to leave our homes alone and empty.* The act of escaping this internal realm at least attests to the existence of it. Even those of us who were given permission in childhood to spend time inside so easily stray to other backyards where the elusive green grass awaits with promises of better, happier times. Unfortunately for some, it's only when the home is in its final stage of destruction that we wake up and acknowledge its existence.

Some people are especially skilled at acknowledging everyone else's homes. Breathing life into another house seems to be the very way in which they feel worthy of breathing at all. They visit another's home with the hope of being seen themselves, as if they only exist in the reflection of another's windows. Often, nothing comes back and so they continue their search, peering through peepholes hoping to see a flicker of life that stirs their own. I call these folks the home holders: "I know who I am through knowing who you are."

There are still others who want to look at another's home only to compare it to their own. In this way they can somehow know if their own homes are good, bad, better or worse depending on their felt self needs on that particular rating day. I've always been amazed that in this comparison game, "better than" ratings never seem to make people feel better than "worse than" ratings. You can only be good as long as the one "less better" still manages to stay standing. If they fall, the mirror that supposedly reflects your "better than" status shatters as well. The trouble is: homes are being torn down and built up much quicker than the self can stay steady. The comparison game makes life much too whimsical and the self much too unstable. Judging and contrasting also separates us from each other. If you are better than me, I need to keep my distance lest you realize this. If you are worse than me, I need to keep my distance so I don't become you. Using others to verify the rightness or wrongness of the self is testimony that the self has not been lived in enough. More often than not, every judgment you hold for another hides something of yourself that you don't like. I've noted in my years of practicing psychotherapy that the best projective test can be found in the judgments people hold about the world around them. For those opinions, rulings, judgments and verdicts possess enormous information and evidence about the things we fear and dislike most about ourselves. In the motion and action of judging others we attempt to give these things away to those bystanders who happen to be within our visual field. However, perhaps in the practice of becoming more mindful Earth citizens, we shouldn't litter the world with our own unresolved angst, but instead begin to focus on becoming responsible for all that we are. Living in the home of the self with full acceptance is the only place we need to be. Once there we may be surprised at how little we need to compare or judge others. Just like our fingerprints, no two homes can ever be alike. One thing is for certain; all of these searching and comparing activities keep us out of our own home. It's time to return.

We are born with a core self, our soul essence, which is very fluid and permeable. As we begin to move through life we gather rings around this core, both for protection and provisions. Information is stored in these outer rings that help us move safely through the world. As part of forming our identities, many of these rings contain internalized attributes that have originated from influential external properties. This ring model is analogous to the rings you see when you cut down a tree. The older the tree the more rings you will see. The ring design is actually found throughout nature. Our solar system is a great example. The sun is at the core of our solar system. The planets form orbital rings around the sun. Gravitation principles keep the orbits intact and continually spinning around the sun. Much as the solar system is its own self -contained system within a larger galaxy system, so too we each have our own ringed system that resides in the larger three-dimensional world. Our soul/ self (our sun) resides in the core and fuels and attracts rings to form around us that make up a whole system called a human being.

As we go through life, we gather layers to this system, some of which tell us who to be, how to be and what to be. In part, we gather and wear these rings to interact and belong in the world. Initially, these layers of rings help us reach out and connect. We are able to identify and resonate with others through the rings we see in them. But soon, we become lulled into the pursuit of rings, for the sole purpose of proving our worth. We begin to believe that our value is dependent on the number and type of rings we can accumulate. The content and usefulness of these layers matters less, as the quantity matters more. We easily begin to believe that our life mission can only be found out there and we quicken our pace at gathering outside material to expand our internal sense of who we are. Our sense of self and soul become dimmer and dimmer as we hone our senses to mine the external fields of goods and gadgets.

Originally, our internal core or soul, stays connected with the eternal or invisible realm. But as we gather more and more layers that surround this core, we become less conscious of this spiritual realm and more conscious of the external three-dimensional world. As our attention shifts towards the external, our awareness of the invisible world lessens and our connection with it fades. We become convinced that reality can only be found and seen in the outer world and so we begin the arduous task of shaping ourselves into the forms and fashions of these outer models. (**see illustration 6**)

In the beginning stages of life, when we've only a few layers surrounding our core, the invisible realm, which is the surrounding infinite world, can still permeate and penetrate the inner core. Children attest to this as they often report interesting experiences with angels, invisible friends, auras and other strange phenomenon. Most adults ignore such stories because they've long ago forgotten this connection. As we become more interested in surviving in the Earthly world, our attention shifts and becomes much more narrowly focused. We continue adding layers of rings to our system until one day it eventually collapses from the weight.

It's my belief that everything in the human field of study can be understood by examining analog situations that occur in nature. If we turn to astrophysics we can see an extraordinary example of the ring model. Type II supernovae are giant stars that have short lives due to their grand size. They collapse because they run out of fuel at their core. In typical stars, an energetic equilibrium is established whereby the star continues to slowly grow outward, creating more gravitational pull inward, towards the core. In turn this pull heats up the core and it's this fuel from the core that pushes material back out to keep the entire system in balance. If the star grows too fast and becomes too large, it becomes a type II supernovae giant star. It begins to run out of fuel and cannot keep up with the steady and larger inward pull of gravity due to the very nature of its rapid expansion. Eventually it collapses, as there isn't enough fuel expanding outward to compete with the gravitational pull coming inward.

This is a helpful explanation of many of our current crises in the human arena. We continue to gather more and more material in our wish to be giant stars. We spend enormous time and energy gathering material: wealth, houses, status cards, relationships, beauty, stamina, etc. But, we run out of fuel, or perhaps we simply have less and less access to our fuel from our core. We begin to collapse because we cannot support the giant layers we've accumulated in our lifetimes. I see so many people running on empty. Yet, still they're unwilling to give up the material that weighs them down. They fear

EXTERNALIZATION

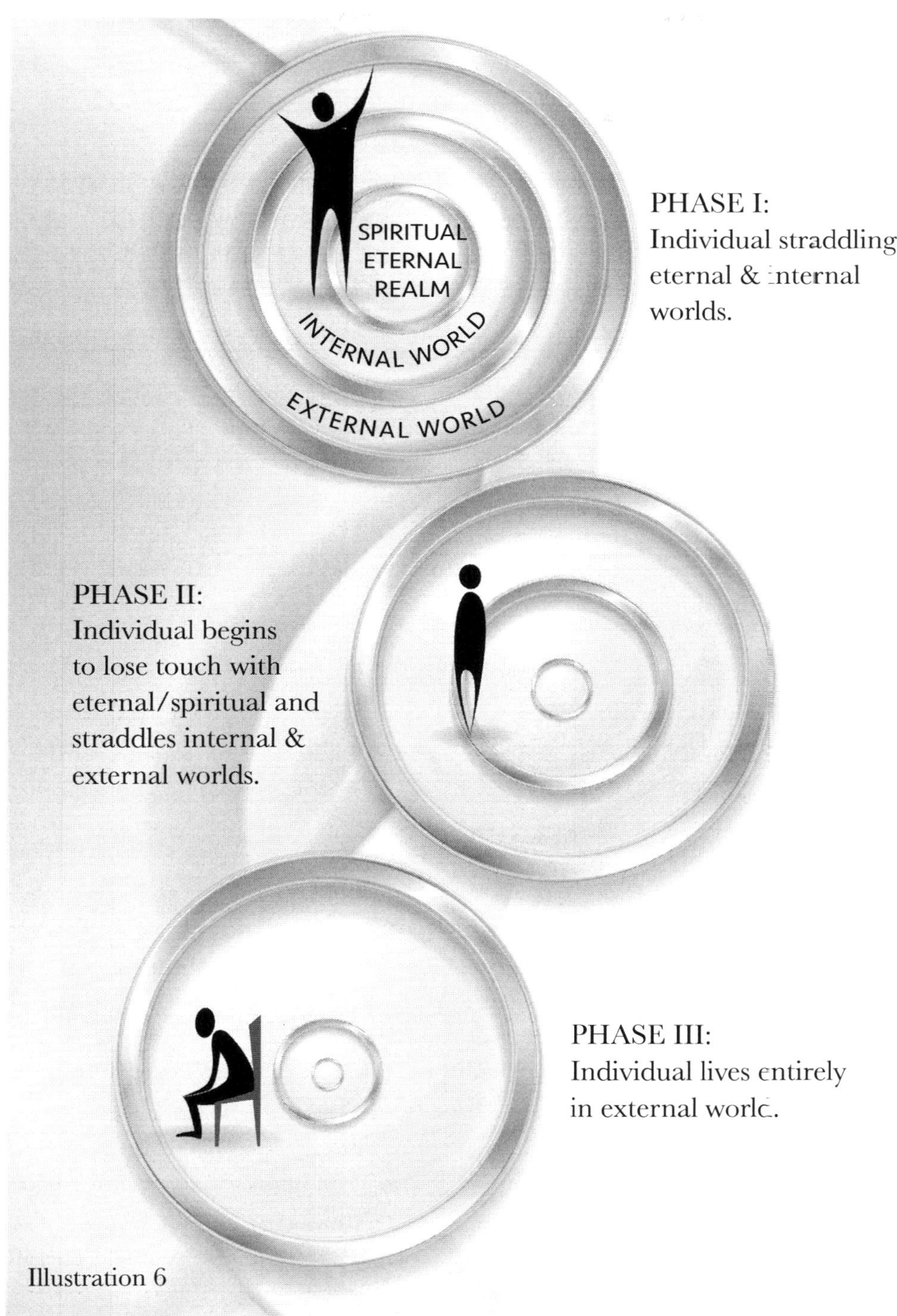

Illustration 6

without all of the material rings they would be reduced to nothing. Ironically, it's eventually the very weight of the rings that causes the system to collapse inward. In this disintegrative breakdown, the layers begin to dissolve and we become free once again to feel our core, our essence, and our soul presence. Paradoxically, it's only when we are stripped of our outside layers that we find out truly how big we are. The catalyst for this collapse often comes in the form of crises, loss and tragedy. Unless we are willing to take a proactive role in delayering ourselves, we often must experience the chaos of collapse. It's actually only when we rid ourselves of outside presentations that we've accumulated in order to obtain love, that we see the powerful essence of who we are and how we can love and be loved. *In feeling our essence we actually have the experience of non-separation.*

As the system caves in, the outer-most rings begin to dissolve and pathways open up that allow the spiritual realm to penetrate our consciousness once again. New and strange experiences may begin to happen. Dialogues with God, visions, psychic phenomenon, and intuitive healing abilities may occur. Some clinicians may diagnose and treat these epiphanies and struggles with medication and "solution focused therapy." Others are recognizing these times as "spiritual emergencies" and are helping people celebrate and embrace the collapse as a transformational, crucial time to walk into a new way of living. It's when our world is crumbling and we are most vulnerable that we are the most open to the incredible resource system in our world within. Rebuilding more cemented layers from the mortar of the external world will only burden and sink our system. Finally, in our desperate attempts to stay afloat, we finally turn inward for comfort.

As our attention shifts towards our internal world, *this very act of attention fuels our core.* As the layers slowly dissolve, pathways from the ever-present eternal realm open up and this also fuels the flames within. Our core begins to expand, incorporating the remaining material from the various self-layers still surrounding us, until we become less and less separate from All That Is around us. The rhythm of out to in also undergoes a change as the core begins its rhythmic beating of in to out. This is the spiritual journey. This is the path towards oneness. (**see illustration 7**)

It might be helpful at this point to take a look at the Internal Resource System that lives within. (**see illustration 8**) The Internal Resource System is made up of many different things. Each person houses both universal elements and unique attributes in the different layers of this resource system. How we each decide to utilize our universal or common human characteristics becomes part of our unique make up.

THE PATH LIVING FROM THE INSIDE OUT

External layers dissolve as inner awareness expands.

In to out flow joining with All That Is.

Illustration 7

INTERNAL RESOURCE SYSTEM: THE RINGS AROUND US

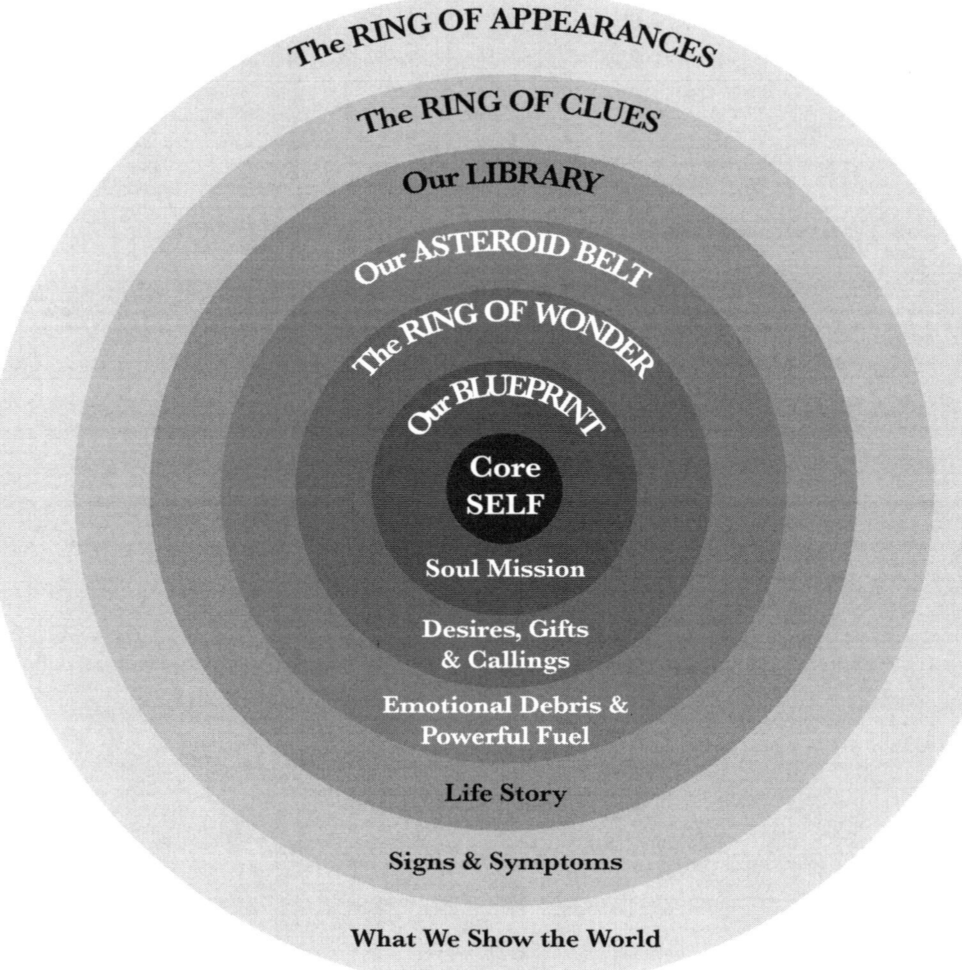

The RING OF APPEARANCES
The RING OF CLUES
Our LIBRARY
Our ASTEROID BELT
The RING OF WONDER
Our BLUEPRINT
Core SELF
Soul Mission
Desires, Gifts & Callings
Emotional Debris & Powerful Fuel
Life Story
Signs & Symptoms
What We Show the World

Illustration 8

The outermost Ring is the "coming out" ring or the Ring of Appearances. In contains those things we use to interface with the world. It's closest to the world and therefore there is much activity in this ring. We are most conscious of this layer and pay most attention to it. It holds much of the wardrobe we use for appearances in the outside world. Many of the things found here have been incorporated from the external realm, and therefore, this ring is very important in helping us navigate through the three dimensional world.

The Second Ring is the Ring of Clues. The ambassador for the entire ringed system lives in the second outer ring. This is a place like an international café where emissaries from all rings converge negotiations occur and decisions are made. We are fairly conscious of the activity in this ring, but can rely on this activity to continue to take place even when we are less mindful of it. Messengers from the deeper rings converge here telling us of things to come. External opportunities for experiencing a variety of things as well as the internal discomfort felt from false appearances held in the First Ring combine to give us glimpses of the things we might be good at but have not yet tried. It's often our inability to correctly interpret these messages that cause difficulty with self-esteem and feelings of worthiness.

Oftentimes, symptoms and signs appear in Ring Two in disguise. We mistakenly try to rid ourselves of them, closing pathways to the deeper layers within. The mental health system has spent much time and many resources on trying to invent new ways of stamping out these symptoms. Sometimes humans are so good at making this ring invisible (through addictions or old wellness programs), they end up living with the illusion that they can be totally self-contained in the first layer of appearances. This is when we might expect more catastrophic illnesses to surface. It's important to note that most of us haven't begun to utilize the healing energetic power that lies within so it's often the symptoms and confusion found in this second layer that are clues to the deeper powers within. For instance, the depression and dissatisfaction felt on the way to a non-inspiring job everyday often are messengers of unseen and unactualized gifts and talents. The dissatisfaction and disgruntled feelings need to be held and felt as they are a path to deeper layers of yearnings and dreams. In addition, the lack of energy and enthusiasm surrounding work may be an important signal that the apparel we must wear to do the job may be injurious to true self-definition.

Many times when I see people come into my office for help, they request symptom relief. But it's through the symptom that I can begin to recognize the real want, desire, fear that needs to emerge and surface. Once this comes to fruition, the symptom is no longer needed and can be replaced by examining and experiencing deeper layers of the Internal Resource System. If I collude with the client and give aid in the destruction of this Second Ring, information is destroyed and the ability to rely on the knower within is hampered. Symptoms are often testimony of the wide world within. If we simply rid people of symptoms, it's no wonder that they become more and more reliant on the outside world, believing there is little underneath. This second layer is also where we begin to look for proof of our intrinsic worthiness. It's important to remember that as we traverse this layer, we often encounter discarded disapproved parts from Ring One that have been buried here. Upon seeing them, we may have the impulse to run back to Ring One, where we are busier and less aware of this revealing inner world.

Ring Three contains our life story…our library. Here lay our patterns of twisting and turning throughout life that are partially determined by both our circumstances and our yearnings. Rhythms can be discovered here that will become crucial in changing our movement and growth from in to out. Our biological, chronological and psychological history is stored in the libraries of this ring, as well as our grandest attributes and our serious problems. Talents, skills and unique abilities can also be found here. This layer is often scary for people as they confront their hugeness and smallness. In my experience, interestingly enough, our grandness is often scarier than our smallness.

Ring Four contains our feelings, inspirations and the fuel necessary for staying alive and well. I call this the asteroid belt, because when people first encounter this ring, they often feel as if they were on a spaceship careening around asteroids desperately avoiding some catastrophic crash. Feelings of a lifetime are stored here and the potential risk of volcanic emotional explosions is always present. The amount and intensity of stored up emotional material is directly correlated to the degree to which we've lived constricted lives. A restricted lifestyle requires by definition more acts of denial. The emotional debris that might cause conflict and confusion in conscious life end up becoming deeply embedded in Ring Four. We often don't realize that this, like compost, can be life sustaining in the most vital and vibrant way.

As we begin to encounter and experience these feelings, we release tremendous amounts of energy that then is available to the whole system of rings. Emotions contain the fuel necessary for change and growth. We know, however, from other energy storehouses, such as fuel trucks or nuclear plants, that these places can be very volatile. So, when we first spend time in this ring, we may feel unstable and labile and therefore feel compelled to leave and go to the outer banks where there is more familiarity and safety. People often use the emotional evidence found in Ring Four to prove they are indeed unworthy, unwell and off balance. However, this ring really holds our passions and aliveness and guides us towards our true nature. *Once again we encounter a paradox: nothing is as it seems, but everything is a clue.* The richness of Ring Four cannot be judged by its odorous and sticky initial appearance. The richest fertilizer does not look or smell appealing at first glance. Yet, it's this fertilizer that causes everything to grow and become what it's intended to be, whether a tree, a corn stalk or a person. Once we learn to navigate Ring Four, our lives can become much more fertile, abundant and lush. The first three rings will feel like black and white worlds compared to the colorful world of Ring Four.

The Fifth Ring, called the Ring of Wonder, holds the essential requirements necessary to sustain one's life. Our deepest needs and desires, including issues related to attachment, love, intimacy, survival and sex can be found here. Unique life assignments and impassioned callings lay hidden in this ring, like gemstones in a cave. When spending any length of time at this level, we may find ourselves pondering questions about life's meaning and purpose. This is where truths have been held that are the least polluted by the external realm's reality. True discoveries of who you are and can be await you here. There is a wide world of wonder at this deep layer of the Internal Resource System. Solutions to many of our world's current day problems can be discovered here.

The Sixth Ring, closest to our core, contains our original blueprint. This blueprint is the map to our Divine design. It holds the keys for our unique Earth mission, our life's meaning, and our truth for this life. All the ingredients we need to carry out our life mission are here. Our original blueprint came with our soul when it landed in our bodies. It contains the recipe for combining the unique attributes of our body, mind and spirit with the universal characteristics of being a human to create a life perfectly aligned with the Divine purpose for this particular life.

In the middle of the ringed system (the Seventh Ring), lies the core self. This is the habitat where the soul lives. All sacred energy is stored here and portals to the eternal realm are plentiful. This is our sun and learning to live in and harness this energy is a lifetime task. *This is where the essence of self never dies and the connection with God always lives.* The soul is the instrument for perceiving all there is within simultaneously with all there is beyond. Soul hears and feels a symphony. Soul sees and feels a sunset. Soul thinks and feels a great cosmic concept. Soul touches and feels the union of great love. The activator of soul is love. Love fuels the soul's fires. Love gently plays this soul organ to the heights of a sublime symphony. This is my truth about soul. It does not have to be yours, but let this take you to you. For you have soul and you have truth and there is nothing greater than your soul (sole) truth.

This ringed journey takes place throughout a lifetime. As we gather the comfortable clothes from Ring One, we can throw out the ones that no longer fit. Attending performances in the external world that feel hurtful or dimming are no longer required. Our appearance begins to take on the forms that come from deeper internal layers of self rather than the external world's notions of self. As we start listening to the clues and messages held in Ring Two, we find the magical pathways that lead to our deeper treasures. At some point the life story of Ring Three becomes more intriguing as we recognize it as our own. The vast libraries here teach us how much we already know, for the information contained here is already part of us. We can then be less afraid to navigate through the emotional layer of Ring Four, as we know the priceless value of the vast fueling system contained therein. As we become invigorated and rejuvenated by traveling through our emotional world, our spark for life only increases as we head closer to our center sun. The closer we come to our core the bigger the pull. I imagine that our sacred inner core holds magnificent magnets that pull us towards it, much like the Divine Mother holds her arms out to embrace us in the night. As we come nearer to home, the rejoicing heart beats with rapture.

By the time we reach Ring Five, we discover what we truly need to sustain ourselves in this world. As we accept our needs and become fulfilled, we know we can walk anywhere in the world. And the most exciting place to wander is in the wonder of our original blueprint in Ring Six. Many lifelong questions are finally answered here. As we set about our mission we spend the rest of our lives becoming acquainted with our soul purpose and soul energy. Working from this inside out position provides us with the ability to bring our truths back out into the world. Thereby, feeding the world with the necessary ingredients to heal it and elevate the spirit in it. The division lines become much less clear between all of our different parts and we become a more integrated system of Internal Being. In addition, we become much less separated from the eternal realm. The soul has no boundaries with the Divine Source and therefore information and communication will All That Is beyond us is more forthcoming and flowing. There is also less need to protect and hide from the external world as our mission becomes clearer in its manifestation. Herein lies one meaning of the oneness of being.

Surrounding this wonderful whirling ring system is an outer formless band or halo of vaporous energy. This halo is composed of changing energies that come from the continuous attention we give to our outer world. It's analogous to the atmosphere of our planet Earth where rocket ships, satellites and space debris float in orbit, circling and held in constant motion by the gravitational pull of our planet. We too have an atmosphere. Here the external energies we chose to attend to, orbit and spin until we decide to jettison them to other places thereby releasing them from influencing our own world within. Imagine for a moment that our attention, like an arrow, focuses on something in the outside world. This arrow of attention begins to form a conduit, a channel, between ourselves and that to which we are attending. As a result, the energy from that outside object begins to be pulled into our own atmospheric orbit. It forms a halo around us and either clouds our appearance or lights it up. Some people have a hazy halo while others seem to have a sparkling star like halo. For example, there are those folks who diligently attend, because of fear-based beliefs, to external potential pitfalls and dreaded dangers. The very act of attention (our gravitational pull) brings the energy of fear into our orbital band, forming a halo of energetic fear around us. Eventually this energy seeps into our more solid layers of rings and we begin to think that these fears are actually part of who we are instead of part of what the world is.

A client of mine had a rather stormy childhood in which she was told that she could do nothing particularly well. In truth, she was exceptionally talented and gifted at many things. However, she began to believe that she was never "good enough" at anything and was afraid to take risks to do the things she wanted to do for fear of failure. She got a safe job and, although she was quite gifted in music, art and drama, she never pursued these activities. As an adult, she continued to attend to information in her environment that was more fear based regarding her abilities to be great. The atmosphere that she created around herself began to hold some of this fear-based energy. She saw the world as scary and unsafe and continued to conceal and disguise her desires, wants, talents and gifts. When she did try to give voice to some of her deeper desires, she carefully scrutinized her environment for rejection cues to ward off evidence of her "not good enough" status. In attending to more fear based cues in her environment she kept attracting fear energy in her halo ring. As a result, even when she was brave enough to play the piano in front of people, unfortunately they heard and saw her through the veil created by this outside halo ring.

There are so many wonderfully talented and gifted people in this world. I often wonder about the musicians and artists who never get seen by the rest of the world. When two people go up on a stage and play the same piece of music, technically flawless, why does one get the part and the other not? I believe, in part, it's due to the halo affect.

The halo affect is the affect we have on people due to the halo of energy around us rather than from the deeper rings within us.

This is the invisible variable that becomes visible in the experience of a person. So, for instance, when we attend to externalized fear (which is plentiful these days), we create a conduit to that fear which builds a hazier halo around us. In turn, we can also attend to the beautiful and lovely things in life, which pulls more sparkly and star like energy into our atmospheric halo. Be careful what you attend to, for it's often this hovering halo that people first see and feel when they encounter you. *If you really want people to know who you are make sure they don't encounter what you are afraid of being.*

For most of us, this Internal Resource System has been less explored and experienced than the external realm of perceived realities. Yet, our greatest assets lie within. The internal world no longer contains liabilities. In fact, our greatest liability is staying outside of ourselves. We can choose to go on this inner journey and commence with the arduous, but rewarding process of delayering and dissolving unwanted baggage we've gathered over the years. As we mindfully and consciously look and live in the various layers, we can decide what we want to keep and what we must discard. As we travel from layer to layer, we begin to weave a much more complex fabric that shapes the sacred self. Instead of a system divided into disconnected and distinct rings, we create a mosaic, a masterpiece of connected currents from all parts, producing a much more holistic, united system of self. Pathways are paved that make all layers accessible to the conscious mind. We now know that nothing in this internal world has to be avoided or denied.

The more awareness we have of operating from within the less restricted we are operating outside!

Energy is available in a much more vibrant way, and new ways of being in the world begin to emerge. As holistic beings, we are able to interact with the outside world from a sacred stance where service and self are indistinguishable.

The figure 8 is a helpful sacred symbol and conceptualization tool to envision this self-evolving process. Imagine that through and around your body lies a sacred figure 8. The middle of this sacred 8 rests in the center of your chest, in your heart chakra. The movement of energy begins from this inner core and moves out through the front of your chest following the sacred 8 over the top of your head towards the eternal blessed realm. Here the energy merges with the Divine, boosting the mystical movement of energy back down the sacred 8 towards the middle of the back where it enters the heart chakra once again. As this powerful merging energy pulsates through your core, you continue to send sacred waves of these vibratory rhythms back out into the external world. This energy continues to follow the path of the sacred 8 traveling down the loop in front of you leading deep within the Earth place below your feet. As the energy rounds the loop, it merges with energy from the externalized Earth plane and again this merging momentum propels further travel up the back loop, once again returning to the heart center. This meeting place within, lying at the very center of your heart, is where *All That Is* meets and merges. This goes on through infinity as the path of the sacred figure 8 connects you to the vibrant worlds within, the Earthly world without, and the Divine world beyond. Being in this flow continually joins us with *All That Is*. The sacred 8 can be a reminder, a symbol for staying on the path of oneness!

It's helpful to note, that as we do this incredible labor of love, this self-work of wonder, we may, at first seem less available to the demands of the external realm. The self, on this inward journey, can go through many different appearances: confusing, paradoxical and deceiving at times. Another illustration of this self-journey may be helpful here. There are five phases of self/soul development: *self-estrangement, self-discovery, self-centering, self-service* and *self-merging*. As we spend time in the outer most rings or layers we actually are in what I call the self-estrangement phase, where most of our attention isn't on the self but on all else in the world. In this phase, the magnetizing arrows from the external world can easily pull our attention away from the rings within, especially because at this point we are most concerned about how we fit into the world. Because we've not developed the true self, we don't have much to offer the world at this stage. Yet, paradoxically, we may act as if all our focus and attention is about taking care of this external world. But, we take care of it, mainly to get the sustaining life force contained in this outer world. In other words, we look for what the world has to offer us by becoming what it wants us to be. Many people, especially women, are seduced into thinking that they must stay in this phase as a way to keep a good enough definition of the self where our sole definition is that of attending to and caring for the outside world. Yet, in this self-estrangement phase we are actually alienated from the self, having little knowledge of who and what we are. Our culture provides us with many self-estrangement activities that lure us out and keep us out of this inside place, this internal home of the self. We participate oh so willingly by feeding from these menus, overindulging in things that keep us too full to awaken to the emptiness within. Drugs, videos, buying, selling, eating, drinking, can all be self-anesthetizing activities that dim our awareness of the home within. Just note whether you engage in routine daily activities that take your focus inside or outside. Is your week full of self-estrangement or self-awareness?

When we begin to transfer our focus from the outer most rings to the middle layers of this internal world, we become more absorbed in the self and may appear less accessible to external callings. This important self-discovery, self-recovery phase is crucial to understand, as many of us return to the outer rings much too quickly for fear of being labeled self-serving, narcissistic or too self-engrossed. In our culture, we don't even let children play in this internal playground for too long. I have often heard the refrain, "that child is too full of himself." If not full of ourselves, then who? If we can understand that this phase must be experienced in order to return to some larger place of being, we might not be so harsh towards those going through it. During this phase, we begin to feel the alluring pull from the magnetic arrows found in our sacred internal core.

Here we begin the amazing task of finding out about this home within. First we have to become aware of the need for the inner self-journey, this inner path of self-work (worth). It would be nice to think that most of us could enter this path of self-actualization through natural curiosity and joy. In my experience this doesn't seem to be the case. We become conscious of the need to travel on this inner path due to some outside crisis, loss, hurt or disappointment. As we become disillusioned by the outer world, we begin to follow the crafty clues and symptomatic signals within. In this process, we unravel the stories of the self, uncovering forgotten parts of who we've been and can be. Many people who have had difficult childhoods may need to spend time doing crucial recovery work here, where past traumas and painful difficulties are healed and understood. In addition, for those who have spent a lifetime engrossed in too many self-estrangement activities, they may need the aid of self-help recovery groups like AA. In phase two, we are retrieving the self so that we can begin to breathe life into the flattened forms within. As a balloon expands, so too the self takes shape, rising up through the veils of constricted awareness. With this clearer, more vibrant view of self, comes the realization that conscious care and nurturance are crucial for further growth and expansion.

As we continue to gather the essential fuel and information from the self-discovery phase and are permeated with more of who we are, we can begin to practice the art of self-centering. This third phase has more to do with balance and alignment than the negative connotations of self-centeredness. In this process of centering the self, we become ready to be in the world, standing firmly on the Earthly ground with our missions of service in hand.

During this self-centering phase, we create our own magnetizing arrows, with energy lines going further in and at the same time back out. These energetic arrows begin to form the infinite figure 8. Self-care practices are crucial here for these are the routines and rituals we develop to nurture and feed the self. Inherent in self-care practices is the ability to see oneself. We can see ourselves, know who we are, and what we intend by how we show up with consistent self-care practices in our lives. Practices can be as simple as being conscious of our breath, taking bubble baths and walking in the woods. Or they can be practices that demand more discipline like daily meditation, bodywork, inspirational reading and conscious acts of kindness. *The most important thing is simply to value your self enough to show up for practice everyday.* Inherent in self-care practices is pushing the pause button on the "life VCR." Most of us are so busy rewinding for missed scenes or fast-forwarding to future scenes, that we rarely pause to see the scene in front of us. When we pause to go within, we access tremendous amounts of fuel that we can then use to finally push the play button! Practices simply help us pause to see the within, value it and bring it back out into the world. Remember, practice is the commitment to show up consistently with activities that make you conscious of the self in body, mind, heart and spirit. In practicing self-care we become centered, balanced and steadier in our mission to be in and with life.

As the self grows and continues to actualize, we begin to feel stronger and more self-assured about showing up in the world around us. We may begin to paint, write, sing or dance and in this outward expression, we begin to have the opportunity to see ourselves in the world. We have proof that what we feel within has in its outward expression a concrete manifestation of its vitality and existence. We begin creating things in the world around us that further validate the world of the self within. This inward-out rhythm of creating self has the power to change the world around us. Instead of having the world define and decide who we are (as in the phase of self-estrangement), we, through our own outward manifestation of who we are, begin to define, instruct and construct what and how the world is. This can be a very comforting stage as we begin to see and feel more self-constancy as the outer world begins to match and be in rhythm with the ever changing inner world.

The self now becomes ready for the most intriguing and invigorating fourth phase of self-service. This is probably the most misunderstood phase in this self-actualizing process. During this phase, the self begins to realize its more Divine origins, connecting with the more spiritual nature of self. We examine questions of meaning and purpose as well as issues of transcendence. Here the self becomes hungry for self-expansion not so much for the purposes of the individual self but more for the purposes of everything else surrounding the self. In our deepest wish to be connected to all and to finally cease the pains of imagined or real separation, we begin the process of offering our unique sacred gifts of self to *All That Is*. Through serving, we become united with the world instead of separate from the world. We become more connected to others through the active motion of giving rather than the waiting stance of receiving. The best gift we receive is this heightened and expanded view of who we are. It's important to note here, that as we offer our services, we don't lose our sense of self, but rather become more conscious of our connection to All That Is beyond the self. As we become more conscious, we become less distinguishable from *All That Is!* Love and compassion easily become the fuel for this service. Often, people will join causes where they share more mutual and common concerns like that of the environment or world peace. Finally, in giving our soulful missions to the world, we become part of global service. As we become united in this global healing process, we offer the biggest gift to the self as well. A figure 8 is formed, whereby our very act of "being self" is nurtured as the unique self/service that lies within expands out into the world. We are fully seen and can fully see the world. We can continuously expand and grow. Our wish to be of service is actually our deepest wish: to be nonseparate and transcended!

The fifth and final stage, self-merging, is where the self merges and unites with *All That Is*. Metaphorically, the raindrop finally drops into the sea and becomes part of the vast ocean of *All That Is*. The human self or ego loses consciousness of itself as the soul comes into full "beingness" and becomes indistinguishable from the Divine sea of sacred consciousness. Paradoxically, it's our individual consciousness and our sense of separated self that begins this journey in life and yet it's our individual consciousness that will take us once again to this merging moment where self-separation and ego dies and soul/divinity merging lives. Typically this has been written about in reference to yogis and masters like Jesus Christ and Buddha. In some mystical way that most of us don't understand, they've let us know that humans are capable of walking this Earth in human form while in this Divine sacred state.

Before you become too overwhelmed with the enormous possibilities and extraordinary difficulties awaiting you in this self-journey, let me share some of my own personal experience. Amazingly enough simply being present with the tasks of one stage creates the necessary fuel for the next. As I discover new things about myself, I naturally begin to do more balancing and centering self-care practices so that I can actually hold more discoveries. As I feel more centered and balanced, I'm more and more motivated to share these discoveries with the world around me. At this point my service intentions become clearer and more enticing. For instance, I have found a renewed vigor for my psychotherapy practice as I'm much more invested and capable (when I'm balanced and centered) in helping others see and actualize themselves. As I have learned about the part of me that is more patient and gentle, I have been able to see new ways of understanding others. This expanded vision of my clients has inspired me not only to hold their "Self-work" more compassionately, but has allowed me to be more present in their self-actualizing journeys. On a personal basis, I have decided to work daily on giving up judgment as one of my services. I'm amazed that as I walk through the world with less and less judgment, I feel more and more a part of the world and less and less threatened by it. In the midst of these services I've had flashes of "soul-merging." At these times, I become acutely aware of the Divine intelligence surrounding everything and for brief moments feel merged with *All That Is*. Because these experiences have been so extraordinary, I find myself more committed than ever to both my self-care practices and my service practices. And so, one stage influences and fires the next.

It should be noted that all throughout life we continue to visit the different stages. Self-evolution isn't fixed in its direction or phase. We can easily be in service one day and become self-estranged the next. We are too complex and interesting to have this self-development process be linear and finite. Rather, it more closely resembles a spiraling staircase that we travel up and down many times in a lifetime. Each time, winding another strand of ourselves until we've woven a bridge to eternity.

So you see, we must awaken from self-estrangement, so that we can begin to use the self as the vehicle to travel back to the oneness of all. The self is the only instrument we have...it's time to "know thyself" so that we might recognize once again the exquisite beauty of being in the oneness of *All That Is*.

Soul Remedies

#3 – The Wide World Within

Take a moment and breathe new life-giving air
into the very center of your core.

Become aware of this world within…
Know this is the most important place for you to be…
For it's the most powerful resource in the world.
Stay with it…don't go away…

Now turn your attention to your deepest layers of energy…
the energy that has been untouched by outside influence.
Let this core place speak to you…
what does it say…how does it feel…does it have
color, tones, temperature, taste, texture, or time?
Understand that this inner core can and will
manifest everything you need and want.

Imagine that your very attention to this core
causes your energy to slowly vibrate and move.
Follow this current, this symphonic movement,
through the sacred figure 8.
Take this ride at your own pace…

Feel the magic of being connected
to the Divine realm and the Earth realm
all at the same time.
You never have to feel separation again.
You are this flow.
You are both self and All That Is beyond self.
Now…put this book down and practice celebrating!

4

The Original Blueprint: Maps from Eternity

"Our deepest fear is not that we are inadequate. Our deepest fear is that we are powerful beyond measure. It is our light, not our darkness, that frightens us. We ask ourselves, who am I to be gorgeous, talented and fabulous? Actually who are you not to be? You are a child of God. Your playing small doesn't serve the world. There's nothing enlightened about shrinking so that other people won't feel insecure around you. We were born to manifest the glory of God within us. It's not just in some of us; it's in everyone. And as we let our own light shine, we unconsciously give other people permission to do the same."
—Nelson Mandela

"I am me. In all the world there is no one else exactly like me."
—Virginia Satir

Each of us came into this life with an original blueprint. It lies deep within and holds our unique design for this particular life. It's Divinely created and therefore, soul directed. This blueprint came from the eternal realm and resides within our soul's knowledge. It holds information not only about our Divine heritage, but also about how to manifest our soul truths in this Earth journey. Some of us never reach the chambers that hold this original blueprint as we have become convinced that the blueprints others have given us are the ones we must follow. We have forgotten long ago that these sacred scrolls exist within us.

As we begin to follow this original blueprint, we come into the Prime Directive for this life. Prime Directive is the overall direction from the Divine universal source. As we build the structures for soul directed living from this blueprint we come into clearer and clearer focus with the Divine Design. The Prime Directive is that calling from the Divine Source that, like a light, shines upon us and activates our original blueprint into full manifestation. Anytime we are following the design from this original sacred blueprint, we are in the light of the Prime Directive. Prime Directive is Source driven; original blueprint is the individual activation of such directive.

Much of what ails us is a direct result of living out of alignment with our sacred blueprint. There are three conscious actions necessary in the blueprinting process: ***attentiveness, recognition*** and ***actualization***. First, through ***attentiveness***, we must realize, know and direct the concentrated energy of our awareness towards these sacred scrolls within. We can choose to become much more attentive towards this process of discerning our blueprint by learning to pause daily to look mindfully and listen carefully to the voices within. Second, we must learn how to ***recognize*** and read these maps so we can take charge of the choices we make and the directions we move. Third, we must learn how to ***actualize*** and manifest our blueprint's intent. Once begun, this process is a naturally unfolding journey where each step fuels the next. At the very moment that we consciously attend to our unique soul design, we begin to recognize and remember various facets of this blueprint. This very recognition causes the manifestation process to come into action.

Before we can learn to recognize our own original blueprinting process, it's important to be able to identify all the other blueprints that we have superimposed on our own. I call this the blueprint overlaying process. Throughout life, we accumulate many external maps for building dreams and achieving goals in life. It becomes difficult to hear the callings from our deepest place within. The most influential externalized blueprint comes from those given to us by our parents. In our culture, we have lived with the popular myth that parents know best and therefore, must mold their children like a wood sculptor carves his wood. We have not yet mastered creating environments that allow for individual blueprint expression while providing safety, care and love. Perhaps, when we are able to each actualize our own sacred blueprint, we will discover more clearly how to parent someone else's blueprinting process.

Most of our parents have lived lives of unactualized dreams where huge parts of their original blueprint were not even recognized, let alone manifested into being. In desperate attempts to realize their own potential, parents often try to give their children their unactualized blueprints. They may feel the presence of some deep prodding, but have never had the opportunity for its fulfillment. They know, perhaps unconsciously, the importance of some inner resource and the process of manifesting its gifts, but have never done so. In their wish to acknowledge this, they unknowingly decide that we should manifest such abilities, talents, goals and dreams. I have seen many people who want to blame their parents for imposing a set of goals and guidelines that don't fit their own, which has no doubt stifled their growth. The problem, of course, is that no two people can have the exact same blueprint. Oftentimes our parents sacred purposes in life have little to do with our own. The hardest, yet most crucial, task for a parent is to provide an atmosphere of self/soul development where the natural blueprinting process that lies within the child can come to fruition without interference. Until we allow for the uniqueness of each one of us, we will hamper this unfolding process.

A parent who was a teenager in the era of the 60's had always had a wish and desire to play in a rock band. He felt a deep inner calling to play the guitar and pleaded with his parents until finally in high school they bought him a cheap guitar. He taught himself to play and consistently practiced until his fingers bled. His parents still insisted that he take piano and trumpet lessons, for these were "acceptable" musical pursuits. There was no doubt that he had exceptional musical talent, but he was never reinforced for the true activation of his inner blueprint. He began to despise his music lessons, because they took time away from what he really loved, his guitar. When he went to college, although encouraged to major in music, he quit playing all instruments. He did ask his parents on several occasions if he could join a rock band, which apparently he had ample opportunities to do. But, his parents insisted that if he did, they would not pay for his college education.

Now as an adult, he has returned to the love of the guitar and plays in a band for weddings and other festive events. His parents, upon hearing his band commented that they never knew he could play the guitar so well! Now, he has another dilemma, his own son seems to have an inclination towards the violin. He initially tried to expose his son to guitars, drums and all other potential rock world instruments. He admitted that of all the stringed instruments, the violin was not something he wanted his son to play. Remembering his own painful experience, he has succumbed and let his son develop what seems to be an extraordinary talent with the violin. What he may not be quite aware of, is that as he gives permission to his son to actualize his gifts, he is also at that moment actualizing one of his most beautiful gifts, his love. After all, love fuels everything else into active manifestation!

All of us also have converging influences from other outside sources as well. There are general blueprint designs that show up in our educational systems, in our communities, and in our churches. We are given blueprints for success, blueprints for learning, blueprints on how to worship God and even blueprints for living and dying. A typical blueprint found in middle America defines a successful home as that which houses a husband and a wife who share similar ethnic and religious backgrounds, children, a two car garage and plenty of material comforts. Yet, many homes were not built with this blueprint in mind and therefore the inhabitants are given messages that they miss the mark in mainstream America. Families are being redefined as we have more families with mixed ethnic, racial and religious orientations as well as single parent families, step families and same sex marriages. Until we are able to honor each person's unique blueprint manifestation as a choice that must be made, many of these folks may see themselves as failures rather than understanding they are forging new territory of actualizing their own blueprint design. Certainly our culture's view of mainstream heterosexual marriages has caused much harm to those who have come to live with same sex partners. We are just beginning to learn how to really love, and until we do, no one can dictate to us the recipe for complete loving.

Another interesting example of group blueprinting can be found in our educational programming. Most of us went to schools where the classroom was set up for left-brain learning. Our left-brain seems especially adept at learning language, solving problems and linear thinking. Our right brain houses our more intuitive skills and creative endeavors. If you happened to be well endowed in your left-brain, you probably did quite well in school. However, if you are particularly gifted in the creative arts or have a learning disability, you may have graduated from the schooling system with the mind set that you're not very intelligent. We have discovered, that in fact, many learning disabled children simply can't process information through the left brain, but are perfectly able to learn through right brain methods and may have exceptional skills that otherwise would go unnoticed.

There are so many examples of group blueprinting processes that have hampered the actualizing process of our own unique designs. One very interesting grouping is that of your gender group. Gender role stereotyping has caused enormous suppression of self-expression and actualized talents. Certainly, in my own generation, girls and boys were told very different things about what they might be good at, simply because they were a boy or girl. Girls were good as helpers and boys were good as doers. Girls were not that good at math; boys were not that good at cooking. Girls were very good in art, and boys were exceptional in athletics. The list goes on and on. Sadly, many individuals have failed to know their most important gifts within, simply because of their gender. I wonder sometimes how many formulas for the cure for cancer have been left hidden in some untapped scientific corner of the female mind. Or, how many formulas for peace lie unnoticed in the hearts of men because they were told to make war not peace. Stereotyping, no matter what group it's aimed at, is one of the most insidious obstacles impeding the self-actualization process.

Meticulously drawn maps for the "God experience" can be found in our churches and temples. Many of our religious institutions have very specific ideologies for mapping our relationship to God including the rituals employed for Divine practices. Unfortunately, so many times these impede our own understanding of our relationship to God. They become substitutions for our own experience with the Divine. So many times these practices do not resonate. Nor do they allow for personal experiences with God. One of my clients related a story that broke my heart. She was attending a Catholic grade school and asked the nun teaching her class several questions about religion. She remembers two specific questions, one: did Jesus ever show up in the Here and Now and two: could God be felt inside? The nun harshly reprimanded her for these questions and in no uncertain terms told her that if Jesus ever did show up he would only show up for the chosen few, namely priests and saints and second God was too good to be inside humans especially in someone like herself. This had a lasting impact on her. It shamed her and devalued the relationship she thought she had been having with both Jesus and God. From then on, God always seemed so distant and unreachable and she never felt good enough to ask for help even in prayer. Many people I see seem to be struggling in their pursuit of spiritual or religious practices. They feel abandoned by their childhood religion while others simply feel a lack of inner resonance. We all have a sacred/Divine part to our unique blueprint that relates to spiritual matters. We must be willing to take responsibility for exploring this part and hopefully our religious choices will then support and strengthen this part, instead of dictate and limit it.

I remember sitting in church every Sunday when I was a little girl, thinking God must be pretty big and austere and therefore seemed difficult to reach. Yet, after church I would ride my horse all afternoon in the country, and find God everywhere. I could see God's handiwork in all the nature around me, and this soon became my time to commune with God. I thought that must be why so many people take car rides in the country on Sunday afternoons. I decided that it must be the church building and the "rules" of the church that made the service so stifling and serious. For some reason, you had to dress up and sit very still. Luckily, I have never thought that God was quite so serious and was probably gently laughing at how still and proper we were all for the sake of HIM/HER. I always believed that God showed up no matter what you wore or how loud you were. Somehow I allowed this bigger than life figure of the Divine to resonate with my own inner sense of sacredness, and together, we were on a path. Fortunately, I have always felt Divine urgings to actualize my unique soul blueprint. Otherwise, you would not be reading this book.

Our inner callings often are buried by the outside demands of the external world. Some of us may be called by artistic, athletic or spiritual endeavors, and if we are lucky enough, we may grow up in atmospheres that foster this calling. Few of us, however, grow up in unconditional atmospheres, where any and all interests, abilities, talents, etc. are reinforced and nurtured. Usually, these callings are shaped by what is reinforced and nurtured. Some may have musical talents or interests but never have exposure to musical instruments. A girl may have unusual abilities in science or mechanics, but never actualize them because she is told girls don't do those things. Others may love to move their bodies in dance and sport, but are told they will never be good enough to make a life income from these endeavors. Yet, some children and adults have such strong propensities from their blueprint that nothing seems to stop them. Nevertheless, the outside world does play a role in triggering and stimulating or dampening and dimming these deep resources from within.

Following the inner passion for individual blueprint manifestation is most difficult against the backdrop of choices, whispers and shouts from the outside world. These external blueprint vendors vigorously sell maps guiding you to plentiful pleasures and unseen treasures. Just be careful when you cannot locate yourself on the map. The external world is an incredible place to gather resources and raw materials for this life journey. However, much too often the external world becomes the life journey. We should visit other blueprinting processes, much like we visit homes when we are thinking of building our own home. We go to see what we might like or what we don't like and to feel what resonates with us. In the same way, external blueprints for living are helpful for a sampling process or a resonance process, but too many times we take on outside blueprints and give up the search for our own.

We also have global and universal blueprints. Our global blueprinting has to do with our status as Earth beings. We have information in this blueprint that teaches us how to be connected to all living things on this Earth. It's here that we begin to understand the interconnectedness of all things on Earth. Unlike other group blueprinting processes, we seem to have lost touch with this vast storehouse of information. Indigenous cultures can teach us much about Earth consciousness and global concerns and we had better listen and learn. Our individual survival depends on this global consciousness.

Finally there is the universal blueprint. The holographic model of the universe suggests that we contain all the information of all universes. In other words, we hold all of the information that is within us and beyond us. This is perhaps the most mysterious blueprint of all. It unifies all and yet holds the unique pattern of each individual living thing. When we are in touch with the maps held here, we are at one with the oneness of all. It's a natural requirement that before we can walk down the halls of these universal maps we must by definition manifest our own unique design. The keys to this universal corridor can only be found in the midst of our unique design manifestation process.

We have so many prescribed practices in our culture for reaching spiritual attunement, physical well-being, emotional health and intellectual accomplishment. We are actually very fortunate that we have so much access to so many outlets and occasions for exploration in this culture. In fact, it's the very depth and breadth of these opportunities that offer evidence of the incredibly vast resource system that lives within us. It's only when these practices become dogma and destination instead of path and process that I think damage is done. All of these activities and endeavors can be utilized to stimulate and vibrate the blueprinting process within. But, in many cases they are used to take the place of, rather than to foster, this internal yearning process of soul birthing. It's not so surprising that our original blueprint has been buried underneath reams of paper designs and mechanisms of architectural dreams.

It's important to remember that when we follow the directions on maps created outside of ourselves, we can, by definition, never feel truly fulfilled. Our feeling of loss associated with this has its deeper roots in the loss of discovering our Divine uniqueness and therefore our true mission in life. In our desperate attempts to honor the designs that have been handed to us by the outside world, by parents, educators, rightdoers, wrongdoers and psychic viewers, we confuse failing to perfectly construct the structures outlined in their plans to mean that we ourselves are failures. We then carry a distinct feeling of being half empty and unfulfilled on our life journey. What a relief to realize that these very feelings of dissatisfaction and incompleteness are not about success or failure in the external world. Instead these feelings are crucial in calling our attention towards the beautiful labyrinth within. Were it not for disillusionment and discontentment, we might never wake to the vision of the golden temples found along self-manifesting paths. The only real feeling of success, or fulfillment, or completion we can possible have is through our own discovery of our internal, Divinely planted blueprints. No one else's plan, no matter how grand, can ever fill our balloon with enough air to keep it afloat. We can only know true expansion as we actualize ourselves from the inside out.

As we develop our own blueprint, we will find different ears and eyes within ourselves that can see and hear and interpret all other blueprints. We have deep within us our own unique perceptual organs that can understand the importance of blueprints from family, race, gender, religion, global and other sources. We will not remain divided and separate from all of these larger blueprints, but can now begin to know our unique role in them. All of these things tell an important piece of the story, but they are not the story. So many times when people come to see me for therapy, they've constructed who they think they are from their stories. They birth themselves from their histories, their life facts and the narratives that narrowly define who and what they've been in their life. Instead we should look at the chronicles of our lives and learn about the nature and design of our own internal Divine diagram. During our lives, we are exposed to a variety of things and with each exposure comes an experience that tells a story about what we hold within. All of these experiences simply prepare us for being on the path of blueprint actualization.

So, just what is it that keeps us from this more natural process of "true self being?" As discussed previously, we must certainly be willing to examine our attachment to externalized blueprints and measure our willingness to explore our internal world of prints and designs. But a more compelling question is: What *internal* fears keep us out? Initially it looks like we are afraid that nothing is really there. We would rather live removed from our blueprint than find out it isn't inside us at all. This isn't so dissimilar to atheists who, rather than think God exists and someday find God does not, would rather believe from the get go that there is no God. Atheists are actually repressed believers, for it's their conscious stance that God does not exist that protects their yearnings for God to exist. So, we may do the same with our beliefs about our internal world. Perhaps it's better to believe that it doesn't exist and pay little attention to it, rather than pay attention to it and find nothing is there. So many clients of mine, shout the refrain, "But wonder if there's nothing there?" I always follow this with the question, "By the way who is asking that question?"

Of course the next fear we encounter, if indeed we are willing to don the explorer's cap and take the risk of traversing within, is, "Okay but wonder if I do find this blueprint thing, wonder if it isn't good enough?" Abandonment fears constantly seem to be lurking around every corner. Finding your blueprint aspirations are one thing, but manifesting them so the world will see them is quite another. Then you really will be open for criticism, judgment and rejection. If you decide to imitate other people's designs, at least then you can blame them if it doesn't look right. If you actually bring your unique design into the world, the world could openly abandon you. I have only one comment to this: self-abandonment can be a life sentence, causing the deepest wounds and most suffocating suffering. Abandonment caused by others is most often time limited and whimsical. Yet, you are still left with the exhilaration of experiencing your deepest places of truth all on your own, freed from all others. Socrates stated this oh so long ago, that to know thyself was the greatest task of life.

Beyond fearing nothing or fearing smallness, our greater fear is illustrated by Nelson Mandela as he stated in the quote at the beginning of this chapter, "Our deepest fear isn't that we are inadequate. Our deepest fear is that we are powerful beyond measure. It's our light, not our darkness that frightens us." We are terribly afraid of our grandness because we have no paradigms for exploring, honoring and celebrating our unique individual grandness. No wonder it feels scary to explore this fairly unknown place within. We are much more familiar with our smallness than our bigness. In addition, our grandness puts us in touch with our expansiveness and the last time we felt so expansive we were not embodied. So interestingly, the experience of expansion and grandness may bring us closer to death fears. We may fear that if we really expand and grow past old concepts of self, old parts will indeed die away, and new parts will expand until the self is lost in the oneness of all. Doing this kind of psychospiritual work does often bring the experience of both birth and death.

Luckily, if you have made it this far, you've probably begun to realize the paradoxical dilemma you are now in. *To do this work of blueprint manifestation, your personality (the old you) may go through a death of sorts and yet to refuse to do this work means certain death to the true self and the soaring soul within.* Welcome to the mysterious world of metamorphic self-spinning transformation.

At the beginning of the chapter, I discussed three important processes for blueprint actualization: attentiveness, recognition and manifestation. I would like to suggest some ways in which to pursue these conscious actions.

Attentiveness

This first is the action of awareness. Your waking consciousness shifts from the outside world toward your inside world. This may sound easy enough, but for many people this seems to be the hardest of the three actions to take. This is where we become reacquainted with our own unique world within. The power of your conscious intentions is crucial here. *For action follows the energy of intentions.*

INTENTION #1: I give attention and awareness to the beauty of my inside world.

INTENTION #2: I give this attention without judgment and with unconditional regard.

INTENTION #3: I make a conscious effort to check in with myself at least three times a day.

By the very act of stating Intention #1, you already have shifted your attention towards your inner world. Don't underestimate the power of this shift. Remember, your attention has been fixated on everything that surrounds you and is analogous to a speeding car traveling down a six-lane highway heading all the while towards some outside destination. Shifting this attentiveness is like stopping this 120 mph car and turning it around. Your ego will scream out, "You can't change directions, we have places we need to go, don't take your eyes off the road you will crash, you will never get anywhere if you turn around!" You are not only shifting the speed at which you have been traveling, but you are shifting the direction as well. At this point you can see how well your outside blueprint destinations have solidified in your mind field and in your personality as your idea of who you truly are.

In order to be successful with this, it's important to carry certain attitudes with you when you make this shift and visit this inner land.

Always pause and check your attitude: remember nonjudgmental and unconditional regard are crucial if the many parts of you are going to come out of hiding. Awareness requires nothing else but alertness, wakefulness and consciousness. When you first begin to see your inner world you will be tempted to run commentary on what seems to be there. Many beginning students of meditation know, all too well, how the mind interrupts the process of silent meditation. Note your attitude shifts as you pay attention to your inner world, constantly bringing your awareness back to Intention #2: nonjudgmental and unconditional regard. When we have really accomplished this for ourselves, we truly will then be able to accomplish this in the world towards all other living beings.

It's important then to set guidelines for yourself in space and time. We are three-dimensional beings and as a result to do live in all three dimensions. Human beings have much difficulty with discipline especially as it relates to time and space constructs. So many people I have seen over the years, comment that they understand the importance of self but have no time to do anything about it. This seems to be quite a contradictory statement, don't you think? The effort we put into bringing these actions into our daily lives will begin to solidify our commitment to actualizing our soul's mission and building our intended soul blueprint. *Without daily practice, actions have no path to follow.* It's crucial to make a conscious effort to check in at least three times each day. This can be as formal as meditation practices or as informal as simply pausing and bringing the conscious thought to my mind: *What am I doing inside right now?* Keep the four check points in mind: body, mind, heart and spirit.

You have enormous power simply in your attentiveness and awareness. You can create everything you want in your life. First, you need to know what you truly want to create. Shifting your attention to your inner world without conditions is one of the most powerful actions you can take to manifest all your dreams.

Recognition

With so much stored inside of us (remember the ring chapter), it's difficult to begin to sort through what material we want to pay attention to. It isn't an easy process to distinguish our own blueprint raw materials from all the others we have gathered over the years.

Here are some clues.

Signs you are not in your native blueprint state:

- Restlessness.
- Feeling unfulfilled, depressed, dissatisfied discontent and disillusioned.
- A deep sense of longing and yearning.
- Short-lived feelings of accomplishment.
- Feeling slightly out of focus even when pursuing "important" tasks in life.

These are just but a few signs that you can begin to recognize as clues that you are not fulfilling your own unique destiny. When you are working or playing or loving, you can use these cues as signals that intimate that you are choosing to focus your energy on things that are at least slightly removed from your deeper blueprint plan. This is just the beginning stage for you to know and embrace your truths. Living in your soul truths is the most precious and inspiring thing a human can do.

Signs you are in your blueprint plan:

- Feelings that you do not want to be anywhere else.
- Feelings of fullness and depth.
- Absence of yearning and longing.
- Feeling as if whatever you are concentrating on has come into sharp and lucid focus.
- Contentment and fulfillment.
- Peace and calm.
- Clarity of mind and illumination.

Again, if you have even momentary times when you experience the above, note carefully what you are doing, where, who with, how you are feeling. You will begin to gather the many pieces of your beautiful mosaic puzzle so that you can begin to weave them together in manifesting your unique design.

Fostering your intuition is absolutely crucial at this stage. It will be your intuition that will be the most ardent messenger of blueprint clues. We all have an intuitive tracking system that we've learned to disregard too many times in too many places. How many times have you gone to an event or agreed to do something even when an inner voice said "NO." Start tracking these inner voices. Invite them to speak to you again, only louder. You'll have to invite these inner voices out, again and again, because you've subdued and suppressed them, and many of them have stopped speaking altogether. We must stop suppressing our inner cues about what feels good and what feels bad. I always ask myself the following questions when I am doing just about anything in my life: *Is this my truth right now? How happy am I with this? And most importantly is this who I want to be?*

It's absolutely crucial to recognize how much you dismiss yourself. Is it any wonder that you're out of touch with your deepest yearnings for life? If you listen closely, you'll begin to know what your body needs for wellness, what your heart needs for love, what your mind needs for fuel and what your spirit needs to soar.

Body questions:	What do I need to eat and how do I need to move today?
Heart questions:	How do I want to love and give of myself today?
Mind questions:	What thoughts inspire my mind today?
Spirit questions:	What uplifts my spirit and how much gratitude do I have today?

Whatever comes to mind as answers to these questions should simply be noted and seen. Too many times we get caught in the how's, when's and where's. For instance, I know what my body wants to eat today, but I don't have time to go to the store and make it for dinner. Even if I cannot follow through with an actual response or action, I have only to recognize the language of my internal world. Perhaps, everyday I will get up and have the thought of being in nature, but the business of my day prevents me from going to the country. Eventually as I *attend to and recognize* this thought, this feeling, it will gather enough energy, enough volume and mass that I will soon arrange a weekend in the country where nature abounds.

We all have of these answers inside of us. We always have. It's simply time to come home again. We no longer have to be afraid to recognize ourselves and listen to the internal voices when they speak. There are vast mapping systems inside that all lead to our unique place in the world. In recognizing these answers, we are one step away from actualizing our lives.

Actualization

This is the fun stage. For it's here that we can begin to "try out" all that we've begun to recognize inside. The biggest mistake people make here is trying to manifest too much too soon. The old models of success, outcome measurements and accomplishments come rushing in as judges for this contest of active participation. The most important thing to remember: *Start with the smallest aspects of the self and life will become beautifully detailed.*

Action is the confirming experience of what you know within. Action is concrete evidence that you have been listening to you. Action is the follow through, the vote of confidence that you indeed believe in your unique design. Failure or success has nothing to do with this process of actualization. It's the active experience of you that is the only measure of actualization. Judging how you did when you tried something is commentary and has relatively little to do with the experience itself. The only true measurement of the action is the experience. Judgment is only a comparison to another person's experience.

So, test out what you like and what you are about. Often, people ask me what books to read and even what music to listen to. Although I certainly have favorite books and music, my choices are more about my experience than anything else. So I suggest that they fuel themselves with curiosity and intrigue and take an intuitive journey to the bookstore. It may be as simple as sitting in front of the section you are interested in and picking out a book by its cover if nothing else calls to you. Begin somewhere and don't analyze so quickly whether you made the right choice. I have a client who has spent her whole life debating over her choices and decisions. She's terrified of making the wrong choice and, as a result, often chooses to do nothing. She still has a hard time realizing that "to do nothing" is a choice she makes and it's this choice that causes her the most pain. To jump, leap, skip and fall is far better than to never leap at all. So follow your whims, even when they make no sense remember *nothing is what it seems but everything is a clue!*

I grew up in a musical family and have always loved music. My sister was a concert pianist and so I always felt awkward about taking up this instrument. Nevertheless, several years back, I decided on a whim to buy a small electric piano with the hope of learning to play it. It sat in a very special place in my study and every time I walked past this room, I would longingly look at the piano, but just didn't ever consistently play it. In fact, I played it very little. I got a lot of heat from the person I was living with at the time, with statements like, "Why do you get things and never use them?" At some point, feeling guilty about my expenditure, I gave the piano to my ten year old neighbor girl, who seemed to enjoy banging on it more than I. Two years ago, I rented a piano for a family reunion, thinking my sister could play tunes and we would all sing around the piano. Late at night I began playing it (even though I thought I didn't know how to play). Tunes came into my mind and then into my hands from "out of nowhere." From that point on, I began making up my own compositions. My mother, noticing how much I seemed to enjoy this, bought me one for the following Christmas. This was an amazing event on many levels. The fact that my mother actually paid attention to a "blueprint birthing" process and responded with such a mindful act was extraordinary. I allowed myself to continue to listen to the creative process within and have composed music without ever taking a lesson. Sometimes, important blueprint actualization processes take time to be birthed. It isn't always easy to respect this with attitudes of patience and faith. Little did I know that in following a whim eight years ago, I was setting the motion for manifesting this creative potential that now results in beautiful musical compositions (at least to me).

That is why it's crucial when you first begin to bring life to your inner intuitions, whims and wishes that you do not judge their value at first sight. This is a time when hobbies should definitely be explored. I've noticed that old dreams and talents come alive again through "leisure time pursuits." When it's clear to me that someone is working at a profession that isn't fostering their unique gifts and talents, I first ask them to pursue an activity outside of work that sparks them. If you don't have time for a hobby, then you probably will never have time to actualize your blueprint!

There's no question that we can be much happier when we are actualizing our unique designs. It's a win-win situation. We are fulfilling our own destinies as well as adding a unique service (through our unique actions) to the world. If everyone were doing this, I can't even imagine what we could accomplish in this world. When I am expanding from the inside out, by definition I am more full. This causes enormous peace and contentment not because of the product I am producing, but because of the experience of being in all of who I am. Every time I sit down to write this book and am concerned about outcome, I cannot write very well and certainly the process becomes tiresome and tedious. But, when I write because it's in the flow of my blueprint manifestation, I feel happy and relieved. Then I'm in the action of my truth. First we must attend, then recognize and then put what we recognize into action. So much of our unhappiness and discontentment is about not being in our unique truth. We use the experience of feeling disengaged and disillusioned to further condemn who we are instead of realizing that we feel that way because we've not been who we are.

Imagine that we are all full of beautiful strings. Each one of us has a different set of strings like no other. Manifesting our blueprint is analogous to these strings resounding all at once, creating an orchestra of beautiful unique melodies. Oftentimes, however, we get such pressure to sound like violins that we distort our strings in a manner to mimic a violin sound. Perhaps our strings are meant to sound more like a cello, and no matter how we try, we cannot make the sound exactly like a violin because the strings are simply different. If we get reinforcement for this, we begin to think that this act of distortion is our life task. Soon, we may even forget the natural shape of our strings and we may think that the sound created from our true strings should not be heard. At some point, we forget we had these beautiful cello strings at all. There can never be a more fulfilled moment, a more realized moment, a more complete moment than that when we begin to pluck our own strings from their natural state which creates their own pitch, tone and vibrancy. In that moment we know from a deep experiential level that this note, this tone, is perfect. Perfect in how it has always been meant to sound and feel. The vibration goes through us and begins to resonate with all the other strings that have been left unstroked and untouched. A symphony begins that has never once been heard before. Although some people have become amazingly adept at sounding like a violin, they will never have the same feeling hearing these notes as when they hear their very own naturally produced sounds. Sometimes we want others to play our notes because we are too scared to play these same notes (the coward), or because we think these notes are so sublime everyone should play them (the narcissist). Each person can only play their music the way it was intended to be played.

None of us can really know what notes another should play until they've been played. If you listen with your 'heart ears' you can tell when someone is playing notes that are Divinely inspired from the blueprint within. When someone is playing their very own song, you know and feel its truth. You feel moved. It resounds somewhere deep within you, not that you recognize the notes themselves, but you recognize blueprint actualization process. You can feel the vibrations that come from this resounding energy that's released when the blueprint is being actualized and is in movement. Recognizing someone else in this unique "truth movement" does not have to separate us but can unite us. Often we feel envy because we may know that someone is doing something we've not done. At this point, we may go into the judgment mode, especially if is occurs to us that we've never heard the exact notes before. We might begin to criticize the notes and decide we don't even like hearing them. After all, the person isn't that good at playing the notes anyway. We may quickly forget the link we felt to the process and only hear the outcome. This is simply one more way we distance ourselves not only from others but, from our own blueprint actualizing process. If you hang out long enough with a blueprint manifestor you will begin to actualize the movement towards your own treasures within. This is one of the most poignant and stirring forces that motivate us to view art, hear music and read books. These are just my words, but let the movement of these words move you back to you! Open, open, open.

Imagine now…that everyone simultaneously played their set of strings exactly how they were meant to played. We would hear an orchestra of sound that has never been heard on this planet before. Perhaps this is the music that people who have had near death experiences have heard. Can we decide that we don't have to wait for heaven to hear this? If the sound from this chorus could cure all ailments in all beings including the Earth herself, would you sing the notes from your uniquely scripted blueprint? Or would you still be too afraid?

The Immersion Process

When we immerse ourselves into our very own blueprinting actualization process, this actually causes the Earth to shift ever so slightly into her own blueprinting process as well. Imagine that when we are thriving in our own blueprints, we actually are doing an enormous service for the Earth. You see, every time I step into my blueprint, it sends out energetic vibrations that call to other people, especially those with whom I am closely connected. This energy, like a magnet, calls up their own blueprint designs. So, when you are around people who are fulfilling their own destinies, it's contagious. It causes you to become aware of the need and desire hidden deep within you to do the same. Blueprint actualization causes on inward out motion within us. We are no longer taking from the world (outward in), but instead we are in the natural rhythm to give to the world. When we are immersed in blueprint manifestation, we create an energy field that can be felt by all life around us. So every time I step into mine, I make small shifts in other peoples ability to make small shifts and they make small shifts in others and so on and so on. Actualizing and manifesting the unique you is therefore one of the most important steps towards world service. This is one of the more intriguing life paradoxes: actualizing myself actually brings me the closest to all other actualized processes.

It's only when we are willing to remove ourselves from the doldrums of previously conceived notions of who we should be and move towards the truth of the uniqueness of who we really are that we begin to feel unified with all there is. In our experience of uniqueness, we will actually experience unification. If you are unwilling to experience your unique design, then you are unwilling to be human. If you are not willing to be human, you will always feel alienated from the human race. The process of blueprint manifestation is what we share. The designs are all different, and they are meant to be. We are all fingerprints of God, each different. The process of going through this is what brings us together. As I am unique, I am unified. Each one of us is a necessary piece to this grand puzzle called life As we bring our puzzle piece to the table, we can begin to see that we fit perfectly into this Earthly design. As we each actualize our soul intent as designed in our original blueprint within, we gather more and more energy from our Prime Directive, the Divine Source. It's my belief that as we take more and more responsibility for this process, we open up channels and become conduits for the Divine light of Sacred Source to join us in actualizing our Earth's blueprint. This is one more experience of the oneness created from simply being in total truth.

Soul Remedies

#4 – Blueprint Living

Relax and breathe into the middle of who you are.
Know that you house a beautiful map, unique to you,
that will guide you towards the most beautiful moments
you will have on Earth.

Take a moment to remember a moment when you felt that everything
was just right, a moment when you thought, life can't feel much better
than this. Perhaps, when you were on vacation, or witnessing some
beautiful scenery or in love. Remember a time when life felt full
and wonderful. Perhaps, it was only a fleeting moment,
but bring those feelings into the forefront of your mind
right now…

Now, multiply those moments a thousand, million times in intensity and
vibrancy and you will begin to come close to what it would feel like
to live in the process of your own blueprint manifestation.
See how long you can stay in this vision.
Breathe it in. Know it's already yours.

As you actualize your own blueprint destiny, your own unique truths,
your life will fill with the wonderment of the truth of who you really are.

And in this truth, you will finally know that life is exactly as it should be
and you will no longer have to wait for brief moments of
awestruck vibrancy,
but you will live in constant moments of
bursting, life-giving energy.

5

Presence As Path

"Don't let a mad world tell you that success
is anything other than a successful present moment."
–Eckhart Tolle

"When we are in the present moment, our work on Earth begins."
–Reshad Feild

"The 'past' is only a memory and the future is only a hope.
It is only the present, the now, that means anything to us,
as presence is what we are…"
–Nisargadatta

"Let the clock and the Earth do their own thing…
Let the comings and goings of life continue…
But YOU stay HERE and NOW!
This exercise is to bring you to the Eternal Present…
Where it all is."
–Ram Dass

The Power of Presence

The most powerful energy and most revealing experience of the universe can be found right here, right now in this very moment. After all, here is where the self resides, and now is where consciousness knows itself. Therefore, *when we lose our sense of "Here and Now," we have not only lost ourselves, but our awareness of ourselves as well.* Through the very powers of human intelligence, we have the ability to propel ourselves right out of this dynamic and powerful place and time called the present. It's one of the most puzzling paradoxes of human existence that we are perfect instruments for being in the experience of the Here and Now. Yet we misuse our most precious tool, our ability to be conscious, to escape this gifted place called the present. We spend so much time actually dimming our awareness of the now by obsessing about other places, other times, other realities. Interestingly enough, the most fundamental aspects of this three-dimensional world, time and space, have taken us far away from this moment, now. Since we have the ability to consciously travel on the continuum of both time and space, we can experience notions of the past, present and future, as well as spatial perceptions of being over there or over here. We seem to think by going to these distant reaches of the "there and then," we will be more capable of living fully now. However, as we search the annals holding past records of present moments, and ponder possible future installations of new moments, we avoid the effervescent now. Certainly, no one would argue the value in understanding past failures and dreaming future successes. Yet, no matter how much we understand the patterns in our own lives, as well as those passed down through generations, we still find ourselves in repetitive waves of struggle and surrender. Even as we plan for some future event, it never turns out exactly as we thought. Life continues to be a surprise, even to the most powerful among us. *One of the most intriguing and difficult paradoxes to grasp is the notion that as we let go and free ourselves of having to know the future in the "now," we are propelled into understanding that "right now" is what solely determines the future.* What we do with the present moment provides the only currents from which the future can be reached.

Furthermore, we may spend hours coveting our neighbor's place in space (over there), but we can't exchange places with another. We seem at least for now, to be forever seated in the space of here and the time of now. Yet, it seems an awesome task for many of us to succumb to momentary living. It's somewhat ironic that our biggest task is to find our way back to our truest home: the Here and Now. The motivation, however, should be deeply stirring, because the greatest energy, the greatest life, the greatest God, the greatest self is always in residence in the Here and Now. We have wasted enough time; we have wasted enough space. Ironically, living in full presence will aid and assist us in wasting less in all other places and in all other times.

Presence, then, is a concept to be experienced both in the here (space) and now (time). The power of all life force can only be found in this present moment and, as our awareness expands into the land of presence, the gates to infinity open. It's only our thinking that refuses to believe that consciousness lives forever. Yet, the energy of eternity lies in this present moment. There's nowhere else it can be found. We have just forgotten. This eternal life force energy is what powers all universes in all places and all times. *We, in our refusal of momentary awareness, have lost our true power.* Simply by becoming acutely aware of this moment, right here, right now, we can begin to traverse the steps of eternal wisdom. Imagine, just for a moment, that you had absolute knowledge that your sense of awareness never dies. How would that change your life? Many scientists say that we only use ten percent of our brains. What if you knew that by practicing the art of presence, you could turn on and open up the rest of your brain field? Would you do it? What would it take to live here, now? Interesting enough for many people, it takes some catastrophe, some life crisis for people to come back down to Earth and "smell the roses." However, in the meantime, valuable resources are wasted and buried in other lands, in other times.

Absence of Presence Precedes Absence of Wellness

In all the struggles I've seen people have, there's no bigger critical crisis than that of learning presence. It's at the heart of every other problem. Relationships dissolve because the participants have not learned how to truly be with one another. Yet most people get married for the gift of another's presence. Peace talks break down because agendas are already determined and solidified before anyone sits across from another. Ears that have been cemented in the past with particles of hate and dogma can't possibly hear another's desperate voice in the current moment. People have lost the art of listening and feeling another person's presence, let alone their worth and importance. We're much more concerned with our own issues and much less curious about another's experience. Life is, after all, lived at a terrifically fast pace and there's very little time to be curious and silent in the pause in between. We find ourselves moving through space with life's lists at hand, barely able to look up at the scenery passing by. Moments of now quickly become barely seen specks of landscape sliding by, lost in the land of travel guides and life diaries. Some of us may even pause long enough to note those fleeting moments as places we actually might want to return to if we ever had more time. However, we remain unaware that the place is less important than the *awareness of being in the place.* We can cover vast territories in fast times, but if we fail to be conscious of the experience itself, we will not remember being there! If we were truly present with our natural surroundings and conscious of the living, breathing planet we live on, wouldn't we be unable to pollute and ravage it? If the man on the bulldozer could pause and feel the vibrancy of the rain forest, would he be able to put his vehicle of destruction in forward motion to dismantle it? Most of us are in such a hurry to get through the forest, we forget to pause and see the active mechanisms of life itself. It's time to come out the den of denial and live in the reality of the marvelous, life-teeming world of presence.

As we traverse this path towards presence awareness, it's helpful to first understand that we often utilize built in mechanisms to purposely recede from the present moment. Sometimes these disappearing tactics are enormously beneficial. In severe trauma for instance, there's a psychological defense called dissociation wherein a person can fragment their attention from the current traumatic moment in order to be less aware and less present. The brain also has the kind capacity to forget horrific experiences so that memories of these experiences simply can't be found. Surprisingly, most of us utilize these tactics on a daily basis when we choose not to be present and forget important details. Anyone who has traveled a freeway probably is familiar with the dissociative experience. As they are mesmerized by their own mind thoughts, they may not remember when and how they took the right exit to arrive at their destination. We can all do this to some extent as we daydream during boring meetings. So, through dissociation, we can fragment our attention to be in two places at once (traveling down a highway and daydreaming) or, in extreme cases, to be entirely split off from the current place, as in trauma. For instance, people growing up with trauma and abuse learn to dissociate in order to save themselves from being too present to horrendous acts of cruelty from another human being. This actually is what helps the self survive! Unfortunately for people who utilize this defensive technique, the self may survive, but is unable to thrive. It's an ultimate paradox – in order to exist, the person must discover ways not to be present. In fact, we know as a result that certain areas in the brain itself begin to shut down and atrophy over time. Emotions, physical systems and the mind all learn to dim down in the presence of trauma cues. However, it's clearly difficult to fully function when systems are shut down. In my years of trauma work, I've understood the importance of presence work with trauma survivors in order to bring their consciousness back to the Here and Now in a safe and therapeutic environment. Sustained positive interactions in the present moment have been crucial not only healing psychological damage from childhood trauma, but, actually cultivating cell growth in atrophied areas in the limbic system of the brain. The limbic system is where our emotions are regulated. This has tremendous implications for us all. For even without trauma, people have a very difficult time staying present with themselves and the world. The ultimate goal of all therapy should be to help people become more conscious, aware and attentive to the present moment. This will lead to ultimate freedom, because when we don't have to disappear from life, the self-actualization process flourishes. Showing up with who we are is crucial for health. Repression, suppression and dissociation guarantee that we will stay incomplete and fragmented; continually held hostage in the world of non-presence.

A client came in the other day and stated she desperately needed to change her life. I asked her how much time she spent fully aware of herself in the moment. At first, she didn't understand what I meant and asked for clarification. I suggested that she keep a journal of the activities in her life that made her conscious of being present and aware of herself. She reluctantly agreed. The next week she came back dismayed and disgruntled stating that the journal had been a waste of time. She argued that the moment seemed such a small place to start. After all, she came to therapy to change her whole life. As far as she was concerned, her life thus far had been wasted. Paradoxically, she was actually feeling the dulled affects of too many unlived moments stored in too many unspent "life banks." Nevertheless, she felt certain that she could not find solutions to the magnitude of her life problems in the small place of one present-felt moment. How much could she possibly accomplish in such a small space of time? So instead, she made lists of all the things she hadn't been able to do in the past and all the things she must do in the future. Again the week had been spent piling further unlived moments on the historic shelves of the self. She honestly felt she had no time to live in "present time." After much persuasion, she began to sit with herself for a few minutes at a time every day. She eventually stated, "After I got my lists out of the way, I actually began to feel me and that sense of "me" guided me out of the mire of my life and into the magic of myself." So many of my clients echo this sentiment: it's just too difficult to be with the self in the now. They concern themselves with foraging future stockpiles of unrealized fantasies or handing out pardons and punishments for past deeds already gone. Yet, the future and past are the smallest spaces of time and anyplace over there outside of you is the smallest space of place. Paradoxically, we spend more time and effort confronting the biggest things in life with smallest portals of time and space, i.e. then and over there! *The smallest details of life lead to the biggest place and the longest time, the place of here and the time of now.* But most of us don't trust that such a simplistic notion of presence could possibly be so powerful in solving our problems.

While learning the art of presence work is difficult, it's the most vital and crucial practice for living well and whole. We struggle and agonize with "now awareness," often because we think we have too much to do, to think, to solve. But our greatest resources for all of our life's dilemmas and dreams can only be found right Here and Now. Through the work of present practices, we can begin to know, to feel, to see the wonder of the world within and its connection to All That Is beyond.

The Rich Place of Presence

The present moment is where we live, regardless of whether we are conscious of it or not. We gather our very breath from this present moment, even as we daydream of future hopes and past pleasures. Imagine, for a moment, that the air found in this place of presence is the richest oxygenated air that can be found. Therefore, the more conscious you are of being present, the more you are able to breathe in this pure, invigorating air. Now, imagine that the future and past are like outposts that are found outside this rich layer of oxygenated air. The further you go out into the past or future, the less oxygen you will have to breathe. In addition, the present not only includes the notion of time, but also the experience of space. So in this ***place*** right here, we also have the greatest degree of oxygen to breathe. If we try to go to some other place over there, the air gets thinner and thinner and we become faint headed and slower and thicker. Staying right ***here*** in this place we are ***now,*** again gives us holy life force air. Imagine time on a horizontal line and space on a vertical line. **(see illustration 9)** We find the present (Here and Now) where the two lines intersect. In other words, it's in this middle area of present time and space that we have the greatest life force power, e.g. oxygen to breathe. Yet, many of us purposely take the trek out to these outposts (future, past, and other places) searching for answers to life's most complex and challenging questions. I ask myself, "Why would I want to ponder such important things with the least amount of oxygen in my brain and body?" The best place to find remedies, replies and resolutions would seem to be in the present moment where the air is purer and bursting with life generating oxygen. This is a beautiful metaphor for understanding the gifted power of the present. As we learn to stay in the present, we will begin to harness this potent eternal energy source and be in more perfect alignment with who we truly are. All other space and time zones will be created from this place.

If we trust ourselves and trust the present moment, we will find incredible resolutions not only for our individual dilemmas, but the very predicaments that threaten the planet on which we live. This is why *the path is learning presence.* If, right now, your consciousness (which is the power and life force of your existence) is somewhere else, you probably will not remember now, later. *If you leave no evidence that you were here, you will not be able to look back and see yourself.* Being conscious of the present expands your reality. The you of tomorrow is

PRESENCE

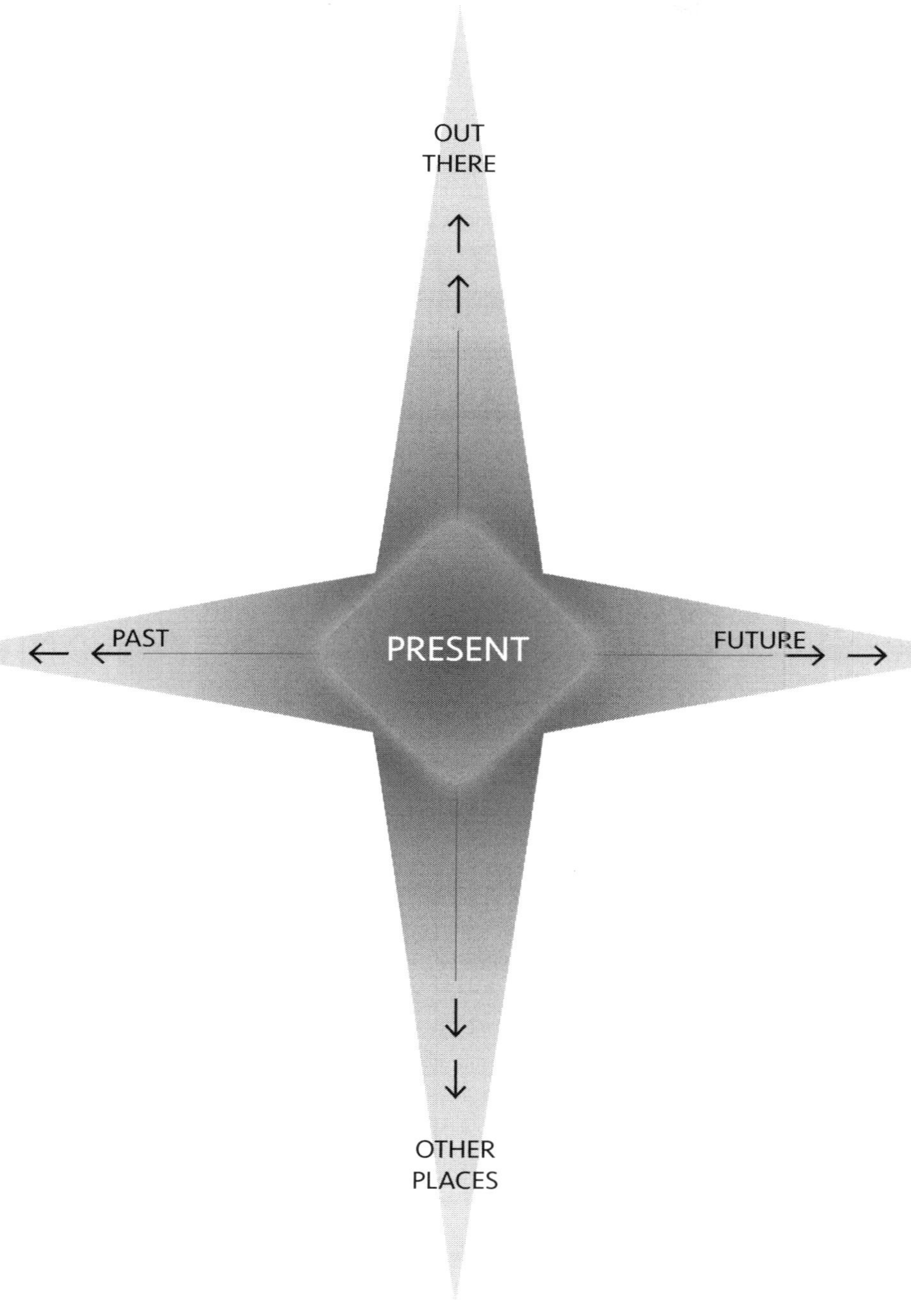

Illustration 9 The rich time and space of Presence.

birthed from the conscious experience you have today. The more awareness you have of your self and your surroundings, the more access you have to the infinite resources that abound before and within us. True conscious living in the present moment pours forth a waterfall of past, future, above and below realities. This blending of time/space travel (all the while never leaving the present moment) becomes an ever flowing blending of All That Is.

Obstacles on the Path

What then makes it so difficult to return to our rightful place of presence? First of all, let's understand that our tools for presence live within. Therefore, our first obstacle would seem to lie in our preoccupation with the outer world and the resulting abandonment of our inner world. As we concentrate on the outside world, we slowly begin the inevitable drift from in to out and with that, our consciousness becomes dimmer and duller. Yet, deep within us, there's a knowing, growing need to expand and self-actualize. We hold sacred, but secret, knowledge that we are and can be so much more, but we look towards our external world for discovery and definition. Many of us are desperate for this filling out process and yet, mistake it for a filling up process. We build enormous appetites that must feed on external notions of satiation and fulfillment. *We look out and become external excavators, consuming enormous amounts of accumulated possessions, all the while, dampening the awareness of life within.* Many of us spend a vast amount of time in these search and seize activities. Searching and scanning our outside environment for happiness, joy and bliss and seizing anything that looks like a likely candidate for such fulfillment. Luckily for us, these search and seize activities eventually cause spiritual seizures. Even then, we try to medicate these emergent chaotic spiking waves, which are crucial messengers of impending soul death, with the Novocain-numbing march of more media madness. Our focus must shift from out to in, but this is an amazingly difficult task.

Externalized Attachments

We slowly, through a lifetime, become attached like flies in a spider's web to outside trappings for feelings of completion, fulfillment and realization. We become convinced that if we find exactly the right thing, person, time, place, etc. we will be ultimately fine, enough, okay and safe. Yet, these very attachments keep us from ever entering the very moment of now. You can hear the reverberations of the attached mind saying, "if only I didn't have to work so much, when I have more time, if only I lived in my dream home, when I find a soul mate, if only I had more vacation," etc. and the list goes on into infinity. We truly become attached to the idea of things and even when we obtain them, we fail to be in the momentary experience with them long enough to ward off the next screen of lists and wishes. It's interesting, for example, that many of us believe that we can only relax when we are on vacation. The vacation is carefully planned, with much deliberation surrounding issues of places and schedules. Finally, after much anticipation, the vacation arrives and the inordinate amount of premeditated activities precludes any relaxation! Often I hear people say, "But I couldn't relax, I was so busy trying to have fun." Relaxation becomes so attached to these external factors, that an internal sense of rest and rejuvenation escapes even the best-intended vacationer. It's no wonder that retirement has been so difficult for so many Americans.

All of these outside pursuits are not in vain. They call our attention to the deeper questing for self-fulfillment and expansion. Deep within we have a profound yearning to fulfill our soul contracts. Learning how to listen will send us towards manifesting our original blueprint and align us with the Divine. We simply confuse the process by which this can take place. We mistake the restlessness within for a need for outside replacements. We often miss the mark in finding true self-enhancement which can only happen when the inner self is the guide and the intuitive voice the navigator. We spend so much time trying to choose various things, places and people in a smörgåsbord of combinations, as if life can be arranged like a Chinese menu. Some external attachments of course match up or truly resonate with the inner self. Our attention, however, becomes too easily fixed on the external world to provide these clues and cues for self-contentment. We begin to focus on the past and future; those outside time spans that are far from the inner now and the inner know. In this process we can too easily lose consciousness and slip right out of the luminous *now*.

Even when we are in a present conscious interaction with some outside object, we begin to believe that the *experience* is less important than the *object* itself. It may feel like one particular object is in fact, endowed with the power of the experience. We worship and adore the object for its empirical value and devalue our own selves. Unwittingly, this actually serves to contract the feelings and narrow the vision of both the experience and the object. It's certainly true that many externalized things open us up to particular experiences, and these occurrences often feel so good, so complete, that we go to great lengths and great investments to continue to keep the objects that are associated with the experience. We may further surmise that the experience itself ***is*** the object and conclude that without the object there's no experience. Therefore, we start to view and judge our very possession of these externalized items as evidence of our own importance and worth. This devilish dance becomes more and more about building position and permanency with the object. *Soon, we are less and less aware of the moving flowing energetic experience of the self in action as we are addictively spellbound by the outer callings of illusionary icons.*

As we become more and more convinced that control lies in the outer realms, the inner self begins to act and feel as if this is indeed true. This automatically leads us to believe that things in the outside world are controlling what we can have and experience. This is one of the core illusions we live with everyday. In reality, the locus of control in life is from the internal world of the self. Once an experience has been felt from the vantage point of the world within, it can always be accessed again. People and places simply bring us home to this experience within. We are such powerful manifestors, however, that if we decide that all control lies in the outer realms then indeed we live as if this were true. Unfortunately, this causes us to wait for things to happen, which takes us out of the moment of the Here and Now.

We love, for instance, the experience of being in love. However, when the loving experience is first associated with a particular person, we begin to think our feelings are directly related and dependent on that person for that loving experience. Soon we covet that person and attachment webs begin to spin. We may spend more time fretting about future ways to keep this love, than just being in that love for the momentary experience of loving. It certainly is true that people, things, places, etc. carry with them very particular vibrational states. Like keys, these vibrations resonate and open up similar states inside of us. However, it's actually this dance of exchanging energetic vibrational states with another person that creates the experience of being in love. It's important that we allow ourselves this exhilarating process of falling in love. In that experience, we know that love exists and further more we know that we are capable of love. No doubt, the person we fall in love with, is certainly part of that, for without their wonderful attributes (all vibrational in nature) we would not be so stimulated inside ourselves. Most importantly, however, loving another person, actually unlocks these deep experiential processes within that might otherwise lay dormant, without resonance, without ripple, without storm.

Nature provides us with similar examples. As you look at a sunset, the sunset acts as a catalyst, a key, a stimulant to activate some place inside that's capable of seeing the divinity of nature. Your ability to know and feel the divinity of nature exists within you long after the sun has set, just like the ability to love exists long after the lover has slipped away in the night. Freedom is living with the understanding that we can experience these things without the blinding nature of attachments. We can know love from many places and through many people, just as we have the ability to experience the divinity of nature from a thousand different vantage points around the globe. We, unfortunately, become so affixed to the objects that open the experience, we forget, that the reality of what we feel, is taking place entirely in our inside world. Attachments actually constrict our ability to enter the exalted experiential realm. And without entrance to this realm our ability to be on the path of presence ceases.

I often hear the questions, "So, what's next in my life? What should I be doing or how should I do this self-actualization stuff? What should I do next at home, at work, in fun, in play?" The search for answers often begins by looking out there. What if the question of what to do next could be changed to "what do I feel right now?" Could we pause in the now and truly experience what is already here? Could we have enough faith that this pause could carry us like a current to the next moment? Instead of looking for a list of things from the external world or from the past world or from your neighbor's world, could you simply see and feel what is present within and let yourself flow with it into the next moment. We know very little about this process of being in the now. *The sentient self resides in the now and it's in this residence that we will find the real clues about what we want to be and do.* When you begin to spend more time operating from the present moment, you have to do much less guess work about what you might enjoy. Instead of waiting for some particular item on your life list to match up with something you actually like, you can simply go right to the item as the inner voice guides you directly to the truth of you. So next time you are deciding on what to do next, simply go within and let your intuitive voice emerge. Whatever is there, be with it, even if it seems like nothing. Even if it feels difficult. Even if it feels intensely bright. Stay with it, and you will begin to move from within. Listen to that voice and you will be intrigued enough to follow it. It will only lead you towards more now awareness. It's in this moment that you can begin to know yourself better and in knowing yourself better you have committed yourself to the exhilarating process of a lifetime. Now is where the self resides. It's the vehicle of the self that moves us towards transcendence. So you see, now is the only passageway to eternity.

To summarize, external attachments take us further and further away from self-awareness and our life force energy. When we focus more and more of our consciousness on that which is external, we starve the inner world of the nurturing light from our luminous consciousness. However, the less attachments we have towards the outer world, the more available energy we have towards self-awareness. And when this happens, consciousness expands from the inside out, joining with the effervescent energy of the universe. One can only imagine the enlightened world of non-attachment. (**see illustration 10**)

As we stretch out our available resources and strangle our own self-awakening process, the process of returning home to our inner world becomes more and more arduous and precipitous. Attachments drain energy from the very core of our life force. So, when we do venture to return once again to our internal sense of core consciousness, it may actually seem dim at first, especially compared to the neon brightness of our outside accessories. But, these outside colorful lights only seem bright because we have imbued them with our life force energy!

THREE FEARS THAT FOSTER NON-PRESENCE

Fear #1: Returning to the Self: Is Anybody Home?

Because the self is the only vehicle for presence work, we must return to this internal domain where self lives and breathes. If you recall from chapter three, we have three main fears that keep us out of the domain of self. The first fear is the fear of nothingness. As we begin to travel inward and loosen our grip from outside attachments, we must face the mind's fear that there will be nothing within that will soothe our wounds of abandonment and deprivation. From the first abandonment from God as we were embodied in the womb, we have had the ability to know separation. Ever since then, we have been desperate for unification in the form of love and acceptance. In our frantic and distracted attempts to reunite ourselves with All That Is, we have become convinced that the outside world must hold this reunification potential. We certainly seem to mistake the search for and connection with externalized objects as some type of amalgamated experience of reunion. We then may associate any attempts to go within as further experiences of separation and division. As soon as we are asked to simply shut our eyes and go within, it becomes a scary experience because it may induce the original separation and abandonment feelings we so long ago remembered. *So, we may mistake this time within as time without.* We may fear that this within process may further separate us by our very own walls of embodiment.

I notice that people who begin practicing more formalized inner activities like meditation or yoga usually find classes or groups beneficial. This may help counter the loneliness and emptiness that people often face when practicing

ATTACHMENTS

Born with
beautiful Life Force.

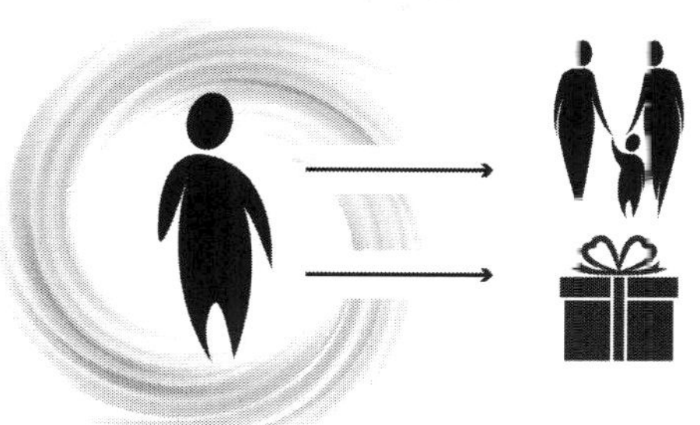

Gates open and energy moves out
towards attachments.

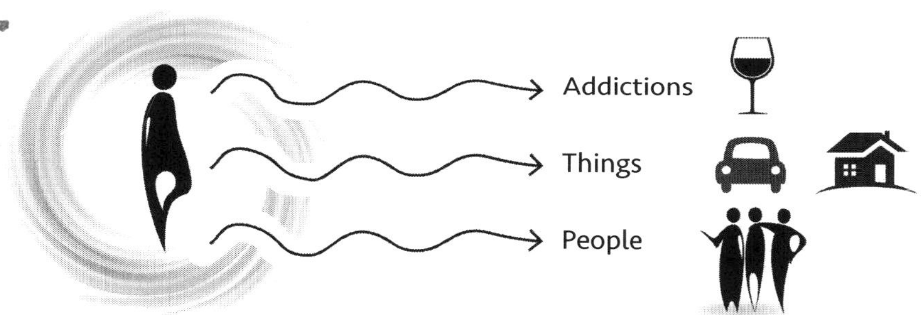

Self less felt as focus is on attachments.

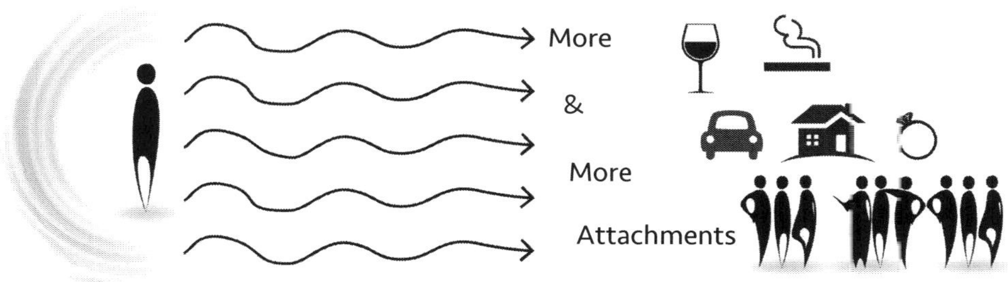

Life force goes way out to outer edges of attachments.
Self+awareness fused with attachments.

Illustration 10

solo activities. Once the world within opens up, however, it's very difficult to leave this world and function in the three dimensional world. The never-ending balance of living within while living without is always present!

As we open ourselves to this world within through the work of presence practices, we will begin to know that it's the vehicle of the self that actually leads to All That Is. *The very thing that separated us at the beginning (embodiment in a self) can now be the very thing that leads back to the sea of All That Is.* Metaphorically, it's the raindrops recognition that it's simply made up of the sea from which it came. It's in that realization that it becomes one once again. The self is indeed the vehicle for enlightenment and yet, when enlightenment happens, the self becomes everything and nothing as it disappears into the sea of All That Is, much like the drop of water becomes indistinguishable from the sea. The road maps to God therefore, lie in the internal world within.

The first practice of presence is to simply become aware of the *who within. Wherever we give our attention, we give our power.* So, if we are to empower the inner world, we must first be *willing* to direct our attention towards it. This takes a conscious daily commitment to the work of presence. The first step in presence training is to simply make a statement of willingness. *I am willing to work on inner presence today and every day thereafter.* It's amazing to me how many people say they want to be more present in their lives, but are not actually ***willing*** to make the changes necessary to be present. Yet, even when we can honestly state that we are willing, and even desperate, for this work, one of the hardest tasks is to simply *remember* this newly defined inner attending. For so many of us, the outer world is so seductive in transfixing our attention that we forget our commitment to the who within as we travel through the daily rubble of outside fallouts. The most important job in having your life is having awareness in your life.

The second task is to discover ways in which to *remember* this most important commitment of your energetic awareness and the process of going within. It's very hard to create these present reminders within our body-mind configuration, and so we need to establish cues and rituals in our outside environment. Start with putting note cards in places that you ordinary look everyday – your bathroom mirror, your nightstand, your underwear drawer, the refrigerator, your desk at work, and even inside the book you are reading. The note cards can state simple mantras for daily remembrance like: "Be within, not without," "Stay Here and Now," "The best in life can be found inside," "Breathe," "Remember." Creating your own mantra will be an important part of this process as well. In addition, take some time to decide what outside things remind you of this work. Nature often is a great reminder for us, for nature is always in presence. I imagine that a tree never forgets that it's a tree, while I can forget that I am me. Anything from nature like stones, crystals, branches, flowers, etc. that can be placed in your home or office can remind you of the task of going in. You can even do a ritual that imbues an object or piece of jewelry with the energy of presence so that as you carry this object around it calls to you to return to presence.

To summarize, the most important question to ask is, "Am I willing to shift my attention inside and can I remember to do so?"

Exercise I

Composing a statement of *willingness*: "I am willing to pay attention to my inside world, knowing that this is the most important way to become present in my life."

Exercise II

Create and design methods for *remembering* the task of presence.

Exercise III

The following is an exercise that can be done anywhere, anytime to shift awareness towards the *self in the now.*

Check-in Practice:

1. Note your breathing and the body…pause.
2. Note your feelings and the heart…pause.
3. Note your thinking and the mind…pause.
4. Note your spirit and the soul…pause.

As you begin this process, you will widen the doorway to your world within. Once you are consciously standing in the doorway, you will be able to initiate the process of inner seeing and inner hearing. Simply shifting your attention to that which is within will begin to empower and energize the body-mind connection. As the inner world becomes more connected and solid in its energetic experience, now living becomes easier and more fluid.

Fear #2: Shadowy Forecasts

If we accept that there may be more than emptiness within the inner walls of individual domain, we also must face our deep dread that when we do find some signposts of our true identity, it will never be enough. That our unique individuality will simply be inadequate. This notion that we house an incomplete, imperfect, self is the biggest motivating factor in the avoidance of being present. This fear of scarce self often turns into a derisory, pitiful and contemptible version of self-identity. When this kind of notion of self is left unattended, huge vats of self-hate accumulate, often bubbling over as intolerance, prejudice and even violence, stinging those within reach of this hot flowing lava of loathing. I've seen many people over the years hold this deep secret of self-hate and inadequacy. Even narcissists, who spend most of their time pruning the appearance of a huge grand self, are really just using this presentation to hide the small, susceptible, inadequate self within. The field of psychology has much to tell us about these self-avoidance tactics especially as they relate to self-loathing, self-acceptance and self-worth issues. Our primary task, our foremost responsibility, is to learn to love the self. Through this process, all other miracles will unfold. Yet, we avoid this work because it involves meeting the shadow parts and learning to hold compassion for them. Instead of requiring perfection within, it's time to behold our imperfections with compassion. After all, if we were perfect, would we have the need to search for God and if we found this Divine Source, would we even recognize the perfections and harmony of All That Is. Our very human nature, even in our incompleteness, provides the backdrop by which we can see this Divine Light. Unfortunately, we have been taught to strive to be perfect, without blemishes. Most of us are only too aware of our imperfections and blemishes. We use this knowledge to conclude we can never measure up, and so we dim the lights of present consciousness as a way to avoid this insufficient, sketchy self. Some of us spend lifetimes hiding these shadow parts; others are simply in denial. However, we often miss the rich value to this shadowy nature. We have the capability to make mistakes, feel pain, strain with struggle, and utterly fail at life's major tasks. We, in our strides to be enough, dim our awareness of those darker silhouettes dancing on the walls of the inner being. As a consequence, we become less present with, and less aware of, the inner light of self-divinity.

One of the biggest barriers to present self-awareness is this self-loathing that results from years of denying the shadow dance within. For most of us, this is a subject matter to be avoided at all costs. However, anything that blocks the entrance to our inner world obstructs our ability to be present with full self. It's this presence that holds our greatest power. Discovering new ways and fresh frameworks for working with the inevitable struggles within is crucial. It's paramount, at this stage of working on the inadequate self, to learn compassion and forgiveness. There's no greater practice ground in all of life than this place of the self within. The struggles, the pain, the self-defacing attitudes and feelings and the lonely inadequate self all are desperate for compassionate awareness attention. It is through this process that healing will occur and the whole self can transform. Instead, we often offer freight loads of fear and hazardous hate to these shadow zones. Imagine for a moment that you are able to fill your pinpoint awareness with compassion and love. You then direct this newly formed laser beam inward towards your pain, your struggle, your smallness, your hate. Imagine being able to hold with warmth and understanding these places, flooding these long neglected zones with sacred nourishment. In that beautiful healing moment, consciousness will light up the path of presence.

It seems very paradoxical that when we are in some pain, or some struggle, we want to do just the opposite as we retreat, run, remove and rid ourselves of it. However, our presence is the greatest gift we can give pain and struggle. Love and compassion can only come through the path of presence. Can we greet the dancing shadows as if they were children playing with the light? Can we love our imperfections, knowing they come from God's perfection? This becomes a curative offering of sacred nurturance instead of starvation and destruction. By giving our present attention to the very thing we want to deny, we will actually heal it, soothe it and move it. This then will be the very fuel for self-actualization.

I recently had a client who felt that if she really became more acutely aware of this shadow zone, she would sink in it, become more of it, be overcome by it and be lost in it. So she developed very clever techniques to avoid it and cover over. She asked, "What good would it do to acknowledge these things except to prove that her mother was right in the first place regarding the bad parts within?" We began to create a new paradigm based on nurturance rather than starvation. She began to treat the pain, the struggle, as if it was her own child whom she could hold, embrace and give offerings of warmth and love. In so doing, she gave herself the love that she had been denied, the love that she had always been waiting for. Together we designed the following statements to call her consciousness to the presence within.

Stay with the inner path.

Breathe into the pain, the despair, the struggle.

Listen to its whispering.

Learn compassion through the shadow zones.

On your way, give up judgment and expand your knowledge.

All is to be experienced, not dissected.

Hold your attention.

Open your heart.

Treat the shadow zones as you would a child.

Hold them, caress them, and nurture them.

She diligently practiced these statements over and over for two weeks. Although at the end of two weeks she was much more aware of the content of these shadowy complexes, she stated that she felt much more peaceful and content, and felt control over her life in inexplicable ways. She added, "Strangely, I also have been noticing more things in the present moment. I had no idea there was so much to see and feel right here and right now."

As we decide to avoid our usual evasive tactics of avoiding the painful inadequate self, we have the opportunity to be with it and finally just become it. Of course, our fear is that we might become so solidly stuck in this half lit place, that we would become indistinguishable from it. Can we find that inner voice that says, "This is the work, this is the walk and this is the path of transformation?" As we are willing to be with the pain and struggle, it's crucial to remember that this pain is not the journey itself, the pain is only the fuel to propel us inward to the path of presence. Pain and struggle are simply the prologue, the call for attention. We've used consciousness to separate us from all the within and the beyond. Now we can use consciousness to unite us with everything we have lost and everything we dream of gaining.

The Divine Source of all creation lives within all living things and all living material. However, humans were given a separate consciousness, one that let them be aware of themselves. This makes humans different from all other life forms on Earth. The flower and tree hold Divine energy, but have never distinguished themselves from Divine Source. Unlike human beings, all other living things have never felt separated (sea-parted) from Divine oneness. While they stay steadfast in their unique living shapes, they also never have lost consciousness with the source matrix. We have a different dilemma, for in becoming self-conscious, we have separated our experience of being part of the oneness consciousness or the source matrix. We have mistaken our awareness of self to mean that we are separate from the Divine. Remember, as the raindrop falls into the ocean, it once again merges with the all-encompassing sea of water. The flower, the tree and all living things are raindrops in God's Divine intelligence. Paradoxically, human beings have encapsulated themselves with this gift of consciousness. Even when the sacred sea surrounds us, we feel separate from all that sacred liquid enveloping us. This has left humans feeling isolated and alone. It's time to utilize our consciousness anew. In order to do this, we must shine it throughout the residence within where we will find our Divine connection. Then, we will know once again that we are of God and can never be separate from Divine Oneness. *The path is presence, the direction is inward.* Stay present, aware and compassionately conscious with everything you find.

We often think that success is measured by the structures we build in the outside world: our house, our work, our bank accounts, our degrees and material possessions. As we put stock in all of these measurable things, they become our measures of success. These visible, tangible belongings actually separate us from everything else. The real measure of success is invisible, and it may very well be that no one else will see it. It's the ability to sit here, *right now,* with our consciousness *turned on* and our inner world *lit up.* Seeing and feeling our divineness within opens our long closed channels to the world beyond. We must accept, however, that the world at large may never see this kind of success because it's a process that takes place in this very moment in the world inside the self. We can have faith that this opens up the possibility of becoming conduits for sending Divine energy out into the world. It will come through our actions, feelings, thoughts and spirit. This will be what makes us know and feel our goodness, our successfulness, our brilliance as an Earth being. As we do this, we will have less and less of a need or desire to be recognized. In the past, we have wanted to be seen so that we might be connected, accepted and whole. Once we are connected to All That Is, we will have no need for building false structures outside of ourselves.

Fear #3: Magnificence Beyond Belief

Although our fear of nothingness and/or inadequacies certainly keep us numb and void of being present, I believe our greatest fear, our greatest obstacle, is encountering the truly magnificent beings that we are. Since most of us haven't had as much practice with this, it will be unfamiliar. However, it's important to understand that through this inner sanctum of sacredness, we unite ourselves with our Divinity and God. From this place, we receive more clarity about our original blueprint, our mission and as a result, our service to and in the world. We often fear this awesome task because as we begin to expand our sense of self, and realize its hugeness, we fear disintegration and/or death. This happens for both for psychological and spiritual reasons. Psychologically, most of us have been taught not to be "too big for your britches," or "too full of yourself." We encounter guilt and shame when we begin to acknowledge our grand gifts of unique self. In addition, the last time we experienced oneness with Divine Source, was before we were in this human body and this particular incarnation. As we go closer to the light of our own magnificence as a human being, we may once again feel like we will die. To realize our grandness while remaining embodied, as a human being is our goal and our birthright. This is when the world will change into a New Age, a New Renaissance of Being.

It's the very *power* of this moment, not its smallness, that keeps us from fully entering its hallways. Unconsciously, we peek for a split second into the domain within and see the bright burning sun of the sacred self and God. We back away for fear of getting burnt. The small or ego self reinterprets this and says, "Oh, *this* one moment, what can it do?" The higher conscious self knows "Oh *this* one moment…you are not ready for it's hugeness yet…you are not prepared to hold it's grandeur." Learning to simply pause and breathe in the light from within is no small task. So when you hear yourself say, "I need to learn more, do more, have more to achieve this now living experience," this will be your cue to do less, think less, be less. *We have not yet learned how to be in the moment of less, let alone hold the miracle world of more.* It becomes crucial to start with the basics and practice simple things in small moments. How about the next 60 seconds? Then we can move towards sitting for five minutes, walking for twelve minutes and eating with the pause of gratitude. We must start small in order to expand both our capacity to handle the explosive energy we house within, and to expand the small now moments into more continuous even moments. The little, ego self may respond, "Well if sitting with the self will get me somewhere grand, then I will sit for 20 hours." The higher self knows that will never happen. It would create an experience too vast for the little self to tolerate. We must slowly build our capacity for momentary living so we can build footholds for anchoring our consciousness in this vast territory of presence. It's important to hone our abilities to be present moment detectives or explorers, so that we can begin to consciously recognize these current moment experiences. There's a distinct signature to these moments.

So simply start with the question, "What am I doing right now in my body, in my heart, in my mind and in my spirit?" Pause three times a day to inquire within and see what the detective sees and hears. You may begin to identify a distinct state of being with the person who lives within. As a result, you may become more aware of all that surrounds you as well. After all, you must step inside to really feel connected to the outside. Living in total awareness of the now offers us a much clearer view of the Divine and sacred organizational principles that abound around and through us. This is when living becomes synchronistic and harmonic.

Being present with the empty self fills the void.

Being present with the inadequate self accepts, heals and transforms.

Being present with the grand self leads to oneness.

Being present turns on the light of consciousness.

I'd like you to imagine for a moment that each one of us is enveloped in a balloon like cocoon. The balloon, heavy in its texture and fabric, covers us like a cloak and for many years lays dormant around the core self. We begin to feel that this swathe of dense material is a safety cloth that protects us from the world. We lie underneath this illusionary cloak of protection, unmoving and small, for much of our lives. So you can imagine that initially before the self is present, aware and conscious, this balloon, unexpanded and lifeless, is heavier and thicker. As we lay underneath its shrouded weight, we are, in essence, more separated from the world beyond us (albeit in an illusion of protection and safety) by the solidifying nature of non-movement, of non-breath, of true self-diminishment.

However, as we begin to experience the true self within, and as we begin to become conscious and aware of this inner world, we breathe the air of sacred life into this deflated balloon. The breath of presence expands the balloon further and the material becomes less dense, more flexible, more fluid. We discover that the material of the balloon is not solid at all as was first thought and experienced. The veil-like appearance of the balloon becomes thinner and thinner as it swells with life breath and the augmentation of self-awareness. As it continues to expand with the bountiful life of the breathing self, infinitesimal holes slowly emerge in the now delicately thin fabric. This allows light to shine both in and out. Breath becomes easier and more expansive causing more light to infiltrate the inner domain of the self. The illusion of separation begins to fade. Eventually, in true enlightenment, as the balloon explodes in soft dissolution there's no longer any distinction between you and All That Is. *Conscious breathing of presence leads to the oneness of simply being.*

The experience of simply stating the mantra, "come home, go inside, be here now," is the path of presence and it's this path that breathes life into this sheath of separation that surrounds us. We must come back to the home within, always steadfast in returning, over and over again. Even when we land in our self-depriving or self-evolving layers, we must heed the battle cry, "Keep going in, go further, go deeper, go home, feeling the truth of the soul once again." The very act of saying this mantra, "Come home and be present" is indeed, what takes us to self-expansion and soul awareness. It's as simple and hard as this. And as we give our authentic presence to each other, we will create the building blocks for creating a world that is filled with love and peace.

Soul Remedies

#5 – Presence Practices

1. PAUSING: ONCE A DAY TO **ASK**
"What is happening right now in my inner world?"

2. PAUSING: ONCE A DAY TO **SIT**
in silence and stillness for five minutes.

3. PAUSING: ONCE A DAY TO **NOTE**
"What is happening in the world immediately outside of myself?"

4. PAUSING: ONCE A DAY TO **ATTEND**
to some struggle within by writing it down.

5. PAUSING: ONCE A DAY TO **HOLD**
some anxiety or worry by embracing it without judgment.

6. PAUSING: ONCE A DAY TO **LOVE**
something within and something without.

7. PAUSING: ONCE A DAY TO **CELEBRATE**
that you have given yourself to presence: 21 times.

6

Self-Love – The Only Way Out is In

"There is but one cause of human failure
And that is man's lack of faith in this true self."
–William James

"How much longer will you go on letting your energy sleep?
How much longer are you going to stay
Oblivious of the immensity of yourself?"
–Bhagwan Shree Rajneesh

"This is your life and nobody is going to teach you,
No book, no guru. Learn from yourself…it is a
Fascinating thing and when you learn about your self
From yourself, out of that learning wisdom comes.
Then you can live a most extraordinary, happy,
Beautiful life. Right?"
–Krishnamurti

The vehicle of the self is the only portal through which we can make our way back towards the sacred. It's amazing how much effort we spend avoiding the very place that will take us towards Divine Source. There has never before been a time when human beings have created so many clever evasive maneuvers to avoid the inner domain of the self. It's time to return to the self and open the gates to our true mission to be able to serve the Earth and return her to her natural glory. As we have moved so far from the house of self, we have forgotten our purpose for living in this human form. The act of returning to the soul-self with love will open the channels of remembering and enable us to revisit our truest nature. The actual experience of soul-self opens a portal to all that is Divine. Contrary to so much of the propaganda, we must find our way back to the self in order to save the world. We each have a particular responsibility to heal ourselves with love. Oftentimes we spend a lifetime waiting for that something from the external world to love us, heal us and ultimately save us. But, as we pensively pause, anticipating the goods to come, we abandon the task we have come here to experience: learning about love through loving ourselves.

The channel to the *Divine Source* lies within us. As we learn to love and take care of this path within, we will become more open and aware that we're sparks made of the *sacred creation,* here to bring light to the world. So instead of asking for service from the world, we will be in service to the world. We have the power to completely heal ourselves on every level, physical, emotional, intellectual and spiritual. As we begin to love ourselves anew, we will open these channels of healing that lie within us. This healing comes from remembering and holding in reverence the spark of the *Divine* that we hold beyond body and form. It's within us and surrounds us. It's the fabric by which we're one with All That Is. Love directs us both to ourselves and to all that is *sacred Source.* Self-hate clogs the arteries to the heart of God. So many of us house huge arsenals of inner loathing and feelings of unworthiness and these in turn become the materials for constructing road blocks that eventually obstruct the very view of the Divine threshold. People have heart attacks, spiritually speaking, when they have filled these channels with so much self-doubt, self-denial and self-denigration that the light from the *Divine Heart* can no longer be seen nor felt. As we learn to love the self, we actually open the channel to the experience of Sacred Source. Love is the roto-rooter…it's the tool of the sacred plumber. It's only in this cleared space within the self that we can find pieces of remembrance that will build the reality that we're really manifested divinity. *Looking outward reminds us that we're Earth bound; looking inward reminds us that we're spirit bound. Living on Earth with spirit-boundedness is the goal.*

Loving the self is the most responsible act you can do to change the face of the world in which we live. We're meant to evolve to the next stage of our human evolution by the fuel created through self-love. For this self-love opens up the creative potential that lies within and will set the path for the future of our planet. This is not about selfishness. It's actually selfish to refuse this work of loving the self. We must understand that until we each take responsibility for our inner domain, the outer world will remain destructive and chaotic. No one else has the key to your treasure chest and this inner treasure houses your sacred blueprint. The act of loving the self creates a key that begins to unlock the sacred wealth that lies within the chambers of soul memory. As you begin to experience self-love, this key is able to turn the lock and a soul window begins to expand and the blueprint for your life pours forth. At this point, higher consciousness is experienced and life wisdom becomes more available. **(see illustration 11)**

Over a lifetime, and perhaps many lifetimes, of unloved practices we begin to accumulate gray thick veils over the true authentic soul self. Love is the only vibrational energy powerful enough to disintegrate these veils. We often go inside and mistake the self for these darkened veils, believing that we're these dark misty shrouds. These cloaked fractions of self not only come from the current lifetime you are living, but are cradled in collective unconscious templates containing the developmental and evolutionary history of the human race. This history alone does its own part in filling our minds with unlovable material about who we have been. Love is the only experience that can create an inner alchemy of clearing out and dissolving personality issues, dramas and historical (hysterical) propensities. It can and will heal all the aches and pains within. As these veils clear, the path is laid for seeing and dreaming true the authentic spirit beings that we are. The self can then begin to see the world anew. In this seeing, the self can create a new world order of harmony and peace. We're meant to be on a sacred mission to understand and actualize the magnificent spirit beings we are while staying embodied on Earth. **(see illustration 12)**

We must see ourselves…in order to see the world.
We must love ourselves…in order to love the world.
We must create ourselves…in order to create the world.

It's important at this juncture to understand the exact nature of this self-love commitment. After all, if we fail to comprehend it, we will not be able to entrust ourselves to it. Most of us have been taught to love things for particular reasons, conditions or relational values. What I'm talking about here can't be based on conditions or values. *It's simply the act of providing love for the experience itself.* The goal is to provide an experience whereby the energetic being within is offered love without attachments or conditions.

Loving, and for that matter even liking, must be about offering an experience rather than a checklist of thoughts, opinions, conditions and timelines. We so often decide we can or can't love the self due to certain attributes and conditions. For instance, often when I inquire about this self-love process with clients, they often recite a checklist of things about themselves that

THE KEY IS SELF-LOVE

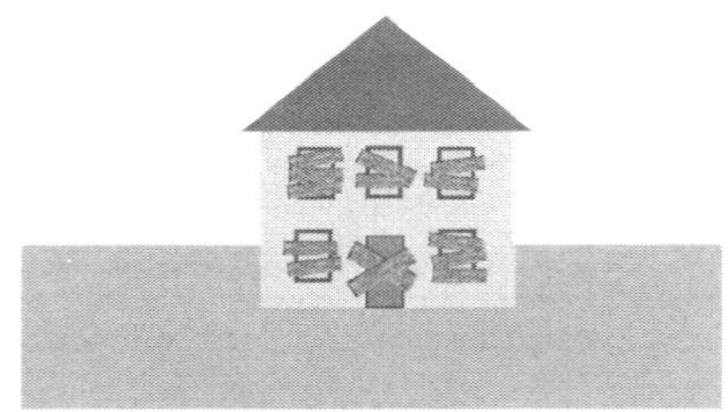

Soul Home without self-love.

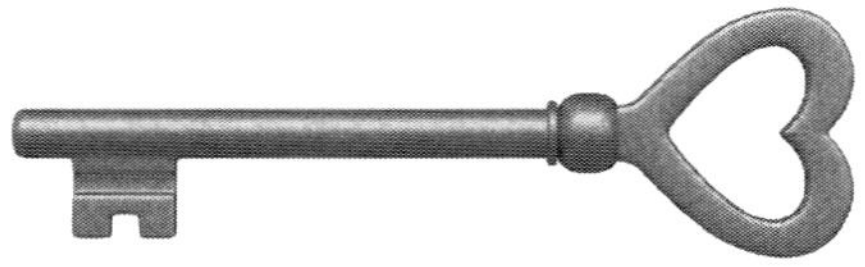

Key to open Soul Home is self-love.

Illustration 11

TRANSFORMATION THROUGH LOVE

Veils cover over self & stifle self.

Veils begin to dissolve from inside out through alchemy of self-love.

Sacred self emerges as veils are removed. No separation from Divine Source.

Wings of sacred love felt from within. Love flows out and world is transformed.

Illustration 12

they love or do not love. I hear things like, "I love my talent for singing, but I hate my fat body." "I might be able to love my ability to be kind, but I really dislike my awkwardness with people." It goes on and on this list of reasons, characteristics and attributes that either deserve or do not deserve to be loved.

Love seems totally contingent on these labels and definitions and is not given simply for the sake of the *experience*. It does not occur to people that both the talent of singing and the fat body could use a dose of experiential love. In fact, there is absolutely nothing in the universe that wouldn't be shifted, healed, and expanded with this dose of love. But we use conditions, characteristics, and descriptions to block the experience of loving the self rather than aid in the process of giving love. We in fact use these states, forms and conditions about the self as evidence of our "unlovability," when indeed the very things that "fall short" are in the most need of love. *There is only one thing that determines our love worthiness and that is the fact that we're simply alive and it's in this aliveness that we find the Divine spark of God.* However, we must first love our humanness in order to find our way back to the Divine spirit within. Some of us would like to cheat by only loving the spirit being within all the while disallowing and shunning the frail if not fragile, fallible human being within. *We must realize that the very act of loving the human self reveals our spirit, our spark, our Divine manifestation of God.* So remember…labels, judgments, conditions, etc. are simply obstacles that prevent the intimate experience of love.

Love must be a felt occurrence not a thought. The *thought* of loving the self may generate some curing energy but the *experience* creates an outpouring of this energy. It's likened to the difference between the light of a single light bulb compared to the light of the sun. So we can't just know that loving the self is important, we must be able to experience it. A sacred alchemy occurs when we're bathed in the experience of loving the human being within. A synergetic energy is created that will not only heal all that is ailing, but uncoil the creative processes of enlightenment. These vibrations, set in motion through acts of self-love, begin to penetrate all the nooks and crannies of the dark, abandoned self and shed the light of sacred divinity. It's only the you that can and will know what truly needs love within. It's absurd that someone else would know. When you turn your attention to the inside, it creates enormous powerful energy. This healing loving energy will shower agony, shame, guilt, bad, deprived, and in this showering, these things will be healed and transform into more light energy. *When the I decides through willful consciousness to utilize the act of love as a technology for healing, wholeness and health can be restored instantaneously.*

We all shout, "I want to save the world," yet we don't realize that the world is within us and so we must first save our inner world. When I bring love into myself I awaken the Divine Consciousness within myself. Love is the key to merging with *All That Is sacred.* We have been given the power of consciousness to willfully choose to love. As I bring the sacred and Divine energy of love into myself, I become the Divine vessel I'm meant to be. As the light of God Consciousness shines within me, I'm both myself and the Divine manifestation of this Divine Light. Oneness is felt. My task is to understand that this is my task. As the negative states within begin to disintegrate with the healing energy of love, I can finally begin to feel and see the sacred being I am. My mission is to come into full consciousness of the spirit being I am while still in human form. Now, I have this to give to the world.

The *self-loving experience* therefore becomes the fuel and therein lays the technology for becoming evolved and eventually enlightened. Through this experience of self-love we're granted the freedom to truly be in activation of our authentic soul self. When we're no longer dependent on each other for this process to happen, we will finally be able to see each other in our more authentic forms. If we're not willing to do this labor of love, we will simply lay in want for others to do this for us. We will never be able to see the true nature of each other, but instead we will only see others for what they might provide us. When we're no longer dependent on each other for this inner process of healing love, the veils will be lifted and we can clearly see the outer world. We will be able to create the outer world according to a loving inner world. This is truly learning to live from the inside out. While we can receive support from each other to be in this process, the real energetic interaction takes place from within, which is your own consciousness becoming alive and well. But we can't afford to dally at this junction of *inner love work* because once completed and even while in completion, we must begin to share this deeper soul-self with the world. It's this sharing that will change how and what conditions we decide to live in.

Part One: Commitment

THE COMMITMENT

I commit to the path of learning to love the self within. I alone am responsible for this path. Loving the self is the path towards sacred consciousness and world service. As I learn to love the self I will begin to actualize my original soul blueprint and in so doing will be in golden service to the world.

It's quite extraordinary how difficult this simple process of commitment actually can be. We can learn all the techniques in the world to be in the "inner journey," but without *conscious commitment,* the techniques will stay on the unspent shelves of the resistant self. We must first understand how committed we have become to the value of the outer world perspective. Many of us have dedicated ourselves to a lifetime of external pursuits, and so to switch our commitment towards this inner journey at times seems impossible. Often, we simply refuse to accept this task of going within and find innumerous ways of staying without. After all, few of us have been taught or given guidance for this task. We have more ways of seeking out than seeking in. My clients often come to my office and say, "Well of course I know it's important to love the self, but I have so many other things that need tending to first. If we could work on these other problems, then maybe I could be freed up to work on loving myself." Often, the battle cry is: "I simply don't have enough time to really love myself." After all, it takes extra time to cook healthy, go to the gym, meditate. Maybe if I lived in a retreat I could go these things, but in real life it's impossible. It's only impossible because we've decided that it's so. That's why examining the truth behind our ability to commit is so crucial. Until we understand that the only path is the path within, we will stay stuck in the seductions of outer world anecdotes to what we think ails us. This task of going within and learning to love is the most important thing you will ever do. It's the only path that will change the rest of your life and everyone else's. I wonder if each of us knew that awakening to our own soul journeys with the light of love could change the world...would we be motivated then? It's absolutely amazing to me how difficult it is to convince people that the work is within. The very resistance to this work is testimony of its importance. I have seen many of my clients become indignant and mad at me for refusing to help them solve their outer world problems. The minute I suggest that the work for them is becoming more acquainted with their world within, they protest and feel as if I've missed the point of what therapy should be. It breaks my heart to watch people disempower and devalue themselves as they protest the woes of their external foes as if this might earn them a place of worthiness and rightfulness. But their resistance belies their lack of self-acknowledgment and their inability to care for the self. It's so paradoxical because so often their biggest complaint is the lack of acknowledgment they have received from the important people in their lives. Yet, they continue this cycle of deprivation and disavowal because they have become the biggest culprits in this process of disaffirming the self.

The Resistance

It's imperative to spend some time examining the energy we utilize to resist this commitment. Although there are a myriad of reasons we invest in resistance, I would like to examine two of the main culprits that divest us of entrusting our time and attention towards this work: our belief systems and our comfort zones. It's a crucial step to observe and study the belief systems surrounding this issue of loving the self because it's in those particular thought patterns that so much resistance can be found. What are your real beliefs about your self, your worthiness, your purpose, your mission? I would like to examine some common beliefs that I encounter everyday in my office and for that matter in the world and offer new beliefs that can change the energy of resistance into energy of commitment.

Belief Systems

1. OLD BELIEF: The outside world holds the key to my safety, happiness and lovability. The reason I'm the way I am is because the outside world hurt me, disappointed me, abandoned me, and it's the outside world that needs to show up and heal me and love me. I will know that I'm lovable and worthy when I get finally get enough from the outside world.

   NEW BELIEF: I have the power and ability to love, affirm and heal the self. It's no one else's responsibility.

2. OLD BELIEF: I deserve to have certain things given to me by my family, my partner, my job. If I'm really okay, then I should have things come my way.

   NEW BELIEF: I deserve to have things given to me by me.

3. OLD BELIEF: I'm so damaged, but when I finally get love from someone I will feel better and then I can work on myself.

   NEW BELIEF: I will be the one to love myself, damage and all. The trick to love is to love what is there now, not what might be there later.

4. OLD BELIEF: I need to find others who have more power and know-how about loving me, then maybe I can learn. I don't know how to love myself.

   NEW BELIEF: I have everything I need to love myself and, in fact, I'm the only one who can love myself in the way I need.

5. OLD BELIEF: It's selfish to love myself. I should be loving others.

   NEW BELIEF: It's selfish not to do the work of loving myself… only when I'm healthier and whole can I be of service to the world. Wholeness comes from this inner process of loving myself.

6. OLD BELIEF: I will be able to love myself, when I get thinner, smarter, richer. When I finally have the things that make me more acceptable then I will love myself.

   NEW BELIEF: The only point here is to love myself for the experience of love and not for attributes or conditions. Love is about the offering of an experience without conditions. If you love because of conditions then you do not love.

7. OLD BELIEF: I don't believe that my particular mission matters on Earth. It's too late for me to have any effect.

   NEW BELIEF: The only mission that matters is my mission. I'm here on Earth to accomplish this mission of loving myself so that I might add to the chorus of love and harmony on this planet. It's not too late; it's just the right time. Fulfilling my mission through understanding love not only changes me but all those around me.

8. OLD BELIEF: If I really love myself, I will have to be more responsible for self-actualizing and in this process I will have to change too many things in my life. This is too scary and unfamiliar.

   NEW BELIEF: As I feel the vibrations of love I will naturally want to become all that I am. As I become more in this self-actualization process, I will discover a new familiarity with the grandness of who I am and the feeling of oneness. This can happen while still embodied...for this lifetime is about remembering this truth and in this remembrance I will know the truth of sacred alignment. This will be the ultimate position of No Harm: spiritual safety, Earth body protection and Divine accompaniment. Oneness.

We have so many beliefs that take us out of this inner process so the first exercise to strengthen our commitment is to examine and take an inventory of those particular beliefs that hinder our vows towards loving the self. If simply contemplating your various beliefs is not enough to confront them, try to do something today that is self-loving and watch what comes up in your thoughts. If you really want to know what your beliefs are look for them in the zone of resistance. The zone of resistance is that place where you can hear and see the thought scripts describing the various reasons you can't tend to the self today. Discover those scripts and write them down on the left side of a page and then begin to write new scripts on the right side of the page. The most important deterrent in our commitment practices is the energy of resistance that our thoughts hold. Most of us have had the experience of waking up on a weekend morning with high hopes and constructive plans for ourselves. Some of us forget those plans within an hour of awakening, some hold on until they are back in the traffic of external events; some actually get to the self-care activity and then become overwhelmed by the enormity of it all. In any of these processes, commitment inevitably wanes as we begin to shift our attention to the shadows of outer movements...away from the luminous inner callings.

The resistance scripts must be revealed. Most of us are automatically and hypnotically guided by these scripts and the behaviors that fit the script naturally follow. You must first decide what beliefs you really have about your life. It's these beliefs that decide the scripts and it's these scripts that decide your behaviors. Unfortunately, it's often these behaviors that decide how you really feel about the self. So, for example, a person has a belief about their body that influences their ability to love themselves. The belief is: "When I get thinner and in shape I will be able to love myself better. After all, how can I love my body the way it is now?" This person feels big on the outside and so small on the inside, but erroneously feels that when they become smaller on the outside they will be bigger on the inside.

It's quite the opposite, the key diet for this person has to be unconditional self-love so that the inside might grow in order for the outside to shrink. When we stay obsessed by judging outside features, we don't have the inner experience of love that would in turn motivate self-loving behaviors. In this case, it might include eating well. Intellectually this person may even know that eating well is good for them, but can't access the fuel (the energy that comes from self-love) within to drive these behaviors. The old scripts instead motivate the behaviors. The old scripts say "Look at you. You're ugly, big and fat and therefore you are not good enough and certainly not lovable enough." This brings on unbearable feelings from which you look for an escape. Food provides that comfort, that distraction, that soothing moment when you forget this unforgiving, unloving place within. Yet, in another moment, this food will provide more fodder for the unloving self.

So the belief must be changed to: *The only ultimate safety and comfort is the path within and the only work within is unconditional love.* I must love myself first and then I can see if the person within wants to be thinner. I will be able to trust that the person within will know better. My first task is to feed the person within with love. This is the first step in eliminating the self-sabotage found in so many of us. We all have methods of disrupting this self-actualizing process. It's absolutely amazing to me how we spend so much of our time sabotaging our greatest assets and our sacred gifts, our soul blueprint. It's absolutely true that our biggest fear is not that we're inadequate but actually lies in remembering, rediscovering and actualizing the grand self. Most people spend more time thinking and doing their inadequacies and much less time thinking and doing their gifts, talents and beauty. In order to change this, we must start with this self-loving process. As we learn to love the inadequate self we will be able to use these experiences to love and actualize the grander, Divine self.

Comfort Zones: We have to begin to rewire our comfort zones because the old comfort zones have such power to pull us out instead of take us in. Initially, going inside and doing the work within can cause feelings of discomfort. Most of us have been well trained to find our comfort zones in the outside world. Notice how difficult it is to settle into a vacation, where ideally we have the opportunity to let go of the external demands of our lives and feel the deeper place within. However, so many people are uncomfortable with this shift and so plan so many outside events that they feel equally unrested, unsettled after their vacation as before. Our outside comfort zones include those external things that entertain us, distract us and in the end separate us from ourselves. After engaging in the work of the self-loving-actualization, we will feel that anything that takes us out of inner consciousness will cause alarms of discomfort. Now, it's just the opposite. Anything that takes us away from our outside comforts makes us alarmed. We will talk about how to establish these comforts later in the chapter, but for now just become aware of what and where your comfort zones are and note how you seek comfort within.

The Remembrance

It's one thing to truly understand the Commitment to this inner journey and it's another to actually remember this commitment. Every time you remember this commitment know that you have turned on the light of consciousness. This light is the fuel for all else to come. *Consciously committing to this process is the most important act of self-love.*

Remembering exercises: Once you have agreed to commit, you have to decide how you are going to remember that you have made this commitment. Often, I see people go to retreats and therapy and have wonderful insights into this process of inner journeying. They make new pledges to themselves and return home refreshed and renewed. But soon afterward, they forget this new experience and with that forget their vows to be on the path of inner renewal and discovery.

The brain is an amazing organ. It's deeply programmed from the beginning of our lives. Imagine that each script occupies a particular neural pathway in our brain. The more you practice the script the wider and deeper the neural pathway becomes. For so many of us, our old scripts occupy so many of our brain circuits and we have in our overutilization of these scripts developed many access paths to the main circuits. So it's very easy to access these old scripts, these established neural pathways. It's easy to remember them because there are so many of them and there are so many on-ramps to them. Developing new circuitry is not easy and requires much diligence.

The very act of remembering to look within places our conscious attention towards this commitment and thus new pathways are constructed in the mind. Over time, we will be able to plant more and more new circuitry in the brain so that the new revelations and experiences of self-love will be the main highways we travel. But first, our task is to develop outside reminders that are readily available in the external world. After all, we're masters at attending to our outside environment and responding to cues therein. We might start by redesigning our external environment to reflect this new task of loving the self.

Take a moment and decide what kind of cues might remind you of this love commitment, this journey within. Look around the place you live and ascertain how many things in your home light up your inner consciousness and how many things take away from it. Many homes today have TVs in every room and often they are all on. Television, video games, and the Internet are all examples of taking our attention outward. Note the design of your home and explore what things you have around you that call your attention inside and what things call your attention outside. Our homes are so revealing about our priorities. Begin to redesign your home in a way that suggests this commitment towards self-discovery. Perhaps you will bring more nature into your home if nature is something that resonates with the deep within. Pleasant colors, smells and textures all can activate the deeper self within. Does your home reflect your self-hate or your self-love? In chapter five I suggested that you write a reminder, a mantra of sorts on 3x5 note cards and place them everywhere. Your mantra could simply be: "I commit to the process of loving myself" or "The only path is inward...discovering my love and my life." Put these cards in your car and at work and find your own symbols that remind you of this commitment. Let these things be your outside circuitry of remembrance and know that each time you remember this commitment you're actually building new neural pathways in the brain. Eventually, your reality will make a shift where your internal circuits become full of cues, rituals and experiences that will anchor you within, calling to you in the day as a dream calls to you in the night.

Practice

Practicing this process of commitment and remembering is what lays the foundation of self-actualization within. It's so important to state this commitment and design remembering exercises in order to keep this task in full consciousness.

You can practice everyday by:

1. Restating the commitment at night before bed.
2. Offering a prayer for remembrance in the morning.
3. Taking stock, at the end of the day, of where and when you were able to remember the commitment.
4. Becoming more aware of the daily processes of resistance.

At this point, you don't have to know how to love yourself, just that you are committed to that process. Often, we skip over this first practice in our rush to get to the goal of loving and actualizing the self. It's imperative that we first understand the powerful act of commitment, remembering and practicing the remembrance. This is like putting new road signs on the inner highways, so that we remember to turn off of the old pathways and turn on to the new.

Part Two: Awareness

So, once committed, what exactly do we do and how do we proceed? First we develop our awareness of what the within is and sharpen our observational skills at viewing this world. We become self-explorers, detectives if you will, of this vast inner domain. This awareness journey necessarily requires a where, when, who and what.

The Where: Seeking in vs. Seeing Out

We must first become aware of where our attention or awareness resides. For most, it's riveted on the outside world, barely ever landing on the inside terrain. In fact most of us would radically have to change our lives in order to have *seeking in* behaviors more prevalent than *seeking out*. If one simply examines for one day the number of seeking in activities vs. seeking out, one would be surprised what would be revealed.

Many people say to me, "Well, I know what seeking out behaviors look like, but I'm not sure what seeking in behaviors are." Often in therapy it's so transparent that the very question, "But how do I go within?" is seeking out the answers rather than pausing to simply go inside and ask the question to the who within. The very act of asking that question to the self within, shifts the where of consciousness from outside to inside. For so many, there's such a relentless search for some outside answer, some outside recipe, some outside instructive manual that will make the initial steps inward clear, pleasant and exciting, because being and sitting with the self is often not. Shifting the where of one's focus (from the outside to the inside) is amazingly difficult. I see what happens in sessions as I support the process of going within. Even with the supportive hand of the therapist, people want to feel me more than themselves. They want to feel the problems in their lives more than themselves. But this message is eventually devastating. Whatever they may be within, they tell themselves over and over not to go there. The conclusion can only be that there must be something pretty baffling, or bad or perhaps just plain boring about this inside place. What we fail to realize is that everything lies within including the thought that my problems are about the outside world.

First we must become aware of shifting our awareness from out to in. Begin to keep a journal or log about your daily activities and note which of these contributes to inner awareness or outer focus. Imagine that you are standing at the edge of outer world attentiveness and inner world awareness. Become aware of slowly shifting your vision towards the inside. Note how many things you do that help this shift or inhibit it. As we look back out into the external world, this often shifts so much attention away from the self, for instance: watching television and video games, focusing on others, working, creating to do lists, addictions and many other things. It's not that some of these things might not stimulate inner awareness, but most of us use these things to numb our inner consciousness. Begin to create thoughts about those activities that might help you shift the focus inward: meditation, yoga, sitting still, pauses in nature, breathing, contemplation. The main thing here is to change the place, the where of our awareness.

The When

The when is of course right NOW, but so many of us feel that the time right now is either booked up or barricaded. Either way, we have a very hard time gaining entrance into the now of inner work. Imagine for one moment that your life is like a notebook page and that the blue horizontal lines on the page are all your activities in life that require attention and the space in between is your consciousness. As the blue lines become filled up with today's to do list, the space in between the lines becomes obscured. Soon, we forget that there's space in between as we hold a vision for only those lines and what occupies those lines. As we look down upon the page of the day, we see nothing but filled in spaces drawn by our own writing in our own spaces and this fosters the illusion that at least for that day we have already run out of time. We're simply unaware that the spaces in between the lines (our consciousness) take up much more space and time than the lines themselves or anything that has been written on the lines. Imagine taking all the blue lines of an 8 ½ x 11 inch notebook paper and bringing them all together on the page. Mathematically these lines would take less than a half an inch of space on this paper. Ten and one half inches would be left as blank space. This is actually how much time we have in one day ten and one half inches out of eleven inches of consciousness. Could we in fact have more time and space for this inner work than all of our outer work? The actual activities or tasks of the lines take up much less space than we think. What are you doing when you are shifting from one line to the next? Where is your consciousness when you are on a line? There is actually more than enough consciousness to live life in full awareness both outwardly and inwardly, but we use the lines of life to avoid and sometimes escape this inner space. Time is just an illusion to stay unconscious and unaware of our own self-journey. *We have enough time…the problem is we don't have enough consciousness in time and so we're unconscious much of the time.* It's not time that's our enemy it's our unconsciousness. If time is our enemy, it's only the time we take to remain unconscious. Before we can live from the inside out, we must first ***be*** on the inside.

Time Awareness Exercises

1. **On the way:** We have more than ample time on our hands as we're going towards some task, some event, some work of the day, whether it's getting ready for work, riding in the car going to work, walking to a meeting, picking up the kids and the list goes on and on. Where is your attention when you are on the way somewhere? Are you thinking about the upcoming meeting, the clothes you decided to wear, the bad drivers on the road or are you listening to a radio broadcast? Become more aware during these times to see and examine the things that take up your awareness space. *Remember that the more things that take up your space the more you will feel that you don't have time.* Be aware right here right now and stay aware of what is going on in your inner world. Use these moments on the way to turn the light of consciousness on within.

2. **During:** What are you doing in your consciousness when you are actually doing some life activity, some event, some task? For instance, what are you aware of when you do the simple tasks of life like the laundry or dishes or cleaning? So many activities don't require our thinking mind so our consciousness can be quite aware during these tasks. Are we fully aware of ourselves during these tasks or is our mind wandering taking our consciousness to some other place and time? No wonder so many of us think we don't have time, we send it away and don't have a clue what's really going on ***inside*** of ourselves.

   Have you ever dialed a long phone number, hitting the wrong pad in the middle only to dial it over again and again? Our minds have been so trained to do this multi-tasking that we can't simply be here for this task at this moment. Next time you dial the phone pause at each number to breathe awareness into the self.

Remember the more things you fill up the spaces with the less time you will think you have. We actually have time to be present in every thing we do. Where are you in your consciousness when you walk to your car, get inside, drive down the road? Can you stay in the moment and become aware of the you that is driving the car.

Even as we work on thinking tasks, we can still keep awareness of the who doing the thinking. As I write these words, I'm always aware of my inside journey, even as I gaze out of the window to watch the falling snow on the stream outside. As I'm aware of the me that writes the words and the me that sees the snow and the All That Is outside my window, I begin to enter the world of oneness. I can't go there without my consciousness, it's impossible.

3. **In between:** How many pauses do you have in a day? Would you be willing to stop after each line and pause and breathe before you contemplate the next item, the next task, the next event? Can you stay aware of this in between place, this pausing task? Can you then, in your awareness of this in between space, breathe the breath of consciousness into this pause and say: "As I breathe in this moment I center my awareness back inside where all my resources lie. I can then take this breath into the next moment to remind me that it's not about time, only about consciousness."

The Who

Who is the being that stands at the door? The who is the observing part of you that's neither the feelings, the thoughts, the body sensations, nor the dancing of spirit. The observer is the part of you who holds awareness of the various internal processes. The observer simply notes without judgment, without commentary, without critical assessments the state of the being within. *When we have a closer relationship with this who, we will finally come to know that truth about who we really are.* It's more difficult than most of us understand to develop this neutral observer. Yet, without this neutral observer, the chances of getting fixated on every nuance, every dark shadow, every less than or more than condition will increase a hundred fold. Once some kind of assessment or judgment begins, observation simply ends and the ego takes control. In addition, your state of mind can be a contaminant to your inner domain. If you're anxious when you begin this process you'll bring anxiety to this inner world and this in turn will act as a magnet to pull anxious material to the observer's eye. For the very act of observation brings an energetic interaction with the domain within. We know the absolute truth of this from the quantum field research in physics. Different results come depending on the one observing. It's crucial therefore that you establish an unconditional, neutral energy at the gates of this inner world. Oftentimes we begin to analyze our inner world with the same tools our parents, educators and peers have given us. These tools are more like vaccines searching for a virus than they are arms looking for bodies to embrace. Neutrally observing this inner domain builds an energetic highway system within that we can utilize to explore the territory where the self resides. Each time we go within and simply observe what is there, we build a pathway and each time we do this, the path becomes easier to travel and moves us deeper into self-awareness. *It's in the felt experience of becoming the curious Who that brings us closer to realizing the grand beings that we are.* The more well-trodden these paths, the more user-friendly they become. Imagine for a moment that as the observing eye turns inward, beams of light are created that shine upon whatever quadrant or part of you that you are observing. These very light beams then become the pathways by which you will travel and navigate. So the more you can observe the What Within, the more you automatically create corridors echoing callings to journey within. At some point the world within becomes more familiar and more natural and is traveled with more ease than the world without. No doubt, this is when the shrouded veils will be lifted and we will once again remember who we are.

This simple ability to observe builds a network of passageways that can then act as a conduit system for allowing various healing energies to travel both in and out. Healing, loving energy can be delivered to various stations or quadrants within and our own various soul gifts of healing, compassion, creative expression can be delivered to the world without. *This Observing or attentive mindfulness paves the way for all else to come.* That's why it's crucial that the one who does the observing remain neutral. Joy and love will then be sure to follow. For if you take a denser energy state with you on the inner journey, that state will often be the material of which the paths are made. So for example if you take judgment, you will leave deposits of judgment in the path. Each new thing you observe will be tainted with the vibrations of judgment. Don't be surprised when the observer begins to resist this task of going within, for who would want to be in the path of judgment. Neutral unconditional observing is crucial so that the paths remain clear of damaging debris and ego clutter. One of the most important reasons to learn the way of the Observer is not only to "know thyself," but also to develop and shape the corridors that will eventually hold the light of consciousness from the higher self and All That Is. The eventual goal is to deliver the raw materials of love and compassion into the deep wells of the self. It's in this process that the inner world of self joins the infinite world of the Divine.

The What

We have four quadrants of experience: mind, body, heart and spirit. (**see illustration 13**) Becoming acquainted with these inner planes of self-existence and experience is crucial. The what involves the four quadrants of our existence and the process observing the what builds the labyrinth that will hold the energy that will make healing, expressing, loving and oneness come into being.

Before moving into each quadrant, it will be helpful to understand how the "what" of our mind/body connection really works. There has been a deluge of new research on the brain/body connection in the last few years informing us about the evolution of our brain/body/heart alliance. In fact, there have been many recent books written on this subject , but I would like to briefly review the most relevant findings for the what of our self-experience.

1. We have three brains, according to neuroscience, the oldest is the reptilian brain, the next most recent is the limbic brain. The neocortex is the newest part of our brain in our evolutional journey and the last brain area to develop in the womb. It's involved with the highest and most complex functions of being human. It's fascinating to know that our neocortex has 100 billion neurons, which is exactly the same as our galaxy has stars. Our brain is both breathtaking in its structure and function and as expansive as our galactic home. As Joseph Pearce so eloquently explains, the smartest part of our brain, the neocortex, still does not govern and reign over the lower more primitive parts of the brain during difficult and high stress situations. The fight or flight syndrome found in our ancestors who faced more do or die life threatening situations was governed by the more primitive parts of the brain including both the reptilian brain and the limbic system. However, even though modern humans have the more evolved and higher functioning new brain, the multiplex of contemporary psychological, global and spiritual stresses we now face seem to have stunted our growth. As we continue to face these more convoluted survival themes, albeit more sophisticated, we call continuously on our other, older parts of our brain, our reptilian brain and our emotionally run limbic system for actions and reactions. So as we face unprecedented individual, global and species survival issues we have

THE QUADRANTS

Illustration 13

less access to our higher problem solving capabilities and wisdom (which lies in the neocortex). Joseph Pearce concludes that we're still governed from the bottom up rather than the top down.

2. Our brain is not the only place intelligent neurons are found. In fact, we now know that we have thousands upon thousands of intelligent neurons in our heart. In fact, our heart is the first body part that grows in the womb and it's actually responsible for developing the neurons that then travel to the area that will later be the brain. Therefore, more information flows up to the brain from the heart than down from the brain to the heart. In essence the heart not only dictates the growth of the brain but also births it with its own essential elements.

3. According to the Heart Math Institute, we have expansive electromagnetic fields (EM) that radiate from the heart that are strikingly similar to the electromagnetic field that arises from the Earth (called the torus field). Our heart's EM field is not only the same shape as the Earth's EM field, but when in a coherent state actually merges with the Earth's Torus Field. Positive emotions like love, peace and joy produce more coherent EM fields and negative emotions like anger and rage produce incoherence in this field. These incoherent EM fields cause interference not only with merging with the Earth's field, but with other human beings as well.

4. The research from the Heart Math Institute has shown that the heart has precognitive abilities and can foresee events that have yet to occur in reality. In addition, when we feel joy, our electromagnetic field expands some nine meters wide and is very coherent. When in anger, our EM field becomes incoherent and shrinks. These intuitive knowings and emotions can cause a near instant corresponding shift in the frontal brain or neocortex. For instance, the heart senses something terrible is about to happen, the EM field not only becomes less coherent, it sends alarming information to the brain. The brain follows suit activating the sympathetic nervous system which readies us for fight or flight responses (limbic system and reptilian brain becomes on high alert). On the other hand, positive felt intuitions trigger the parasympathetic nervous system in the brain producing more coherence, signaling all is well. The neocortex is not surprisingly more awake and activated in this state. In other words, our heart,

through intuitive channels or directly felt emotions, strongly influences our brain heart coherence.

5. Our brain produces different wavelengths of electric energy. The faster the wavelength the busier the brain and in waking states most of us produce strong beta wavelengths. In high stress, we not only produce "bad" chemistry for our bodies, but we produce very fast but less coherent electrical activity in our brains. Dr. Joe Dispenza has shown that when people actually meditate on love and compassion the whole brain becomes coherent and not only produces healthier chemistry but slower more coherent electrical activity, which ranges from alpha waves to theta to delta, which is found in deep sleep.

6. Dr. Dispenza further explains that we have something called the thalamic gate in the brain that transmits frequencies from the deeper subconscious parts of our brain to the world outside. These transmissions tend to search for like frequencies or resonance in the external world. For instance, if you have deep seated anger issues that have been stored in your subconscious, you may inadvertently transmit these anger frequencies outward towards your environment searching for resonance and likeness. If you have a negative view of yourself and the world you will probably see and feel the negative parts that are both within you and outside of you in your external surroundings. In other words, what is found within you shapes and determines what you find outside of you.

7. Instantaneous Connections: The world of quantum physics is turning our view of time and space upside down. We now know that photons that were once connected in time and space are still instantaneously connected even if 600 miles apart. This is called entanglement theory which Einstein called "spooky action at a distance." This theory implies that all particles of life that once were compacted tightly together will forever be connected, not by space or time but by the act of entanglement. We by definition are intricately connected and perhaps our psychic abilities such as telepathy, clairvoyance, remote viewing and intuitive knowing come from that field of entanglement. As David Wilcock states, what we do, think or feel affects the field of all life at all times.

Summary of the Research

Although we have great capacity to be governed by the amazing part of our brain called the neocortex, we're still victim to the lower more primordial parts of the brain that often cause great upheaval and ill health to our system as a whole. Our neocortex holds the power of some of our greatest gifts as humans including creativity, compassion, social cooperation, problem solving, intuition, expansive thinking and spiritual enlightenment. Our modern day stresses continue to activate and trigger our primitive brain, activating incoherence and chaos. We're in essence bottom feeders instead of top feeders. In addition, we have lost touch with our hearts and the amazing wisdom that lies therein. We must start with our heart intelligence, which then can guide the more evolved new brain, the neocortex, into becoming the leading source of cognitive creativity and transparent coherence. With this we will become resonant beings that shape and merge with All That Is vibrant in and above this world.

So, one can begin to see the crucial importance of examining the What Within. *For it's in this process of taking responsibility for clearing out the old paradigms of fear and fright and replacing them with new paradigms of love and light, that we truly will move into the golden age of the human/spirit revolution.* We have only begun to understand that this is paramount for the survival of our species and of Earth herself. The external world is only a snapshot of our internal world. It's in the rich, fertile ground of the internal world where we will make the necessary strides towards eternal consciousness. Bringing the potent sacred energy of love to this inside human world is not only crucial to our individual healing but also ascendant to the opening of our multidimensionality.

Throughout this book, we have talked about the lure of the outer world and the tremendous power it has over our inner world. Strangely, the external world only holds what we already have bestowed upon it and therefore there is nothing new in these outside paradigms. As we remain fixated on these externalized paradigms of old, we have become rigidly locked and quite compartmentalized in viewing the What Within. It's crucial to understand that when we look out at the world, we naturally become more entrained to our fast beta wave world. In addition, the outer world seems so adept at triggering our frightened sympathetic nervous system. It's actually the outer world that continues to activate our lower reptilian brain and emotionally laden limbic system. We now know that when we shift our attention to our inner landscape we're more apt to slow down, producing the calmer and slower alpha and theta wavelengths as well as activating the parasympathetic nervous system, which sends calm chemistry and more harmonic messages to our whole system. When we focus on the What Within, we can begin to eventually slow down our brain wavelengths, correct our chemistry, feel love in our hearts and heal what ails us. This process of finding the sacred self is the most important process on Earth.

Unearthing the What Within is paramount to activating the new inner renaissance of the *sacred self.* As we learn to apply the paradigm of love to all the parts of the What, the compartmentalized blocks of body, mind, heart and soul will be dissolved so that wholeness and expansion will be the energetic signature of our growth and wellbeing-ness. When the self is clear, open, fluid and full of sacredness, it will no longer be attached the outer world for antiquated definitions. Without a clear self-vehicle there can't be expanded consciousness. As we birth the sacred self through love, we will electrify the manifestation grids necessary for co-creating with the Divine a new world, new age and a new external paradigm. *The externalized world, as we know it will no longer create the inner land of What we are, but we will create the outer land of where we live.*

The Resistance

Before we move into the quadrants of the What, let's explore once again the tremendous resistance we will meet on the way in.

1. All of us at some point experienced not having enough whether it be love, physical comforts, psychological encouragement or spiritual guidance. Part of our resistance lies in our refusal to give up our attachment to the idea that the outside will give us enough of whatever we think we don't have enough of. Because we have these injuries within, ironically we still seek the healing solutions from the very place that these injuries occurred, the world outside of us. Most of us don't have a clue how many templates we have internalized that are unloving and unkind. When we look to the outside world for healing, we don't realize that the outside templates haven't changed because we have not changed. So the beat goes on in the same dull, sluggish rhythm that created our unworthy, unloving self in the first place. We haven't been told the truth about how incredibly magnificent we really are. We have the internal power and creativity to change what we are and therefore what the world is. It's time for a reversal of action. Love the inner world so that it might create Love in all that surrounds us.

2. We must be willing to *grieve* this process of letting go of the old externalized paradigm of remedies. This may include a lifetime of ideas about what it really means to be human. It's simply reality shattering to understand the truth about who we are, thereby giving up the outside blueprints prescribing who we thought we should be. It may mean grieving the very foundation upon which we have lived. This may include our religious beliefs surrounding sin and salvation, our family beliefs about what we can and can't do, our educational beliefs about our true intelligence and our political beliefs about freedom and sovereignty. Grieving truly means we must face that we alone can save ourselves. *It can cause great despair to realize that you and you alone are your greatest lover. Yet in this exalted moment of truth, you're finally free to be all that you truly are.*

3. Finally as we courageously go within, let's face it, meeting the inadequate self isn't fun. We have been given so many beliefs regarding the emptiness and/or the inadequacy that lies within that it's no wonder we keep our conscious vigilance and awareness elsewhere. At the very first entrance to the self, you may find pain, emptiness, anxiety, and reams of not enough scripts. These are not our enemies; they are only our guideposts directing us towards that which needs awareness and healing attentiveness.

It's imperative to understand that one of the most important missions now is to reveal our shadow parts and dance them into the light. Discovering the dark side of humanness is not evidence of sin, it reveals the phenomenon of being human. It's not to be used as evidence of imperfection, but rather as evidential proof of spirit coming into consciousness with the truth of our mission. We're here to hold and learn anew from these lower self-projections. As we learn and hold, we can also release and evolve. People who are on the spiritual path tend to want to get further and further away from these shadowy segments of self and so they become less and less conscious as denial becomes a great deceiver of the truth. Instead, we must think as spiritual warriors and realize that we must continue to take the path inward towards the shadowy parts that lurk just below consciousness. It's often these nebulous, murky places within that cause the most havoc outside. Without befriending, understanding and loving these parts, we will forever be lost in the shadows of the obscured self. We must not leave this work behind in favor of more lofty and etheric work. This is one of the reasons we're all on this planet at this moment in time. We're here to lead the negativity of human experience into the light. We should feel so lucky to be engaged in this soul-evolving endeavor. We're indeed imperfect, and this is our birthright as humans. As we release the dark we have come to rescue, we can know the spiritual experience of being human. *We have forgotten that we're really spirit, housed in a human vehicle, not a human trying to become spirit.* It's in fact this concept of *human to spirit* that has gotten us in so much trouble, because this has made us feel we indeed must be perfect, as perfection has become a sign of some spiritual ascent. But, we're already ascending as we are and always have been spirit consciousness. We've just agreed to come into human form and take a wild ride without remembrance of the place from which we come.

Let's remember that this compulsion to be perfect is the human ego trying to reach spirit. The acceptance of being imperfect is spirit reaching and touching the human experience. Only the ego needs perfection. From the ego's point of view there is no realization that the Divine Creator has created everything in perfection even the perceived imperfections. It's through these often-stormy misty fallibilities that we encounter our biggest lessons. Our imperfections and shadow parts were perfectly designed to point towards the areas that demand reconfiguration for the new dawning of the New Human. If it weren't for a problem you might not stop, if it weren't difficult and painful you might not feel. The dramas and traumas of life are simply attention getters so that we might for once stop, look and listen to the deep voice within. So many of us use these struggles to complain, hide and seek. That injurious energy in the outer world just represents the injury to be found in the inner world. Let this be a call to return HOME. If we'd been home all along we probably wouldn't have been so easily injured. So if we're not fully anchored within, we can become prey to fear all too easily. Remember, the more you are anchored within, the less the anxieties and dictates of the world can flood you and determine your mental state. Next time there's some nighttime insult from the cranky, edgy outer limits use this as evidence that the work lies within. Don't distract yourself by going to these outer limits and doing the arduous and exasperating labor in the old oppressive paradigms. Come inside to the place that your energy can dance the perfect dance of love. Taking responsibility for the What Within is the most empowering thing you can do. This is where the neoteric archetypes for the *New Human* will be found. Loving the What Within is the most sacred action you can take.

Soul Remedies

#6 – Self-love

Sit quietly…
Breathe in…
and bring your attention to your inside world…
the world of you.

Just pause in this place of wonder…
without judgment…
without comment…
without condition.

You have been away from this inner landscape for too long.
Feel the relief…you are finally home once again.

Make a commitment right now…to return to this inner world every day.
Whisper this promise to your "self" three time,
all the while breathing deeply and calmly.

Now, in your mind's eye,
think of one thing that might remind you
of this commitment…
a word, a symbol, a note, nature.

Bring this to the forefront of your mind…
and know how you might place this reminder in your life.

Remember how you might be found:
Where: Inside
When: Now
Who: The observer…the one who is simply aware
What: Body, mind, heart and spirit.

7

The Quadrants of Experience

"Knowing yourself is the beginning of all wisdom."
–Aristotle

"There is only one corner of the universe you can be certain of improving, and that's your own self."
–Aldous Huxley"

"Your work is to discover your world and then, with all your heart, give yourself to it."
–Buddha

"All wonders you seek are within yourself."
–Sir Thomas Browne

How exciting to begin the most important and revealing work in the journey of life. As we discover the world within, we will be able to finally create the world beyond with our own image of our highest hopes and dreams. Exploring the "what" within has long been ignored in most of us. So it may seem arduous and formidable at first sight. The first obstacle is the illusion that there is nothing to gain by going in. The second stumbling block is the chaos and unrecognizable terrain we may find in the landscape of these inner quadrants. Rest assured, these are just bumps in the road to test your resolve. The truth in this inner journey is both miraculous and liberating. As you discover yourself, your world will expand beyond your imagination. Pause for one moment and breathe deeply. The wonder and magic of your life is about to reveal itself.

INNER ACTIONS WITH THE WHAT

QUADRANT 1: THE BODY

We're here to be in total awareness of body as we expand in consciousness. We often think this is an either or choice. Either I'm in higher consciousness or I'm in body. But truly, we're meant to feel spirit embodied. This is the miracle of Earth living. I think, however, that when we begin to recognize the importance of being in body, we also get closer to our fears of physical death. To avoid our fear of death, we dim our awareness of being in body and stay disembodied. Of course, the risk of disembodiment is spiritual death. This presents quite a paradox.

The relationship we have with the body is crucial; either it can be a barrier or a conduit to higher consciousness. It's actually our most amazing tool for understanding our heart/mind connection. It's the physical body that holds the reverberations of coherence vs. incoherence, calm vs. chaos, expanding vs. dimming. So, as we know our bodies, we know exactly what is needed for fluidity and wholeness. Our bodies become the container for experiencing and launching our expanding consciousness. The body is, after all, an amazing path towards spirit.

I. The Sacred Beholder

a) The Neutral Observer

To become a Sacred Beholder of the body, one must take the unconditional awake who into the landscape of the beautiful domain of the body. There's so much guidance available in our body, so many subtle cues and signals that can lead us to higher consciousness and peaceful harmonic relationships with all other things. We often miss these cues because our body also houses our anxieties, fears, emotions, ailments and histories. We've been told many untruths about our bodies and we carry our deepest shame in our bodies. All lifetime trauma eventually takes up residence in our bodies. These things often skyrocket us right out of the body and into the outside world. We look for things to calm and numb our bodies so that we don't have to deal with our dense material embodiment. But, the body is quite adept are getting our attention in spite of our attempts to quiet its callings. Oftentimes these attempts are painful and disconcerting and so we continue our search to dampen these places of wisdom in favor of finding places outside of our body that dumb us down and make us weak and exhausted. Becoming an observer, a detective, a Sacred Beholder of the body is no easy assignment.

First we must learn to simply sit with the body and observe without the judgmental winds that confuse and catapult one out and not in Sitting with the body requires a commitment to turn your attention inwards towards the whispers of your *body deep*. The work of the breath is often a wonderful way to begin this observing practice.

Find a quiet place and a comfortable position and begin to simply shift your awareness towards your breath. Watch as you breathe in and you breathe out. Follow this breath with neutral attention. Notice your in breath, the pause in between and then the out breath. Begin to slow this breathing in and breathing out until you can count five times in and five times out. Let yourself stay with this breathing in and out for five minutes. Whenever you feel anxious or stressed, return to this breathing…this reassurance that you are alive…that you are pulsing with life. Know that it's in this breathing that you'll discover all else that lies within and beyond. Becoming a beholder of your breath will light up your body consciousness and help you begin to feel all that your body offers.

Learning to do body scans where you let your breath take you to each part of your body…where you simply note that part and perhaps offer soft greetings that say, "Hello, I see you now and want to feel you once again." Noting tension or pain but not getting stuck in any analysis or fear, but simple awareness.

We have the power within us to heal everything that ails us; we're just not masters of this yet. We can't become healers of things that simply escape our awareness. So the first step in body recognition is awareness of the body. In essence, these body-sitting practices are opening lines of communication and understanding from the observing self to the body self. In essence, we are saying, "Hello I'm here and I want to know more about you. I do not see you… body…as my enemy but my friend and mentor. I want to learn more about you, be in the experience of you and integrate you into the whole of me." Simply giving conscious attention to your breath and your body parts is healing in and of itself. Wherever we direct our higher states of consciousness receives the benefit of the healing light vibration that comes from that place.

Observing these practices will prepare you for the deeper work of loving and healing the body. Learning to be compassionate with and in the body is a most incredibly difficult task.

b) Loving the Body

Neutrally observing the body is crucial but it's also as important to become conscious of the messages you're sending to your body on a daily basis. Do you stop everyday to note what is going on inside your body? Do you know what your body is carrying for you? It's important to become astutely aware of what we carry with us to this place of body. Are you aware of the subtle messages you have about your body? Does your body secretly disgust you? Do you think your body is the reason for your misfortune? Are you engaged in patterns of behavior that undermine your body's vigor and wellness? Do you even know what these are?

The second part of this practice is to become aware of those whispers of disapproval and judgment that haunt the halls of body degradation. Are there particular body parts that you shame easily? Do you have less of a relationship with certain parts over others? Becoming aware of how you talk to the body is crucial. We can't change something we do not know exists. Are there traumas hidden and held by your body? Understanding patterns and conditions we hold for the body is crucial in the healing process. We hold old paradigms of beliefs in our body and if we're ever to be a clear conduit for higher consciousness we must dissolve our body blocks. For most things we think and feel eventually land in our bodies.

c) Healing the Body

As we begin to have a deeper relationship with our body and the various beliefs that we send swirling down the corridors of our biological system, we can begin to get in touch with exactly how our body is wired, whether to be a fear/chaos sequencer or a love/harmonic sequencer. It's most compelling and pivotal to realize that we have the power and the responsibility to revamp our circuitry in order to make a place for the renaissance self to reside. We can begin to explore how the brain/body connection really works. Your body tells an incredible story about where you get stuck in old blueprints and how you might begin to mend the worn out pathways of fear and fright.

Recognizing the signs and symptoms of the sympathetic nervous system (SNS) and the havoc it wreaks on the body is crucial. The SNS is great for alerting the body when to fight or flee, but in most situations these days our survival isn't based on fleeing or fighting. We often have to stay frozen in place as our SNS careens out of control increasing our heart rate, blood pressure, muscle tension, stress hormones like cortisol and the ever so fast high beta brainwaves. While our electric and chemical systems are on high alert, we have nowhere to go to dissipate these reactions. If you are worried about your financial situation, or a job conflict involving your manager or a combative crisis with your spouse, you may not necessarily be able to run away or stay and fight, and so you may just hold the stress within your body. We now know that most of our disease states have been linked to stress. So, how we handle stress in our bodies is paramount to health. Understanding our biological wiring and the survival mode most of us are in much of the time helps us begin to know how to reroute the rutted neuro/bio pathways of our bodies. So much of the time our primitive reptilian brain and emotionally laden limbic system are on overdrive due to our urgent and overwrought lifestyles. It's so important to be IN our bodies so that we might know what the brain is actually up to. As you begin to recognize that the wire has been tripped for stress responses, you will then have more control over deciding how you actually want to respond. As the first indication of biological signs of stress and/or fear runs through our body, we can begin to make subtle changes and actually create new pathways of wellness and calm. Simply becoming a bio/body detective, and noting with refined awareness how and where the body carries unease, apprehension and distress is the first significant step in the process of revitalization of the body.

II. Compassionate Enfolding

This is possibly one of the greatest keys for healing and rejuvenation. We've learned so much in the past few years about the healing energy of compassion. In experiments where Buddhist monks sat in compassionate meditation, sending this energy to the research subjects sitting in the next room, amazing results occurred. It's important to understand that these subjects were unaware that this was happening and yet their blood pressure, heart rate, breathing and feelings of anxieties all decreased, inducing a state of calm and peace. We now know that when subjects are in a meditative state themselves, the stress response decreases and brainwave activity becomes more coherent and slow, thus allowing once again the subjects to feel calm and peaceful. When mapping the brain it's clear that the reptilian brain and limbic system are not activated during these meditative states and the neocortex (the new brain) is turned on, activating feelings of wellbeing and what I will call compassionate holding. In addition, there have been studies where a group of people in one city deliberately offers compassionate prayers during meditation over a month's period of time. Amazingly, the crime rates in those cities significantly decreased during that month. On a different note, have you ever noticed that in stressful situations, it's not specific solutions we want from someone, but compassionate understanding of our experience? As a therapist, I've been told many times, it's simply the act of feeling another person's compassionate presence of listening and holding that becomes the healing moment in the hour.

All of these things demonstrate the intrinsic healing power of compassionate energy. What's most uplifting and amazing is that we have the power to generate this in our own bio/body system, which is both restorative and curative all at once. But for many humans, it's even difficult to recognize this compassionate experience.

a) Bathing the Body in Compassionate Experience

It's first important to understand how we can generate this compassionate energy. It takes place in the heart and neocortex in the front part of the brain. It starts with heart breathing which is breathing and opening from your heart. It might help to remember a time when you felt especially compassionate about someone or some situation. Remember this and begin to bring this state back into your experience. You will probably remember that your body was calm and your mind was filled with understanding and your heart was full of love. It's imperative to practice this remembering and this ability to conjure up the compassionate part of your heart/mind/body. When you begin to feel this compassion, you are secreting the good chemicals in your brain, slowing the electrical wavelengths, opening neuropathways to the higher states in your brain/mind and filling your heart with the soft vibrant energy of love. As you begin to experience this, you can send this energy to your whole body without judgment without prejudice but simply imagine sending this compassionate healing energy to all body systems. You might want to script a few words to go with this tenderhearted state of being, like, "I love every part of my body," or "Thank you for working so hard for me" and "Now I want to give you the medicinal energy of love." Do this exercise once a day for a few minutes, by simply bringing the compassionate experience to mind through the heart and sending this to all body components. Watch how your body rests.

b) Holding Body Patterns with Compassion

As you begin working more astutely with your body, you will notice patterns that may be difficult. Usually, most people have particular body areas that become most affected by stress. Perhaps you hold pain in your lower back, or anxiety in your stomach when you meet some unease and apprehension. Note your patterns of holding stress and use the compassionate exercise to send waves of restorative energy to those patterns, those habitual pathways of stress response. In order to change these patterns of responding to the world, first heal and soothe these old templates of body sequencing.

c) Enfolding Pain and Struggle with Compassion

Perhaps the most difficult exercise is to actually send compassion to body pain and illness. Most pain and illness trigger further fear and stress compounding the problem. Think how many times, you've had an injury or physical pain and you thought to yourself, "Oh maybe this will never go away or maybe something is really wrong, or maybe I will die." As you think these thoughts, stress hormones are activated and sent to the very areas that are in need of healing. If you became an incredibly astute observer of subtle body states, and were able to send the compassionate healing energy from your heart/ mind complex immediately to these physical fields, you might never get sick. At first, you might not believe that we actually house these enormous healing reservoirs within us, but practice offering this compassionate experience to the smallest ache and strain and watch and feel what happens. Remember, this has to be an experience, not a thought, not an intellectual understanding, but a knowing and intuitive action that inspires consciousness to infuse the body with this elixir of compassion. Many researchers are beginning to believe that even medical miracles are evidence of this innate ability to heal ourselves even if we think it comes from some outside phenomenon of miraculous cure. Our belief is clearly crucial in this process. So take a close look at the powerlessness you may feel regarding your body. The first hypothesis you may want to adopt is that you have the healing and restorative power within through compassionate enfoldment. Before we can move into the new era of body renaissance, we will have to utilize this therapeutic reparative process to remove our old blocks housed in our somatic house called the body. And in this way our bodies can return to a holistic system that works harmoniously and resonant with All That Is within and without.

QUADRANT 2: THE HEART

As so many ancient spiritual traditions as well as indigenous cultures have stated, our heart is our most important holder of wisdom. Yet, we often mistake the heart as housing only the torrents of human emotions rather than a place of immense intuitive intelligence. *If we're going to become a species sanctioned with heart primacy, we must first understand the true nature of our emotional fields as they house the greatest blocks and stepping stones to knowing the intuitive insights that are fruited from the heart.*

The human heart houses one of our most important assets – our ability to feel emotions and experience love. This is, no doubt, our greatest gift, and yet it's our greatest challenge. Living with our feelings while not becoming them ...letting them guide us without cascading out of control on the rapids of strong emotional currents is no easy process. Our emotions can be the main thread of connection to All That Is. We can use feelings to understand others, love others or repel from others. Our emotional content, more than anything else, determines how closely we live with other living beings, the world and the Source of All That Is. These heart sentiments help us understand the deeper needs and desires we have as human beings and are the very pathways to our intuitive wisdom. Yet we become so enveloped in the frenzy of feelings that we become stuck as if in a blinding snowstorm and raging winds. In order to have more mastery over this incredible powerful force, we must learn to utilize these winds to navigate through the tides of life to honor and strengthen the greatest gift that comes from our heart and our humanness...love.

I. Sacred Beholder

As with the body, to become a Sacred Beholder of the heart, one must take the unconditional awake who into the landscape of the beautiful domain of the heart. Perhaps the first step in becoming more aware of this domain is developing the ability to establish an identification system for this complex system of emotions. Often, feelings come in mysterious shapes and sizes and we react to things in the world without fully knowing what our feelings are. It's important to pause and do a heart scan, asking the question, "What am I feeling right now?" Of all the quadrants, this one has the most confusion attached to it. Emotions cause us to spring into action before we're fully aware of the exact nature of the emotion in the first place. Emotions also alert us to danger, crises, and emergencies and so we've learned to respond to certain feelings with stress reactions before we even know the authentic and genuine feelings driving the reaction.

We've developed antagonistic and sometimes harsh scripts pertaining to our emotional world that are discouraging to our feeling identification endeavors. We've been told not to feel or that we feel too much. It's rare to be told not to use our minds or bodies, but we're often told not to be so emotional. It's important to distinguish what we do with emotions and how we behave with them versus the experience of simply having them. Our first task is to consciously make a special invitation to the heart. Perhaps the invitation can be, "I will commit to simply listening everyday to my heart quadrant and will be open to all that I might learn about myself…knowing that my most vital life force energy resides here."

First exercise: Pause once a day for five minutes to identify your feelings and simply note them. Watch and listen to your judgment and commentary as you identify what you feel. The object here is to observe this with unconditional regard and curiosity. Also, notice whether you have access to language that can distinguish between different emotional states. Note your gross states of emotional being…happy, sad, anxious, calm and your more subtle states of emotions…uneasy, discontent, melancholy, remorse, inspiration, zest, affection and others. It's so hard for people to distinguish and identify the more subtle emotional states, which may seem less significant or more obscured than the more obvious generalized feelings. Yet these subtle states influence our behaviors every hour every day all year long.

In addition to identifying more specifically our emotional states, it's helpful to identify the situations that cause certain feelings. Become a detective to the when, where, who phenomena. This will help you become more adept at pattern recognition. You can use patterns to identify that certain people, events and places cause similar feelings. Simply becoming aware of this inner activity is crucial to knowing who you are and what you really want. Identifying is very different than responding. Simply noting and becoming aware…this is the goal. Are some feelings more commonly felt on an everyday basis? Often we have patterns that point to habitual emotional responding. We begin to respond to many cues habitually, even becoming unaware when the cues themselves change. We may drive into a parking garage everyday and see the same parking lot attendant who typically may be cranky and unresponsive and so as we begin to go into the garage we inadvertently prepare for this by feeling protective and unavailable emotionally. We may so habitually do this that we don't notice the day that the attendant seems happy, and is smiling. We've developed habitual emotional responses to so many external things in life that it's crucial to become aware of these habits or patterns if we're to have more conscious control.

Are there themes to your emotional material….do your beliefs come from your emotional patterns of responding? Note your commentary about things that make you feel. For instance, you might hear yourself saying. "Today is going to be a bad day because of the staff meeting…I always feel bad and defeated after these meetings or when I see so and so…I always feel jealous and deflated." Can you become more aware of the various situations or people that cause certain themes to be generated? What do you start to believe about yourself because of your particular emotional patterns? For instance, "Large groups of people make me feel uncomfortable...I don't do well socially...I'm an introvert...I can't take a job that requires extraverted skills." Observe the patterns of emotional frequencies that live in your heart. As these patterns make themselves known you will have power to not only change these patterns if you so desire, but you will become acutely aware of the amazing power that lies within your heart. Your heart feels and intuitively knows all, and thus determines the flow of felt abundance in all other quadrants.

II. Compassionate Enfolding

As discussed earlier, we now know the intrinsic healing power of compassion and love and so we must engage the emotional life of the heart quadrant with the healing action of compassionate enfoldment. Difficult or strong emotions that cause us to sit up and take notice that the self exists are the very emotions that often take us on a wild goose chase in the outside environment. We quickly abandon the self for some anticipated redemption found on the roller coaster of external events. Often, we're better at finding outside reasons for our emotions than we are at simply staying around and keeping our emotions company. For instance, when we get angry we become astutely aware that the self within exists as we feel the reverberation of the energetic anger signature rebounding throughout our internal world, however, we immediately look outside of ourselves to see who's to blame. The amazing thing about feelings is that they turn a light on inside and say, "Hey something is happening." But, the bad news is we look to the outside world for the reason for these challenging and burdensome feelings. In doing this, we create a path to leave the self. Thus the paradox appears: the very emotional experience that begins the process of knowing the self is the very experience that takes us way outside of the self to the event, person, object that seemingly caused the emotional experience in the first place.

This seductive loop that brings us back outside once again, causes us to leave the inner world of self when we need to be there the most. As we leave our inner homes, we often find further injury in the streets of our very own impassioned neighborhoods. What we must understand is that the blemished energy in the outer world just represents the afflictions that lie within. When there is some perceived insult or injury in the outer world let it be a call to return home. Remember that the worse time to leave the confines of your inner sanctuary is in the middle of a storm. *Perhaps, we're not quite evolved enough to be ghost busters in the outer world, as we first must be spirit soothers in the inner world.* We can learn to go to these often-blustery feeling states and hold them with the indubitable dynamism of compassion. Producing this sacred compassionate dialogue with our emotional states is paramount to health and wellbeing.

Guidelines for Compassionate Inner Actions

a) Noting and Holding Difficult Feeling States

Don't look for the peripheral causes in the distant lands of the extraneous world, rather, direct consciousness to the solutions of the inner world where the sacred voice says: "I will stay with not against, attend not abandon, embrace not shame."

Embracing our emotional states with unconditional love leads to dissolution and letting go. It's an amazing process to experience the healing that comes from holding a feeling, exploring its manifestations whether in the body, heart or mind, and simply being curious about it. It often changes in the middle of such conscious examination to something else all together..

Remember: the feeling that often gets our attention is not at the heart of the dilemma that lies underneath.

b) Creating the Sacred Voice of Compassion

Invent loving scripts such as: "I see you are hurt, angry, jealous, shameful and I hold you with love and compassion as if you (the feeling) are a child in need of an embrace." So, next time you are in a difficult feeling state create a compassionate Mantra that states: "These are my feelings...only I can soothe them."

Shower them first with the breath of your inner sacred heart. This new template of the sacred voice will begin to penetrate your consciousness so that you now have two choices at the juncture of the next emotional predicament. It will be easier and easier to return to the sacred voice template, because it feels better. You will begin to create the inner loops of wellness and power. These inner loops are self-contained by definition. You have the power to calm all emotional storms. You will never have to be dependent on the outside world again for calming. This inner loop of wellness is paradoxical because as we stay self-contained by compassionate enfolding we will be better able to offer the world more of our deepest healing tools, thereby creating a brand new world beyond the world of inner loops.

This is the fashion by which we come to create the world beyond us by recreating the world within us.

c) Listening to the Story of the Feeling Scroll: Following the Secret Maps Hidden Within

All feeling states have meaning and therefore provide us with pathways to the deeper realms of the self-experience. Following these pathways will take us closer to manifesting our soul's reality of mission and purpose. Let's take a look at the meaning of some of our more potent feeling states.

Shame

Shame is the greatest feeling suppressant we have. It's a heavy cover that secrets away the truth about being human in a spirited world. It keeps us in our place without movement without flow and when we use it as a tool to hide our imperfections it eventually drains all life force. It's the last layer of self-degradation within. We often hold shame where there has been some humiliation, some odium that triggered the unworthy self. When given by others, shame is often utilized as a tool of oppression and control, as the part of us that is disgraced often goes underground and remains repressed in sticky censured places within. Most incidences of shame do come from externalized blueprints of what is "appropriate, normal and approved." Shame always seems to be predicated on the assumption that, left to our own devices, we would certainly be religious sinners, out of touch with social etiquette and out of control with dangerous impulses. My belief, however, is that without these outside controlling, shaping forces, shame would probably be replaced by the organic process of discovering the higher self within, sometimes by trial and sometimes by error. So, it's crucial to understand that shame is a great signal that we're getting closer to the hiding places of the stuck self, closer to some realness, to that place on the outer rim of the deepest core self within. Instead of hiding our discredited places, we might instead explore them to see what they might reveal. Shame is the best place to begin loving the self. It's here that we keep our deepest beliefs about what the perfect and most acceptable human is. So it's here that we can truly practice loving our broken, defective imperfect human parts. This is one of the greatest missions on Earth at this time. If you don't accept the end goal of love, you can stay stuck in shame and blame for quite a long while. Instead, we need to see shame as a light pointing the way to what needs love. *Shame points the way to loving ourselves, and blame points the way to loving others.*

So next time you feel some shame about some act or thought or deed, look into the eyes of the shameful child within and hold her/him with the grace of total acceptance and see for just a moment what lies underneath. Plan to be surprised.

Anxiety

What person has not dealt with moments of anxious fretting, if not torrid whirlwinds of overwrought fears and worries? Anxiety, in all of its forms, often propels people to go to their doctor's office seeking medications to anesthetize this difficult emotional state. Instead we could see this fretful state as a signal that guides us to what needs our attention and love. Many times anxiety is telling us about our unfulfilled soul promises, it nudges us to get our attention. The problem is when we first feel the signals of anxiety we begin to frantically scan the outer world for the reasons for our anxiety never knowing it's simply a deep calling from within. We either anesthetize the symptoms of the anxious calling or search for the antecedent in the externalized world. As we begin to frantically scan the outer world for the reasons for our anxious state, unfortunately, we find there are plenty of things to blame for our feelings. In this way, we become further detached from our inner callings, convinced that if we procure and prosecute the outer culprits, the inner world will be safe once again. It's important to remember that anxiety triggers the more primitive parts of the brain, the limbic system and the reptilian brain, and therefore readies the individual for fight or flight. This, by definition, directs our concentration towards the unsafe dangers in the externalized world. It's very sobering to truly understand that we can eliminate these cascading responses by shifting our attention inward at the first signs of anxious callings. That's why meditation and other sitting practices are so crucial. We know from meditation and brain mapping research that meditative practices create new neural pathways in the new brain or neocortex. Once these pathways are constructed, they become viable alternatives to the old brain paradigm. My clients often conclude that they should be able to utilize meditation only to quell these storms without laying the groundwork through consistent practice everyday. Again, we are a shortcut culture. *We want relief now not later and we don't want to have that relief come from our own efforts of changing our very consciousness.* Anxiety is a great teacher for this very reason. It's these relentless and constant anxious, stressful states that eventually drive us to the only place where there is true resolution and that is the world within. *Thus another paradox: the more our outer world predicaments seem in disrepair and unsolvable, the more we will have to reach to our inner depths for illuminated solutions that will create a new paradigm for harmony, peace and the avant-garde world to come.* So, next time you feel some anxious jitter in you body, mind or heart and you can stay within, you just might open yourself to the miracles of self-revelation. Perhaps, anxiety simply means we've not been spending enough time within.

I had a client who had been through a myriad of relationships that were all unsatisfactory in the end. She'd never spent more than a month without being in some kind of relationship. As soon as one ended, another began. In fact, if she even felt the relationship might end, she would start finding a replacement so that she wouldn't have to be alone. Her first explanation was that she was a believer in love and family and was looking for the right kind of guy to be part of this life journey. She just had trouble finding this right kind of guy and didn't want to waste time in between, so she excused her refusal to take time for herself. Eventually, we started talking about what it was like when she did have moments alone and she began to tell the truth about the enormous anxiety she encountered when alone. She began to realize that being with another person was a tremendous avoidance of being with herself. At first, she truly thought that the anxiety felt when by herself simply confirmed her wish to be with another. When with another, she was indeed distracted from this anxious inner calling. However, this avoidance of self soon propelled her into so many painful collisions with others, she had to finally stand still for a moment and look within. She began to realize that this anxiety was just the first layer of the emotional sediment that had disguised the truth about her real meaning and purpose. After some initial painful moments, she began to understand that she had spent a lifetime avoiding the self within, looking for others to fill in the spaces of self-felt worthiness. Needless to say, she finally began spending more and more time alone with herself, discovering anew her passions and creative endeavors. I will never forget when she came to a session and said that she loved her own company as much if not more than most others. She changed careers and through her new job, she actually met a man she ended up marrying. She stated that this man was not a filler for her life but someone who resonated with her deep new found self within. Anxiety is a signal to go within.

Jealousy

Oftentimes when we see another person in the midst of some actualization, some abundance, it brings up feelings of jealousy. We feel their state of abundance and we want it. Not because we want exactly what they want, but only because we know deep within we've not lived fulfilled from the inside out. I had another client once who would often visit her friends and become overwhelmed with jealousy and envy. She would see her friend with an art studio in her home and so decided to go out and purchase paint supplies so she could have them fill her house as well. Later she would visit a family member and observe that they had a musical instrument room and so once again decided she must pursue music. She finally realized that she lived in a house with rooms full of other people's dreams and actualizations, but meanwhile she still felt empty. She was overwhelmed by feelings of jealousy and deprivation, but didn't realize that she was actually resonating with other people's energetic signatures of fulfillment and zest. What she really wanted was this same experience of dynamic vibrancy. She mistook the content of their dreams for the experience of that fulfillment. Jealousy eventually helped her get in touch with her own deprived state of being. This in turn led her on an inner journey for her own unique creative manifestation process. Living in the deepest place of truth actualization at any one period of time is the truest joy and the deepest fulfillment one can have. The prescription for this resides in each individual and is unique to each soul. When we live in our truest blueprint mode, we can't feel deprived and thereby jealous. All deprivation is separation from our deepest blueprint manifestation, which is ultimately from Divine Source. Therefore, all deprivation is directly aligned with feeling alienated from that Divine Source. *That's why the road back is through self-truth through self-love.* Once again we see that our emotions, in this case jealousy, become our greatest teachers.

1. Can you invite these feelings in to be your teacher?
2. Each feeling holds a particular lesson that leads to soul truth.
3. How do these feelings extinguish your light as well as others?
4. Can you dance these parts to the light through compassionate enfoldment?
5. And finally can you see the creative manifested dreams lying beneath?

QUADRANT 3: MIND OBSERVATION AND AWARENESS

While the emotional quadrant may seem fickle, elusive, whimsical and yet powerful and even scary, the mind quadrant most definitely presents us with a never-ending choice of tangled websites that can capture our attention with the blink of an eye. While the body and emotional quadrants do change over time, thoughts change as fast as lightening strikes. I often think our thoughts are like monkeys on amphetamines…jumping from one thing to the next without necessarily understanding the transition in between. It's also easy to get caught in a particular thought channel, repeating it over and over without ever finding the doorway out. Thoughts skip as easily as they get stuck. Awareness of this domain is absolutely crucial if we're to have any control and creative powers over our thoughts.

Most of our beliefs come from our thought quadrant. Our memories are stored here....our history...our experiences...our ideas of self and all else... Staying oblivious to our thoughts is like living with an intruder in our homes never aware of its presence. *Our thoughts are enormously powerful and the first step in harnessing this power is to become more aware of the presence or absence of our own consciousness in this quadrant.*

I. The Sacred Beholder

Oh to behold the inner domain of our thought tanks! For within these reservoirs of mind reflections and ruminations, we could lose our sanity. Often our thoughts are like pinballs bouncing off walls, flipping here and there, eventually dropping into some underground chute, ceasing movement until the next random tug frees it into action once again. *We engage with our thoughts as if they were dictating the truth about some outer reality rather than realizing that for the most part they are a reaction to a reality that we've already created by our previous thoughts.* This paradox eludes us. Often, we become our thoughts and in that becoming we create the reality of those thoughts. This is actually quite the miracle of our minds and will be further explored in the chapter on Manifesting our Reality.

a) Thought Noting

We have so much commentary in our brains it is amazing we can step through life without more trips and falls. We can be so absorbed by our thoughts, we think we ARE our thoughts, but of course we're not. Until we have full consciousness of our thoughts, they're only the shadowy movements on the stages of our minds. Before we can become aware that we are much more than our thoughts, we must first become more intensely aware of our thoughts. Shining consciousness on our brainwork is like lighting up the mental stage bringing the obscured umbrage into clear vision.

So many Eastern traditions talk about developing the ability to note one's thoughts without becoming one's thoughts. This is a very powerful method to begin meditation practices. Simply noting your thoughts without being seduced by them is a very difficult process. Take a moment right now to simply sit outside of your thoughts. Imagine that you are sitting on the banks of a river and your thoughts are the various boats traveling down the river. The trick is to simply acknowledge the various boats while allowing them to pass by. So many of our thoughts wave to us, beckoning us to come aboard so that we might know some interesting, perhaps crucial piece of information that may be critical for the next moment or for that matter for the rest of our lives. I often think that my thoughts can become like dogged and gritty carnival vendors dashingly persuading me that I must enter their particular wagon of various freakish exhibits. So many times, I'm caught in this frenzy of persuasion and enter eagerly with curious hopes that I will be entertained and enthralled. Usually I'm most disappointed and quite often appalled. The most upsetting part to it all is the freakish energy I then carry for the rest of the day. I have learned to be much more discriminating and am not so quick to jump on boats or wagons that seem to be urgent in wooing me to their ports.

Active awareness would allow us to say, "Oh yes…that boat….yes that is the party boat or the worry boat or the boat of lists or the boat that carries the most important anxiety for the day…but I'll simply note the boat and let it pass." There's nothing more important than staying on the shore and observing the parade of boats passing by. The most powerful place is on the shore in the place of simply observing. I can't sink on shore, nor can I run amok. It's surprising to realize that simply noting the passing thoughts allows for the calmest waters. Rough waters only really affect you if indeed you are on the boat. Choppy waves are spawned by the ruckus created when you climb onto the boat. Once you arrive in one particular thought, you may start to believe that you are that thought and may get stuck for quite awhile exploring that terrain. The best place to be is on the shore, although you may want to visit some of the more irresistible thoughts, first it's crucial to develop the ability to simply observe. As you stay on this shore, you will begin to develop more discernment about what thought you might want to explore. In addition, it's important to develop your intentional strength of will so that you can not only explore a thought but also know when to depart from that very same thought pattern.

The key is to take five minutes to pause during the day and begin simply noting your thoughts. What are my thoughts right now…as I let one go what other thoughts fill the screen of my mind. Can I begin to develop more comfort and safety in the zone of observation? Begin to keep a journal of your free flowing thoughts…and note which thoughts are most seductive and which thoughts do you attach to most readily.

b) Thought Patterns

If we look closely at our individual thoughts, we will begin to see patterns that eventually form habitual pathways of thought processing. Some people are negative thinkers: they always have the down side to every situation. They'll always find the worst that can happen in every event. Others will see the world with fear based thoughts and may end up with crisis based thought patterns. Then there are those who may see the best in everything or the positive point of view. We all have patterns of thinking. Observing these patterns and habits is most revealing and interesting. It's also important to note the particular environmental climate that created your mind patterns. In other words, what was the atmosphere of your thinking landscape… cloudy, calm, stormy, windy, sunny? Simply noting the climate and content patterns of these seemingly disconnected random thoughts will tell you an enormous amount of information about the design of who and what you think you are. Our patterns of thinking most often determine the kind of life we will have…whether fraught with fear or filled with abundance. We believe that we are what we think. We become so absorbed in our thought habits that we become them. In this familiarity, we think that is who we are. As we experience the ride on the road of these familiar patterns of thinking, we can feel the relief of recognizing and being ourselves even if the road is rocky and rough. The power of observation is crucial here so that we create a distance, a separation between the who – consciousness – and the what – the thoughts. These habitual reflections on life and self create the reality from which we approach all else. For instance, if you have a tendency to think that the world is a bad, unsafe place and people do hurtful things, you will begin to live in that thinking paradigm and see only those things that prove it correct. What you habitually think shapes what you see and feel. Our thinking paradigms keep us imprisoned in the old historical data of our lives. Our mind quadrant is probably the trickiest place of all, because we're lead by our thoughts every second. What we don't realize is the creative potential that lives in our minds. We have ideas about life that we feel are true and correct and absolute, never knowing that we've created these realities over and over by our own thought patterns. By simply shifting our thought habits we're capable of creating any world we want. But instead we're lead into future lands by our thoughts, which by definition are from some past place. Most of us are not creating anything new but living in the ruts of old pathways created long ago keeping us in tight spaces and limited places. Once you begin to realize that you're not your thoughts, you can begin to use this consciousness from the deeper you or the highest self, to create anew your thoughts, feelings and body spaces.

At the end of every day, take a moment to note what thought themes you came into your mind today. How much of the content of your thoughts flow into similar themes. How often do you have the same thoughts repeat themselves? What are the categories of my thoughts…work, play, love, health? You'll learn and understand so much about yourself simply observing these themes and patterns. If you have repeating patterns, you're probably living life in a restrictive narrowly focused fashion. If the climate of your thinking is turbulent and stormy, you'll probably live life going in and out of crises, predicaments and high stress points. In addition, the thought scripts you have regarding the self will tell you not only how you really feel about yourself but will also reveal your abundance quotient. If you have thoughts of shame, degradation and unworthiness, you'll indeed feel life is full of deprivation and hardships. When the self is not enough, it's very difficult to feel the abundance in life. Distancing from your thoughts, and pausing to observe them is crucial in understanding what we believe and what we are. Observing these thoughts with compassion is the first step in regenerating new scripts and new life.

It's important to note here that as we become better trackers of our conscious thoughts we will begin to become more aware of our subconscious thoughts. Remember, it's our subconscious thought domain that tends to dictate our hold on reality. This subconscious terrain is where all our past history is stored including past events, traumas, beliefs and conditioned blueprints from our families, culture, religion and species. Most of our conscious thoughts arise out of this deeper field of energy signatures. So our task is to stay awake, alert and aware in our mind fields so that we may learn to ride the streams of conscious thought inwards towards our deeper realms of mind and matter. It's often in these less conscious cinema complexes that we find outdated movies running with abandoned attention, long past their relevance to present living. But these movies influence how we construct the present day world both inside and out. With the tool of compassionate consciousness we become explorers into the inner domain of our minds.

II. Compassionate Enfolding

In learning to observe our thoughts, we can begin to separate ourselves from our thoughts. It's in this separation that we can begin to understand that while we're not our thoughts we have, in fact, created our thoughts. We certainly have help from the outside world, but in the end we decide which thought to put into action in the slideshow of our minds. It's important to understand that when we can't distinguish ourselves from our thoughts, we lose the ability to understand our own generative power in creating thoughts. The first step is to realize we can just observe our thoughts and thus we begin to know we're not the thoughts. The "I" that observes is then in a position to know that its power is to become the creator, both directing and producing these movies on the landscape of the mind. Before we can become renaissance thought creators, we must first anoint the hardened thought scripts with the soothing power of compassion.

a) Holding with Compassion

When we first truly observe our patterns and themes in the mind arena, it can be quite startling especially if we see the harshness by which we judge the world and ourselves. Often, our mind arenas are more like horror movies than spiritual adventure films. We can take advantage of our distant directors chair, and begin to judge and criticize what we see on the stages of our minds. I had one client comment that he didn't know what was worse, his negative thoughts or the negativity and judgment he felt when observing his thoughts. You may discover as you become better at noting your thoughts, that the world of your mind is filled with more clutter and debris than you expected. Then, this produces more thoughts of judgment and criticism for the self. I have clients keep a journal of their daily thoughts and it's quite sobering to read pages of thoughts that are negative, fatalistic and despairing. We live the pages as if they are not only the truth, but have been given to us by some outside ruling force. The first step in this process is to simply allow and hold with compassion the thoughts that become our mind habits. Creating a sacred dialogue for your thought scripts is crucial. This generates new neural pathways, new choices that will begin to compete with the old ego dialogue that has taken up residence in your mind. It might sound like this. "I see how these thoughts make you feel so bad, wow what a burden you have carried for so long as you travel down these harsh corridors. You are not these thoughts; it's only your ego that feels it must hang onto them in order to prove your separateness, and worthiness. These thoughts cause you to suffer greatly because you believe that they are your reality. You've endured them long enough because this is part of simply being human. I'm here now to hold the thoughts in greater compassion and love, without becoming them or judging them. In this pause, you will begin to be something new."

b) Creating Dialogue Anew: Thought Generation

Just as we can generate compassionate scripts to acknowledge and recognize our current thought habits, we can actually create radical new mind patterns that have the potential to advance the status and the direction of our very lives. *Most things we think come from a past moment or time, and so we do not realize that we're thinking the past rather than creating the future anew. Therefore most of us birth the future with past data.* What has been will be. When we understand that we're not actually our thoughts and begin to sit in the seat of this higher self-consciousness, we're in a position to create brand new paradigms of thinking. Clearly we've not solved the world's problems or our own from these old vantage points. As Einstein stated, "We cannot solve problems by using the same kind of thinking we used when we created them." So it's time to sit in our soul's director chair and write new scripts, create new stages and imagine new vistas of thought consciousness.

To understand how powerful our thinking really is, consider an experiment sited in Michael Talbot's book, *The Holographic Universe.* College students were divided into two groups, one where they were given amphetamines, and the second group were given sleeping pills. However, one student in each group was given the opposite drug. In other words, in the first room where nine of the subjects were given an amphetamine, the tenth subject was given a sleeping pill. The situation was reversed in the second group.

The question was: What will take precedence, the pharmacology or the thought? In both situations, the tenth subject who took the opposite drug behaved exactly as his companions did. Even though, in the first group, the tenth subject had taken a sleeping pill, he still acted as speedy and animated as his cohorts. In the second room, the subject who had taken the amphetamine actually fell asleep along with his fellow students who had actually taken the sleeping pill. Indeed it appeared, that our thoughts about our chemistry are more powerful than the actual chemistry itself. What we think dictates so much of our reality.

I'm reminded of a miracle story in the medical literature of a man who was paralyzed in an accident and couldn't move at all, couldn't breathe on his own and couldn't even open his eyes. For all practical purposes, the doctors and nurses thought he was in a deep coma and were certain he would never recover.

What was so amazing about this case was that even though he could hear everything being said about his dire condition, he decided that he would never think a negative thought about his potential recovery. He began creating what I would call sacred dialogue about his recovery story. First, he told himself that he would be able to open his eyes, breathe on his own and some day, walk out of the hospital. He took each step in his mind with only positive thoughts because positive thoughts were the only thing he could do. Most of us would never have been able to stay in this positive, healing arena in the mind, but he did. Lo and behold, he was able to open his eyes, breathe on his own and eventually walk even though the doctors had no medical explanation about how this was possible. He now travels the world speaking about the miracle of positive thinking.

It is hard to imagine the steadfastness required for such a feat. I notice that even when people begin to invent new scripts, their expectations tend to diminish the returns of such new thinking. Again, we live in a culture that has taught us that we should have solutions and feel good NOW not later. Unfortunately, so many of us have not developed the stamina to create new scripts let alone stay with the germination process long enough to produce seeds that sprout.

So the first step is to begin to create mind scripts that will bring positive, healing, regenerative energy to the self-system. Often it's helpful to write old mind habits on one side of a page and write new scripts on the other. Make sure these new scripts are written with compassion and joy, rather than disgust and upset. Let yourself feel your own compassionate heart and within that energetic field, begin to create new mind dialogue. What is the dialogue you might want to create in order to have abundance in your life?

c) Practice, Practice, Practice

We now know that as you practice repeating these new scripts you actually create new neural pathways in your brain. The stronger these networks, the more choices you will have in the future. These new networks will become the new mannerisms of the mind. *You will begin to shape reality with your consciousness as your consciousness creates thoughts of this new reality.* Remember these new highways of thought traffic take time to build. Each time you rehearse the new script you begin to commit to new direction, changing the energetic fields in your mind. It's helpful to have the new scripts in front of you so that you can read and memorize them. In that way, when you have stage fright, you might access these positive healing scripts from the recesses of your mind.

QUADRANT 4: SPIRIT

This quadrant at first presents the most etheric and vaporous of all quadrants. Yet it runs through us, in us, around us and beyond us as surely as the air we breathe. The one who observes is made up of spirit…for this who is neither thought, body nor emotion. While the little me can be found residing in the body, mind and heart, spirit resides in the higher self, the neutral observer, in the sacred voice within. Although etheric in nature, spirit's always turned on, always present, always observing even when the little self is oblivious. Spirit knows no separation. Spirit holds the knowledge of the existence of the individual human being while holding the wisdom that this human being is never and has never been alone. With spirit, ultimate safety, comfort and oneness are finally known. *Higher consciousness is the human manifestation of spirit in form.* Spirit is transcendent. It simply transcends body, mind and heart. It lives within while also stretching out to All That Is beyond. Spirit is the fabric in you that is connected to the web of life that is all around you.

There is a growing body of evidence from medicine and contemporary science that this consciousness transcends the physical body and our normal sensory perceptual mechanisms. This is now commonly referred to as non-local consciousness and is the backdrop for all transcendent experiences. Non-local implies that our consciousness is not localized to specific places of space like our brains or bodies and is not anchored to specific time points. *This consciousness field of spirit is the sacred zone where all possibilities lie.*

I. SACRED BEHOLDER

The dictionary tells us that spirit is "a vital force that characterizes a living being as being alive." The definition also states that spirit is "somebody's will, sense of self or enthusiasm and energy for living." It seems to be a paradox that while this quadrant gives us our very life force, we may indeed be the least aware of it. Becoming aware of the fabric and feel of spirit may be the most important undertaking we do as humans. If we hope to be in the truth of who we really are, we must not only discover spirit but also live in it. Our spirit is the conscious vibratory force that runs through our veins, keeping our hearts alive and our bodies moving.

a) Noting the Inside

To begin to behold this, it will be important to pause each day to check and feel your vital force, your aliveness, your enthusiasm and energy for living. Where is this spirit for life? How easy is it for you to access this? Simply begin to note the you who is not body, mind and heart. This is your consciousness and in this consciousness spirit can be found. What moves you? What inspires you? What enlivens spirit within you? Take a moment to contemplate what transcendence means to you. How do you contact spirit? How does spirit nudge your consciousness into being? Note that as spirit is felt, all other quadrants may begin to feel the ripple of spirit moving through. I often find that as my spirit is acknowledged, my heart fills up, my mind calms and my body feels enlivened.

Simply sit with a notebook and contemplate what spirit means to you. Write whatever comes to mind and begin to chronicle how spirit shows up in your everyday life. How active are you in dancing with spirit? How often do you invite this into your life?

Could you commit to spending more time here in this place of spirit? How would this change you? At this point, these are questions simply to spur you into becoming more familiar with this often misty, mysterious place called spirit. Just the effort of bringing forth these questions of spirit, immediately washes you in the vibrancy of spirit. *Although spirit can seem to be intangible and elusive, of all quadrants, spirit needs the least nudging to come into action.*

b) Noting the Outside

Looking outside yourself, where do you see spirit in the world?

Can you see the vital force that lives in other life forms? Who do you know that exemplifies the fires of enthusiastic living?

Go into nature and see where spirit seems to be residing. It's hard to see a sunset and not feel the strength and beauty of spirit. All things in nature have spirit. So nature is a great place to notice the vital life force of all things. When you see a mother looking at her child with love, can you see the beauty of her love emanating from spirit? When you see a kind act, can you see the fundamental force of spirit acting and moving through the heart? Spirit moves all quadrants into grace. As the mother breastfeeds her child, spirit moves and dances between them. Look to see where you notice spirit move in the world. How often do you look for this sacred dance in the world? Make a commitment to increase your awareness of this powerful life force that surrounds you everyday. As you increase your awareness of this, note how this affects your mind, body and heart.

c) Noting the Connection Between Inside and Out

The communion created by our inner spirit feeling and touching the spirit beyond generates an experience of being in and of the unified fabric of All That Is. The greatest example of this is love. As you look into the eyes of your child or lover you will feel both their spirit and yours and in that you begin to know oneness. The movement of the figure eight becomes alive with Divine grace as the energy of your vital life force dances in this connective fabric of spirit.

God lives in and is this sacred connection. How can you secure yourself in this sacred architecture that is infinite and momentary all at once? How do you keep yourself separate from this vital dance? As you begin to recognize the Divine sparks within yourself, you will more readily recognize those same sparks within another person. *Ultimate intimacy between two living beings is this conscious intention to sit with another, willingly opening to the flow of this sacred figure eight where spirit dances and divinity rejoices.* This beautiful ballet of sacred connecting can come in many forms and experiences. Musical notes, painted brush strokes, the call of the loon can all create this invocation for spirit dance. Begin to note the experiences in your life that create this synchronistic interweaving. Also, note how you might increase these sacred opportunities. Begin to keep a journal chronicling these sacred moments where your spirit connects with all-else. Know that it's in these moments that your life is blessed and filled with grace.

II. Compassionate Enfolding

a) Healing a Dampened Spirit

In these troubled and crisis filled times, it seems that so many humans have lost their spirit. Just surviving takes an enormous toll and the zesty life force within has been diminished if not vanished. It's enormously sad that the real truth of who we are: spirit beings in a human body, has been forgotten. Our consciousness has been dampened and in this process our connection to the Divine has been stifled. While it may be easier to hold the body, soothe the heart and quiet the mind, it can be most challenging to renew the spirit. So many people are walking around feeling little aliveness as they face enormous obstacles in Earth living. But sadly, living here on Earth without spiritual awareness is barren and life defying. As our human form feels the weight of the absence of spirit, we become more compressed, denser and less able to breathe spirit into our form.

Our consciousness is a conduit for the vibrational zest of life that lives in the universe. As consciousness fades, the channel becomes smaller and smaller and eventually we're cut off from the aliveness of universal experience. Imagine that in the womb we had an etheric umbilical cord from our solar plexus area stretching out into the cosmos to the Divine mother of all creation. This beautiful cord was an open channel for the breath of spirit to come streaming forth into our humanness. Imagine further that as we grew older we began to dim our consciousness and our recognition of the spirit frequencies that lie within us. The cord begins to atrophy, becoming narrower and less fluid in its design. Eventually it may feel to some that they actually become detached from this sacred cord, feeling totally separate and devoid of spirit, losing vibrancy from Source.

The first step in this renewal process is to acknowledge the depth of loss, holding this loss with compassionate understanding. We must not only have compassionate regard for our individual selves but the whole of humanity as we've lost our way as a human species. It's critical to breathe the frequencies of love and compassion into this channel or life cord to once again light up its sacred circuitry. We're here on Earth to learn not only that we can survive, but that we can thrive with the invigoration of spiritual recognition that we're in fact spiritual beings. The sacred consciousness of this awareness will help us know that we're infinite and unified all at once. We're here in human form to remember the truth that we're so much more than that form. It's with compassion that we offer our spirit, our higher consciousness, freedom to soar from the depths of our being to the heights of soul manifestation. As we surround our dampened spirit with compassion, we can begin once again to feel our aliveness, our passion for life and everything in it.

b) Enlivening Spirit

We spend more time in a day giving attention – both positive and negative to our bodies, our thoughts or our feelings than to our spirit. Yet the most dangerous quadrant to ignore is the one where spirit lives. We forget to invigorate this place and we run the risk of forgetting that we're here on Earth in a grand experiment of remembering. We're vibrant beings temporarily housed in a human body. We can become so absorbed by our form, our feelings and our thoughts, that we have spiritual amnesia. When we're fully awake in this quadrant, the Earth will shift into peace, prosperity and harmony. We must not only acknowledge this place but also enliven it with the breath of our own consciousness. Remember, if we're not consciously attending to our spirit quadrant it's like depriving it of the necessary oxygen to remain vibrant and alive.

What do you do in a day to enliven your spirit? What do you do in a day to be in a state of higher consciousness? It's important to note that what often enlivens one quadrant also brings life to other quadrants. If you take a walk to wake up your body, it will lift your spirits as well. As we take care of one quadrant it has a magnifying effect on all other quadrants. But enlivening spirit, has the most electrifying effect on the rest of the human domain. Let's examine some of the avenues for such rejuvenation.

Creativity

Any creative endeavor calls the spirit to participate. Whether it's in the field of art, music, gardening, cooking, building or making something new. Creative activity brings a proclivity for passion, zest and aliveness. As we create sound into music and paint into art, we can vision and experience the flow of spirit within. Creativity helps us see ourselves in movement, in sync with life rhythms and synchronicities. Creative endeavors bring our consciousness to the ever-expanding moment of the NOW. As we create, whether knowingly or not, we emanate Divine Source consciousness. We come closer to the manifestation process of creating something out of nothing. In this we are co-creators with the Universal Source of all creation. So create something today even if only a new thought, a new configuration of some kind, a new recipe, a new note, or a new stroke of paint. Feel spirit awakening as you do this.

Connection

Allowing ourselves to feel our connection to other beings outside of ourselves as well as to nature is imperative for spirit revival. As we allow ourselves to feel, connect and touch one another with our hearts tenderness, we feel the invisible realm of spirit stream forth between and within the various layers of our humanness. It's this connection that gives rise to the intuitive knowing that we indeed come from the spirit realm. Through this connective power, we gain the rejuvenation that comes from the hope that we are all more than we seem. As we feel part of the web of life, our aloneness, which surely is the greatest dampener of spirit, diminishes in its power and loses its ability to judge the world and our humanness. As we feel that we're indeed part of a larger network of life, our sacred cord opens and flows with renewed light filaments from All That Is beyond us. This includes our connection with nature as well. For as we see ourselves as part of the natural design, we understand that we've always been and will always be a part of the Sacred Blueprint of Divine Source. This experience of connecting to the web inspires spirit to soar as it comes home once again to truth of oneness. So connect today with someone, a sunset or even a tree and feel the flow of spirit abound.

Compassionate Conduit

As we allow ourselves to hold the frequencies of compassion and kindness towards other living beings, we turn up the volume for spirit to be heard. As we sit in these higher frequencies of love and harmony, we give space for spirit to show itself. It stirs the soul to watch someone offer a hand to someone else who has lost all hope of ever being touched. It awakens one sense of being alive to give hope to someone who has been lost in the dark. When we experience the higher frequency vibrations of kindness, gratitude, love and compassion, we soul surf the waves of spirit in motion. As we become conduits for this grace of spirit, we raise ourselves up towards the light of manifesting Divine presence on Earth. So go today and find a place or person where you might become a conduit for higher compassion and graceful loving and you will feel your life force quotient increasing exponentially.

c) Spiritual Practices

It's important that we have daily practices that feed and nourish our spiritual life. Meditation, yoga, relaxation, sitting in silence and walking in nature are a few of these practices. The positive effects of meditation on our sense of wellbeing have been well documented by both spiritual practitioners and scientific studies. Meditation not only lights up the positive areas in the neocortex but also opens channels to the transcendent pineal gland. By the very process of accessing our vision to the beyond, we experience the higher frequencies of our own consciousness. Spirit lives in our consciousness and as we give space and time to spiritual practices of being in this higher state of consciousness we give spirit breathing room to feel itself. Feeling this beautiful state of spirit, we know for sure the truth of who we are. So engage today in a spiritual practice…a practice that brings breath to your soul. And in this experience you will feel and see the face of God in yourself.

Soul Remedies

#7 – The Journey Inward

Take a deep breath.
Know this breath goes to the very depth of your inner world.
Pause in this place of wonder and send love and compassion
to this home within.

Let the truth of who you really are reveal itself.

State the Mantra
I am wondrous beyond my imagination.

Make the Commitment
I will remember this process of going inside,
even when I'm caught on the outside.

Create the New Belief
I have enormous power to affirm, love and heal myself.

Once a Day: Do a Quadrant check.

Body
What are the sensations in my body?

Mind
What is my mind saying?

Heart
What is my heart feeling?

Spirit
Can I feel the sacred life force in my spirit?

8

The Emerging New Human

"The essence of a person is not the clothing she wears or the things he does. People who love them do not stop loving them when they change clothing or do other things. Your essence is not even your history, culture, race, or what you think and do. It is your soul."
–Gary Zukav

"You have to grow from the inside out. None can teach you, none can make you spiritual. There is no other teacher but your own soul."
–Swami Vivekananda

"True religion is real living; living with all one's soul, with all one's goodness…"
–Albert Einstein

Healing and transforming the *Earth bound human* offers the opportunity and opens the gates for the New Human to emerge. It's such a paradox that we come to Earth to feel the human experience through the soul's eyes and yet, the very act of being in this human form often blinds our vision and erases our memory of the sacred Source from which we've been created. We mistake the fortified field of the human self for the seat of the soul. The longer we're here on Earth the more we identify with this self-fortress we've built. In this human made citadel, we truly believe we're separate, desperately hiding behind these walls of protective mortar to keep others out so that we may be safe within. Inside these fortress walls reside all of our Earth/human blueprints that we've gathered over a lifetime, and probably many lifetimes. Our patterns of thinking, feeling, perceiving and believing are stored here as well. All of this is mistaken for the self. The good news is that beyond these fortress walls, the most authentic you can be found. Your mission, purpose, beauty, wisdom and truth reside here. This is the birthing place of the New Human.

After all, you're a sacred spark, a creative manifestation of the Divine Creator, and you've been many places throughout many times. You have access to all the libraries of wisdom from all places and all times. You will not find these libraries outside of yourself, for the opening to these wisdom annals can only be found in the fertile field of the soul. Each time you're aware of your breath you send ripples of movement towards these openings unlocking these channels towards multidimensional consciousness. Once you understand this, you're absolutely FREE. As you begin to breathe, taking in the fluidity of each breath once again, your awareness shifts to the deepest recesses of your inner domain. In this shifting process, you begin to know that movement and resilience come naturally without boundary or limits. Once again, you feel the presence of your higher consciousness as your soul blueprints begin to take flight. The technology for this transformation is love; the place is in the heart. This is the birthing process of the New Human.

Opening the Gates for the Unveiling

In order to emerge in this New Paradigm of Renaissance Living, our first task is to dismantle the gates that we've so arduously erected to make ourselves safe and protected. We've spent most of our time behind the gated community within. Many of these gates have been closed over time, and we find ourselves even more captive and imprisoned in the domain of the unactualized self and unfelt soul. Paradoxically, living behind these gates fosters the often-terrifying belief that we're indeed alone. We build gated communities, fostering the belief that being sequestered in locked quarters will protect and make safe one's life and belongings. It also reinforces the belief that it's dangerous out there. The very act of blocking incoming traffic may make for a sense of protected shelter, but it also restricts notions of what is safe. This certainly solidifies the idea that gates are indeed important in protective living all the while limiting and separating ones sense of self and well-being. This living in separation and hiding behind the gates has far reaching ramifications. It fosters the idea that we must hide not only from the dangers outside, but also hide the within from the outside. We acquire so many gates in a lifetime that we've forgotten what it's like to be gate free. We often mistake the gates for our sense of self. The withholding motion actually begins to feel natural and

part of the landscape of the self-experience. How many times do you hear yourself say, "Don't say that, don't feel that, don't do that ?" We're constantly monitoring and making decisions about *who* we should be, need to be and even want to be. In this process, the flow of the who ceases and the designed architecture of our conditioned self takes over.

We're different things to different people at different times. Our personality structure over a lifetime dictates the stops and starts of what flows out and what flows in. We establish gates, not only to keep unwanted things out from the external world, but on a deeper level, we begin to understand that we need to keep parts of ourselves from the exterior world. As we live in this insulated environment, we not only diminish outside in flow, but more importantly inside out flow.

It's through the experience of flow that the highest self is revealed. In total flow experience, we're no longer burdened by the sickening notion that something is not quite enough. *If we're willing to allow the process of creative birthing of the New Human, then flow must be accepted as the natural state of being.* Nothing held back, nothing scrutinized, nothing analyzed for final viewing before self-movement can be felt. Movement is the goal rather than content contained in the movement. It's only *In Flow* that there is total integration of soul self.

A word of caution, opening the gates at first can be startling because humans can appear scary and dangerous. After all, who hasn't encountered this in themselves? This is part of the breakout process because as we try to escape our poisonous prisons, we actually look rather depraved and perilously perverted. Remember, the flow has been severed long ago. This break out may not be a pleasant experience for either the holder or the beholder of it. In the first clearing out of the constipated inner state of self, the obstructions, blemishes and impurities seen in the torrential flood of discharge may not seem pretty. When we don't flow, we begin to hold in enormous amounts of debris from life and the debris itself creates substances *that were never ours to begin with*. When we first open the gates, the debris is carried out and deposited on the shores of the outer world. Don't be dismayed by this process and don't spend any time examining the debris for evidence of your worthiness. *The content is less relevant than the movement.* Initially, in any unrestrained movement, there is the startling action of the self, crying out to free from the confines within. What's seen first is not the true self, but the pieces of the remnants of *break away gates of confinement. We've not had enough practice passing this waste matter because we've forgotten the significance of maintaining flow rather than maintaining waste.* Actually, the majority of the material in the external world is made up of sediment deposited by too many constipated selves. We look at the condition of the world and gasp with horror. *We've forgotten that our very self-confinement has created the world in which we've become imprisoned.*

So, for example, when we finally tell someone how angry or hurt we've been, it often comes off rough and edgy. We're quickly told that these emotions are simply unacceptable. Unfortunately, this negative take on our emotional expression can, once again, convince us to go back behind the gates to quell the echoing expressions and stay safe. The initial dam breaking may look scary and overwhelming, further reinforcing the gated system within. As a therapist, I've had to learn to be less concerned about the *form of breakout* and more curious and holding of the *process of movement* that's created by the breakout. The elements that are revealed in the break out are simply clues to the various gate systems that lie within. We often get more caught in the structure of the gates than in the dismantling process itself.

A Review of the Gate System

Let's examine some of the most important gates that restrict our flow.

1. Embodiment

Simply being in a human body stops the flow.

Earlier in the book, we touched upon the fact that the soul comes into the body and the connection with All That Is momentarily stops as the confines of the body are felt. This new embodiment impedes the process of felt flow *with* and *from* Source. This creates the master gate that produces the illusion of separation in the very beginning, and closes us off from the ultimate Creative Source and dims our awareness of Source within. *In this process, we forget that our natural flow of self is full of flow of Source.* Our higher soul/self has come into the world of lower densities to remember the Divine flow, master it, become it, and create the world with this flow. It's only our consciousness that can open this gate.

2. External Blueprints

We're given scripts and instructions almost immediately by the outside human world, defining and prescribing the rules of flow management. It starts at the get go, when we learn when and where to stop and start our elimination body processes. Throughout life, we're continually taught to master how we act and speak, holding back the process of organic flow. Several gate systems emerge for controlling our flow. Some examples of flow stoppers are below:

a. Culture: Rituals, customs and beliefs that help us feel a sense of belonging to our social, ethnic or age group.
b. Education: Studies in how to think, succeed and speak. We quickly learn to quell the questions that come from flow and memorize the answers that come from structure.
c. Religion: Beliefs and rituals that encourage and enforce what we must do and say to get through the gates to everlasting life.
d. Family: What is expected in behaviors, thoughts and feelings to be loved and attended to.
e. Personality: Our own self created ideas about how to make ourselves safe and sound in the world of all other gated systems.
f. Species: Expectations about what it means to be human.

Fortunately, this is an incredible time of change and discovery so many of these externalized gate systems are being dismantled and demolished. Ironically, the hardest system to dismantle is the master gate that determines what it means to simply be human. It takes practice in higher consciousness states to understand that our very humanness is a vehicle, not an obstacle, to immense soaring in the flow of all life. In the dismantling of these old ideas, we begin to come back to our roots of cosmic consciousness and the ability to travel in multiple dimensions, all while remaining in human form. *It's the resolute unwavering flow of breaking out, that we break in to the remembrance of who we really are.* As we feel this movement, this fluidity of soul fire, we will be unable to return to the gated regions of the old self. Only then will we live fully in the resilience of the spontaneous surging of new self-states of being. The state of resilience is the capability of returning to an original shape or position after having been compressed. While human life is one of initial compression, it's forever after a battle between the expansive resilience of returning to Source Flow versus the constrictive compression felt in the towered walls of our gated structures.

3. Flow Attachments

Our yearning for the flow is so strong that even if we stop our fluidity within, we become consumers of extraneous exercises that provide some semblance of the flow outside of ourselves. We become addicted to these activities, places, and persons in order to stay close to the possibility of creating this flow from inside out. After all, the world provides us with a smorgasbord of flow experiences and we're drawn to them like a moth to light. Some examples are:

a. Drugs and substances that disinhibit the brain so that the gate-keepers slumber.
b. Exhilarating activities like sky diving or skiing down a steep mountain where attention is riveted on survival and the surge of adrenaline. The gates are blown open by the winds of danger and excitement.
c. Falling in Love: Riding the loop of merging heartbeats where the chemistry of love blows the gates wide open.
d. Nature: God's blueprint opens the gates.
e. Magic and Enchantment: Soothes the gates open through wonder and awe.

These things can be very helpful in lighting up our *flow circuitry* and inspiring further exploration. However, the danger here is our propensity to believe that we must wait for these outside things to occur (passive stance), become over attached to these events (addictive stance) or are simply not capable or worthy enough of creating these flow states ourselves (powerless stance). Deep within the caverns of our minds, we wait for some outside force to anesthetize or annihilate the gate-keepers, so that we might once again be free to cross the thresholds of self-imprisonment to feel the world and the Divine through the portals of the self. The empowerment that comes from actively opening our own passageways is beautiful and sustaining in our life breathing New Humanness.

In summary, *the flow* can best be described as the fluid movement of the spontaneous creative elements of the integrated soul/self in the effervescent moment of now. This unbroken continuity flows from Divine cosmic Source into self and from self into the exterior world. In the ideal inner world, this figure eight is never broken or paused and each new flow of creative self-expression brings new life and new breath to further grace this sacred current of All That Is. This then is Being In the Flow.

The New Human in the Flow: The Gates Open

1. In Flow Produces Creative Expression

When we're *In Flow* and allow our true organic being, we honor our birthright to be co-creators with life. Creative endeavors including music, art, poetry, and movement, stimulate flow in the human species. Listen to the notes of music and you're moving through sound. See the strokes of paint on canvas and you're inspired by beauty. Hear the words of poetry and your heart moves with beats of joy and tears. In the process of creating, the in flow experience is felt, spontaneous expression occurs and something is often manifested in the three-dimensional world. We love to be part of this creative process whether it's ours or someone else's. This gives us proof of the powerful truth that, in this self-actualizing process, our soul is connected to all of life. In this truth, we experience and understand that our true natures are higher and wider and vaster than we ever imagined.

2. In Flow Offers Transparency

When the totality of the person is flowing from the inside out, nothing is withheld and everything becomes lucid, apparent and perceivable. Being with someone who is *In Flow* is calming and safe, because you don't have to guess at their truth, which simultaneously aids in the fluidity of being yourself. It's hard to imagine a world where we would not have to question someone else's motivations, feelings and beliefs including, for that matter, our own. We would most probably have an enormous amount of energy to construct other, more interesting realities than those of our fellow Earth travelers. This ability to be in the present moment is the ultimate experience of trusting that the soul *In Flow* is the highest place we can be. As we're more transparent to each other, we can hold, embrace and support the most important parts of each other, so that we might begin to fulfill our soul contracts here on Earth. This will change how we interact with each other and the very planet on which we live.

3. In Flow Engenders Manifestation

The most potent fuel for manifesting your dreams and your mission is found in the energetic streams of light created by being *In Flow*. Manifestation is the process by which something is revealed and made visible, emerging from the quantum field of all potentialities. By consciously interacting with the quantum field, we create an even stronger current that spins something from nothing. *The beauty of manifestation lies in the fact that being in the flow with the creation process itself becomes more exhilarating than any particular thing created from it.*

4. In Flow Stimulates Imagination and Invention

We will never discover anything new in old places and closed-off spaces. As the gates open, we gain access to so many libraries of wisdom and creative knowledge. *In Flow* allows us to imagine ourselves beyond ourselves. All new discoveries and inventions come from the quantum field of the flow force. All That Is beyond can be accessed when in complete flow, without blocks, gates or walls. Infinite creative intelligence is seen, felt and heard as *In Flow* provides channels for new sensory-perceptual modalities to open up and be experienced. For instance, we will develop the ability to see beyond the current known visual spectrum and know things from our newly opened psychic abilities. We will discover that our imagination is the channel where we have full connection to the infinite information center of the Universe. Imagination is a blessed act of joining ourselves with the sacred. It's not a feat of producing something out of nothing, but rather bringing what was unknown to the realm of human consciousness so that it might be known. Being in the state of imagination, allows us to touch and feel the unified field of Divine Source, where all inspiration and instantaneous creative invention can be found.

5. In Flow Sustains and Replenishes Love

There is nothing worse than being stuck in the entrenched ideas of what you, or others, need to be or do in order to be in the flow of love. As you're in flow, your heart can manifest love in the fertile fields of the present moment, untouched by past or future needs, and undaunted by old concepts of self or other. Love is the dancing energy of your own Divine spark igniting the heart to spin threads of light that embrace and inspire *In Flow* being. This creates a healing experience for the New Human Being, as it shines a light on the truth of who we really are. Simply put, there is nothing not to love.

6. In Flow Excites and Stirs our Memories of our Source and Cosmic Origins

Memories of our soul and cosmic being merging with Source are made possible through the *In Flow* experience. Once we feel this merging, nothing can stop the connection to All That Is. In this connection, we once again remember our cosmic birth, as we've come from the stars and are part of a living intergalactic Universe. *In our consciousness, we understand that living in separation never existed in the first place.* Gated communities are replaced by expanded vistas. Discovering who you are is more exciting than hiding who you are. Sitting behind the gates waiting for soul salvation is a thing of the past. Spiritual redemption is the act of being *In Flow.* Being in this flow becomes a way of living and the feeling that results is the liqueur of living.

Being In Flow is the Oneness of Being.

The experience of the authentic soul/self can be found in this inner sanctum of the *In Flow* experience and once experienced, the self-fortress vanishes into thin air and soul/self rises in freedom and lightness. The old remnants of conditioning, rules, and blueprints of the old self are no longer vital nor required in the courtyard of higher consciousness. This experience of authentic being is so elevating that the need to be safe simply dissolves. We no longer need the storage space of the fortress, nor the protection of its gated walls. All actions, thoughts and deeds are created from this beautiful sanctuary within. This sanctuary was already created from Divine Source – we're simply remembering this sacred place, taking up residence in the presence of our soul. In doing so, we're no longer stuck in form, but instead we become fluid in flow. We identify soul/self as that unique energetic higher consciousness experience that's felt in the residence of the seat of the soul. Without the fortress walls between us and All That Is beyond, we begin to feel the unified field of consciousness without losing the unique sense of our soul/self. In this vibration of soul resonance, the experience of *Oneness* can be felt.

Sacred Technology

It's important to recognize that this sacred evolution is different from our biological evolution. Our sacred evolution is that pathway of expansion that's created by our consciousness manifesting our *greatest Divine blueprint*. On the other hand, our biological evolution is about the system of our physical form and is more connected to the external world. Our bio-evolution is responsive to environmental changes, creating mutations when necessary to adapt and survive. However, without the guidance from the sacred self, we wouldn't be able to activate our highest DNA potential to take the next step in our cosmic evolution. Bio-evolution ensures that we will remain actively responsive to the outer world, while inwardly passive to transformative factors. Our sacred evolution, on the other hand, is highly influenced by the inner environment of our consciousness and thus transformation is not dependent on the external environment. As a result, spiritual transmutation has the potential to be less helter-skelter, more coherent and Divinely inspired. With the guidance of our higher consciousness, we can change our genetics, our bodies, our minds and hearts and the very Earth on which we live. We can sculpt our world through this Sacred Evolution, instead of having the smallness of the three-dimensional world shape our sense of reality. *We will create from our sacred consciousness in order to change the world, rather than change through mutational processes created by the world.* This is the New Human. We're in a revolution of soul awakening and remembrance, and the technology lies in the activation of the renaissance body, mind, heart and spirit.

The Renaissance of Self: The New Human

As we learn to be *In Flow* and practice the sacred technology, we will come closer to becoming the New Human, experiencing the renaissance of soul living. Let's take a look at how the New Human would be, act and look in this sacred evolution of soul/self by examining anew the quadrants of human experience.

The Renaissance Body: Shifting the Body Paradigm

A. New Beliefs and New "Scripts" for the Body

1. I'm not here *in spite* of my body, I'm here *because* of my body. It's through the process of embodiment that I have come to Earth. I'm here to know and feel the love and joy of this particular body incarnation.

2. I delight in my conscious relationship with my body every day. The most potent medicinal prescription I can have comes from the tablet of my own consciousness lighting up the pulsing network of life within. The degree to which my body is vital and well is the degree to which I can relate clearly with high intention to all else and experience higher and more expanded consciousness.

3. My body has everything it needs to heal and be whole. I came here both self-contained and other connected. Therefore, I hold in my self/body containment the keys to the holographic library of healing wisdom and, at the same time, I understand that part of my life force

quotient is contingent on my ability to connect to All That Is. Both are true all at once.

4. Listening to the subtle shifts in my body prevents gross aberrations of dis-ease and pain. I can alter the tiniest system imbalance through my conscious awareness. However, if this awake energetic experience of body awareness disappears, it may take gross impairments to recall the light brigade of healing and regenerative energies.

5. My body houses many pleasures and extraordinary experiences. It's a joy to eat well, exercise, meditate and be sexually expressive as these pathways enliven my awareness of the body beauty. Repression and withholding snuff out the light in the body temple. The Earth experience provides a banquet of sustaining and augmenting methods for celebrating the body whole.

6. My body houses the technical knowledge to build bridges to all other internal systems (heart/mind/soul), as well as all other external systems. This includes other living beings, the Earth, herself and all other galactic bodies. My body invigorates and allows the heart, mind and soul to be in their fullest state of evolution. *In a sense, my body is the embryo that holds the fertile ground necessary for the swelling of consciousness amplification. This seeds all transformative life within and its interconnectedness with all life beyond.* After all, my body comes from the material of stars and therefore holds the knowledge that I'm part of a larger whole, a larger galactic state, a larger universe in a multidimensional world of all possibilities. This figure eight is the basis for the Oneness of Being.

7. Earth is a living body, just like my own, and the more peace and prosperity I give to my body, the more I will understand how to offer this reciprocity to the body of the Earth.

B. Creating the New Human Body Experience

In the old paradigm, we have so many familiar experiences with our body where we're neglecting it, numbing it or just hating it. These experiences have developed known corridors that we walk down with ease, never opening the unmarked doors to new experiences of joy and invigoration that can be felt from having embodiment. We must commit to providing new experiential templates that we can recognize, so that we may have a new renaissance relationship with our bodies.

These new pathways include how we feed our body. It's said that yogis are so in tune with their bodies that they know what nutrients each organ needs at any one point in time. Wow. As we learn to have more discerning and sagacious awareness of our various body systems, we will learn to provide them with more abundant wellness experiences. We will become more adept at our relationship with the Earth and how she provides us with all the nourishment we need. Our interactions will change in that we will become adept Earth gardeners, working in conjunction with, not against, so that we will unlock all of the secrets of sustenance both of ourselves and of the Earth. We will begin to have a renaissance relationship with the Earth, where her livelihood and survival is equally important to our own. It will be revealed that her body is more and more like ours and so we will be in a partnership with her to ensure she is vital and well.

In this process, we will also discover the wondrous nature of what she births in her belly for our vibrancy. Some of this certainly includes a myriad of resources that we've not yet fathomed. We've been so good at stripping her of fuel resources, mining her underbelly, and laying waste to so many of her most lustrous riches and reserves. Not unlike the process we've undergone with our own bodies. We've been willing to do this at the expense of losing the very residence in which we live. We must seem quite strange to other inhabitants of the Universe. As we upgrade our beliefs about ourselves and begin this new evolutionary period on Earth, we may indeed have a renewed relationship with Earth.

Crystal technology will certainly be one of those areas of profound discovery in the decades to come. It's amazing that the Earth holds within her belly these beautiful jewels of energy that are so healing and generative in their natural state. As we become more crystalline and translucent in understanding our own body, we will indeed have a more lucid and cooperative relationship with the Earthian crystals. The nurturing symbiotic nature of the Earth/human relationship will become a more rhythmic intertwining of body energies making love, the most potent bridge for living together in harmonic convergence.

Creating new experiences within the body that are vibrant, peaceful, calming, healthy and whole is critical in establishing the foundation for all else to come in the New Human. These experiences will create the new electromagnetic, biological and neural pathways and genetic blueprints that will call us day after day to continue laying the ground work in the body. This preparation will make the new anatomy for holding a higher vibrational state and birthing the New Human in the revolution that's at hand.

We must commit to invite these new experiences in, while not being seduced by old paradigms, familiar pathways and shrouded body states of being. Feel the body in movement, feel the body stretching, feel the body in stillness, feel the body in nourishment, feel the body dancing, feel the body laughing, feel the body in joyful expression, but whatever you do, feel the body in its beauty, not its ugliness. Think of this as body building exercises. These experiences will become the new templates for expanding consciousness. Let your body breathe anew. Feel its breath. Feel the life pulse, the chi within. Then promise to never abandon this again and begin this new relationship with body with a life affirming experience. You already know what these experiences are – you just have decided to turn your back on them. Revitalize, revamp, rewire, rejuvenate but most of all, remember the long lost experience of being in body with love and awakeness.

C. New Patterns and Habits

As we begin to allow new beliefs and new experiences, we can initiate the process of new bio/genetic patterns and habits. The very act of creating revitalized patterns and new habits will create a new web of life within. We will certainly begin to activate and change our DNA, turn on the dormant areas of our brain, open our heart's knowledge and electromagnetic fields and feel the wellspring of liquid chemicals that heal and change the very structure of our bodies.

New Habits:

- Taking responsibility for our own bodies.
- Nourishing and replenishing on a daily basis.
- Rehabilitating not debilitating through thought and behavioral patterns.
- Daily body practices that turn up awareness within.
- Communing with Mother Nature and all she provides for us.
- Practicing gratitude and reverence for the Earth experience.

Whatever new habitual networks you build, know that these are conscious choices you must make every second, remembering that at any moment you might fall prey to past debilitating patterns that have slumbering effects on both your body and mind. The renaissance self is constantly aware of these new choice points and stays diligent and vigilant that this path is the only path.

The path of the New Human is defined by this awareness and awakeness that totally rewires and revitalizes us, so that the tired body of old no longer causes the dimming and slumbering energetic signatures of past paradigms. The labor involved in staying awake to all of these choices dissipates as the awakened mind invigorates the aroused and animated body. There is no longer a choice point, only a path. The steadfastness is palpable; commitment is the energy of the new body. Consciousness is a felt body experience and this experience in the body begins to guide everything else. The body is the most dense materialized part of the self-experience and when it carries the momentum of the New Human forward, all else becomes lighter and higher. In the New Human, there is no longer debate about choice points, because the experience of high wellness creates a euphoric state, unparalleled by the old paradigm trappings of body panaceas that are really body exterminators. We will experience increased longevity as the human body will be more vital and capable of living for much longer periods of time. Death will no longer be a feared anticipation nor an avoided event. In fact, we will learn to not only experience our full body capacity, but we will also experience more out of body experiences that will be aided by the soul's manifestation in the New Human. This will help us understand that our consciousness does not die and therefore paradoxically we will be able to be more fully located in our bodies.

The Renaissance Heart: Shifting the Heart Paradigm

Unfortunately, we've forgotten, in our ego-driven state, the miracle of heart technology. We've lost our way in the minefields of the old paradigm of heart suppression and separation.

Some of these darker, suppressed fields include:

1. HATE: Strangles us and freezes our inner resources.
2. JUDGMENT: Confirms we're separate.
3. BIGOTRY AND PREJUDICE: Keep us separate and stuck in dualism.
4. ANGER: Is a hormonal state that keeps us in lower consciousness reminding us that we're bodies, shackled to our need to protect and defend which by definition supports separation and division.
5. DISHONESTY: Hides the truth, and continues the cycle of division and disconnection. This feeds the notion that we're unacceptable and unworthy.

6. GREED: Takes from world abundance and keeps the sacred self totally deprived.
7. SELF-CRITICISM: Alienates the human self from the Divine self. Once we're informed by our Divine self we will no longer be a violent culture.

It's important to remember that these darker, denser fields of self-experience, by definition, live in the third dimension. In order to change, it feels like we have to go into this denser reality of form and matter. Unfortunately, old paradigms and programs can be reactivated quickly in this mire and the heart once again becomes impotent. Most of us are not evolved enough to resist such temptation. The good news is that we no longer have be in the darkness to transmute it, but instead we only have to utilize the alchemy of love and unity found in the New Human heart.

The New Human heart utilizes emotional states as keys to inner peace and well-being. Feelings are signals to deeper stories of self-journeying. How we deal with the negative is crucial to the process of building a world that's positive. As we learn to create new pathways for allowing, holding and infusing compassion into our emotional states, we will make room so that we might awaken the hearts libraries of infinite wisdom. So many of our blocks and compartments within have been created by our emotional states. So much of our survival now in this era is not about physical survival but more and more about emotional durability and vitality. We live in a world where the emotional self has been suppressed, dimmed, censored, quelled and concealed. Yet, it's this emotional self that holds so much of our life force quotient. Our emotions can lead us to our most exalted experiences in life. Without the beating of the hearts rhythmic tides of feelings life would be without zest, without gusto, without meaning.

We can create vibrational sets of sacred heart technology that include noting, holding and dialoguing with the painful affects within. These sacred vibrational sets create new bio/genetic pathways that compete with the old survival network of fright and might modalities of the antiquated human. This new sacred circuitry opens the energetic field of the heart creating not only new emotional experiences, but forging a relationship with the old that renews and rewires.

A. The New Generator

The New Human utilizes emotional states as keys to inner peace and well-being, becoming a Generator of emotions rather than a responder. Emotions tell the story about whether we feel we're responders to life or generators of life. Do we simply respond to the happenings of life with our feelings and perceptions or can we be in a position to generate our own feelings and reactions? Generating emotions is part of the process of living from the inside out. As we learn to master our emotional domain, we will be able to create emotional states of well-being that will not only heal us, but take us out of survival mode and into the mode of thriving.

As we become more familiar with our emotional world, not only will we understand the lessons, but we will rewrite our very ideas about what these feelings states have to offer. Most of us run from our feelings, denying them and developing life stories to protect them. They create a stormy chaotic place of residence deep within, taking the heart's beauty and wisdom far beneath the recesses of our consciousness. As compassion becomes the explorer in these mists, we will befriend these places transforming them into stories, lessons and healing rooms. As we see the restorative value in our emotions, we will take the first step in trusting this domain of the heart. Once in these feeling rooms, we can then have dominion over them. As the old feelings heal, we can decide what new emotions might take up residence. Feelings of calm, peace, love, okayness, kindness and even bliss might then make their way towards our hearts residence. After all, it's not just the tough events of life that cause suffering, but the feelings that these events engender. Can you even imagine, the next time a difficult situation occurs that you might have a choice over how your body responds and what emotions are felt? The first step in this process is practicing inducing emotional states in calm and nonstressful situations. Meditation, yoga, experiences in nature and a kind act all prepare the body and heart for these higher states of emotional being.

Identifying the emotional states that bring you a sense of a prosperous and thriving heart is crucial. We know from the research done at the Heart Math Institute that love, peace and compassion expand the electromagnetic field of the heart several meters wide and produce a coherent vibrant state. This in turn triggers similar states in the brain, activating the neocortex rather than the more primitive limbic system. Feeling states have enormous power to create a synergetic response in the total mind/body system. It's quite startling to understand that the feelings most of us feed on every day, create a diet of disarray, chaos and ill health. Generating the higher emotional states of the heart can bring us into balance, harmony and salubrious reciprocity with all other human quadrants. The New Human not only knows what these emotional states are, but has learned to generate these states on a daily basis. These higher vibrational states of being live in the ***Spectrum of the Emotionally Evolved Heart (SEE♥)***. This spectrum includes such emotionally charged states as: love, exaltation, passion, bliss, kindness, compassion, joy, peace, zest, rapture, warmth, calm, reverence, happiness and grace.

Exercise:

1. Make a list of the higher emotional states of the heart that you have or would like to experience.
2. Design a sitting practice where you generate one of these emotional states at least once a day.
3. Identify the situations and people in your life that seem to generate these states.
4. Redesign your life to invite more of these *emotional energizers* into your life.

For instance, how do poetry, art and music affect your heart quadrant? What happens when you walk in nature? Note the feelings that come from this. What kinds of people are you drawn to and what kinds of feelings do these interactions generate? Are there certain rooms in your home that trigger calmer states? Can you begin to design your life so that you create heart openings, feeling expansion and emotional well-being?

The wonderful thing about our feelings is that they actually change quite quickly. It's our awareness that needs to brighten with the light of turned-on consciousness. As we turn up our awareness, we enable ourselves to have more choices, creative power and direction in generating the emotional world in which we want to live. It's such a paradox that we're most unaware of the very emotions that have the most power in determining our state of being. Identifying them, understanding the wisdom of their patterns and currents and learning to be an active creator in generating them are key components in this awareness training.

B. Emotional Shapeshifting

In mythology, shapeshifting is usually described as a transformational experience whereby a person can physically transform into another form or being. Emotional shapeshifting involves consciously and instantaneously transforming one emotional state into another. That's why it's so important for the New Human to know and utilize a cache of inner experiences of the evolved heart. You can't consciously transform a lower state into a higher state if you remain unaware of the higher spectrum of emotions. *Having those tracer experiences, those tracks formed by emotional footprints within, is crucial so that we have familiar inner resonance with the quest for the outer transformative realities.*

1. Past grooves: Remembering and bringing into vibration (actually feeling the memory) of some past state of being where you experienced the *Spectrum of the Emotionally Evolved Heart (SEE♥)*. Perhaps, you're experiencing some agitation and frustration driving to work and you remember that you can emotionally shapeshift in a heartbeat by simply remembering the last time you felt invigorated with happiness and contentment. In this memory lies an experience and the bridge to this experience is your heart consciousness. Allow this to be felt in the center of your being, so that it may radiate out into your body, quieting the mind and soothing the soul.

2. Future grooves: As the heart can remember the past, it can also jump a beat and anticipate the future. It simply requires bringing to mind a time in the near future where you will be in the *Spectrum of Emotionally Evolved Heart (SEE♥)*. For example, you might be sitting at a work meeting where you're feeling anxious and stressed. You begin to imagine the next time you will be doing something that will elicit a heart soar moment. Perhaps you're going hiking in the coming days at your favorite spot in the mountains near you. Imagine what that will feel like and simply feel it. Congratulations, you've just emotionally shapeshifted. Of course, it's not easy at first to leave the old worn out paths of dense emotional debris. Many people do this all the time when they are bored and begin to daydream of more enticing life offerings.

3. Outside grooves: We can easily utilize outside situations or persons as well. Have you ever noticed that when you're around a calm peaceful steady person, you begin to feel safer and calmer as well? Or perhaps you're around someone who is full of zest and life force energy and it feels contagious to you as you begin to feel the same. If you're in a situation or with a person who is vibrating in the *Spectrum of the Emotionally Evolved Heart (SEE♥)*, you can consciously make the choice to join that vibration and in so doing shapeshift into that emotional state.

For example, when many of us attend weddings, we automatically do this as we tear up at the very moment when two hearts are soaring in love.

4. Parallel grooves: Transforming our present state by jumping into a parallel reality of our own life. Here we must presume that indeed, we're living several parallel lives all at once. If this is the case, unless we're fully evolved, we're not living in the highest, most evolved track of possibilities at this moment in time. However, somewhere in the vast sea of all our potential destiny paths, we may be living a life that's entirely in the *Spectrum of the Emotionally Evolved Heart (SEE♥)*. We can begin to use our imagination and our heart's wisdom to take the quantum leap into the Spectrum of the Emotionally Evolved Heart, even if for only a brief moment of time. This is emotionally shapeshifting at its best.

C. The Intuitive Wisdom of the Heart

As we become more masterful orchestrating the energetic signatures that live in the heart, we can begin to access the wisdom that can be found underneath and all around these signatures. Some energetic vibrational states encourage heart expansion and others restrict it. Being in the *Spectrum of the Emotionally Evolved Heart (SEE♥)* creates, not only coherency and health, but in the afterglow of such signatures, an opening to the vibrant library of heart technology. (**see illustration 14**)

1. Energy Fields of the Heart

All of our states of being create energy fields in the heart. Someday we will actually be able to see these fields with our eyes, just as some people today can see auric fields around the body. But, through the heart's vision, we can learn to feel and intuit these heart spirals of energy. When we first dip into the heart field we often feel the vulnerability that lies right on the surface and so many of us switch to mind operations in order to avoid this felt liability. I hear many people say, that they feel so much heartache from the grief and loss in life and as a result, spend enormous amounts of time blockading the path to the heart. I actually think more heartache comes from this shutting down process rather than from the enlivening experience of being human. Whether it's the abandonment felt at the moment of embodiment, or the loss of many loves or the grief from forgetting the soul's existence, all of these memories can be found in the heart. *We must not mistake this grief for pain and deny it, but rather see it as an awakening towards our soul's blueprint manifestation.* Soon, this new breath of light

SPECTRUM OF THE EMOTIONALLY EVOLVED HEART *(SEE♥)*

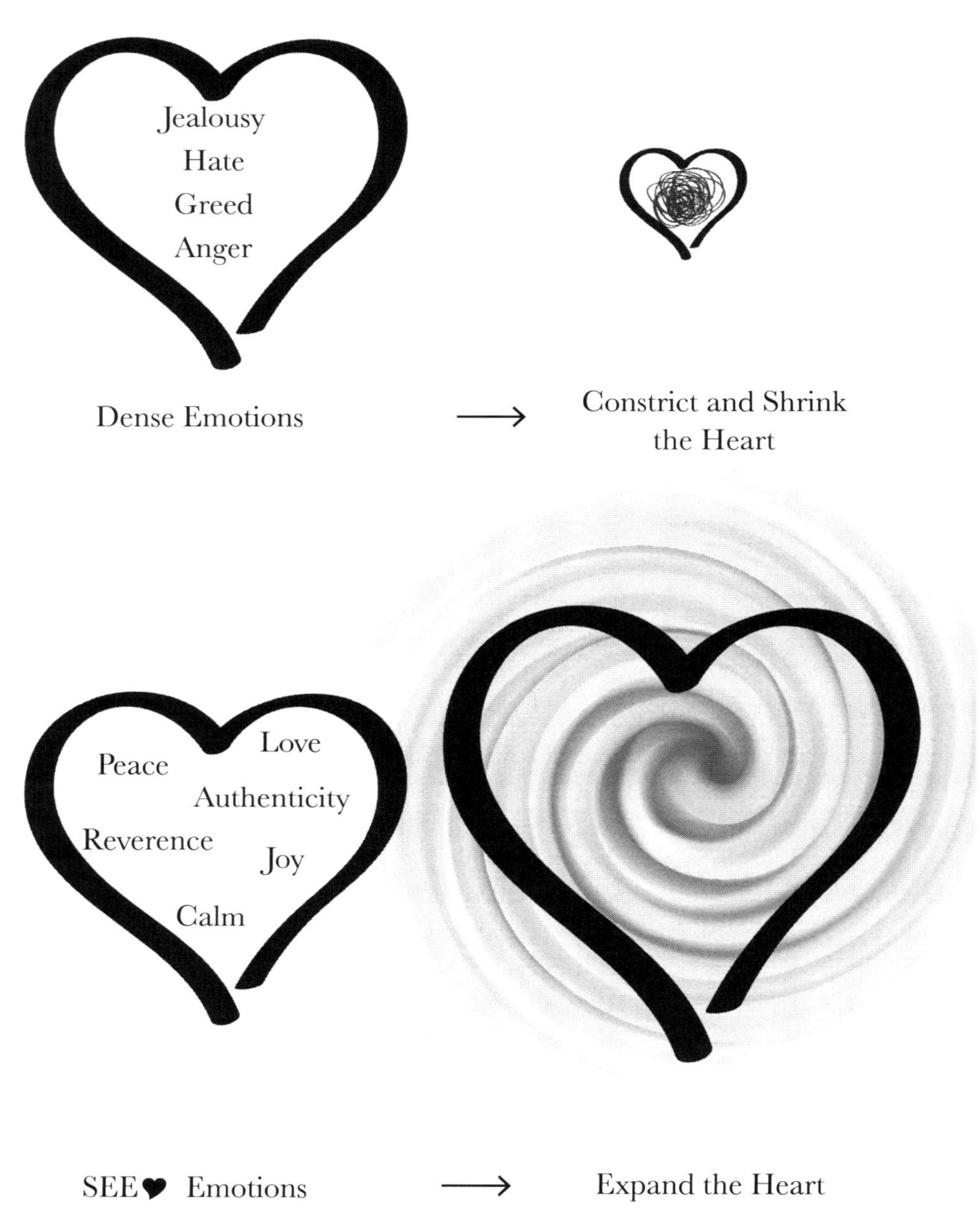

Illustration 14

invigorates the life within and movement becomes a *state of being*. As we begin to become more comfortable in this human heart, we will then discover our cosmic heart. As we do this, oneness becomes our *experience* instead of our goal.

Imagine for a moment that there are inner spirals of light fields in the energetic expanse of the heart. (**see illustration 15**) Each field holds experiences, lessons and information crucial for self-evolvement. Traversing and moving through these "heart spirals" is the crux of soul awakening.

Here are some energetic light fields of the heart:

a. Vulnerability: Our beauty lies in the vulnerability of the heart's light.

Our beauty lies in the vulnerability of the heart's light. The first energetic light zone of the heart is the spiraling field of vulnerability, and it's woven in all other spirals of the heart realm. As we travel into these soft, sensitive and unguarded passages we, by definition, leave our hard, edgy self behind. We soon come to know that without this hard edgy self, we can travel much faster and farther. When we feel this vulnerable place within the heart, know that the constrictive, egoic, frozen self has shifted to a soft liquid movement of self-discovery. This liquid awareness spreads into unknown lands and is finally free to flow. Safety no longer can be found in these aged compressed boundaries, but instead is felt in the beauty of vulnerability.

Vulnerability is a sign you've entered the lightness of being, shedding the shrouds that have covered over your beautiful heart. There is no way to enter and know the heart without the guidance of vulnerability. Rejoice in this, it's here that we're open to all else. This opening is so magnificent we often run for cover for fear that this newly lighted path will blind us. As we stay in this spiral of beautiful light, it will create new visions of the truth of who we are. After all, our hearts hold the sacred technology for consciousness revolution.

b. Humility: We know so little, not so much.

We don't have to protect ourselves when we understand we know so little, for in this understanding, we actually expand the boundaries of what we're capable of knowing. When we *feel* the gracefulness of humility, it helps guide the way towards the sacred libraries of wisdom. *We cannot know this pathway if we think we already know this pathway*. We can only enter this pathway when we're experiencing the state of being that's created from knowing very little. This is humility and is a crucial experience if we're to move from mind knowledge to heart wisdom. *It's through humility that we actually abandon the old paradigms of*

LIGHT FIELDS OF THE HEART

Illustration 15

information and knowledge and declare openly, if not softly and gently, that we're on the path of unknown, so that we might know.

Humility is simply the feeling state of not defending what the mind knows. The first step in this process is to surrender these egoic shields of protective armament that come from the knowledge and information derived from the three-dimensional realm. This grants us a ticket of admission to enter a state of being where we might access and know the multidimensional libraries of sacred art and wisdom. To stay in the limited corridors of third dimensional truths, facts, ideas and principles is to show our ultimate ignorance. The very act of humility allows an opening, an empty space, and it's in this space that the potentialities of all other dimensional intelligence can be known. For in that act, we come out of what we do know and sit on the edge of what we don't know, and in doing this, we begin the journey of ascension.

c. Compassion: Unification and oneness come from compassion.

As we learn to be in the experience of Compassion, we begin to experience the merging of one to another. If anger is the elevator to our lower self, compassion is the skyrocket to our higher self. Compassion unifies, and in this merging we take a quantum leap through the field of consciousness to higher domains beyond this time and place. Know this feeling, request it, lie in it and watch your heart grow in strength and spirit. In this place we will also know and be able to practice empathic states of being, where we can feel, identify and understand feelings and inner states of all other beings in life. Empathy becomes the active channel for compassion. As we ascend, we will come to know, that our biggest strength, our biggest *soul asset,* is our ability to be in compassion for All That Is. In this compassion, duality ceases, merging begins and we will remember the truth of our sacred inheritance. In these higher lighter states of being, keys will appear and they will unlock the infinite truth of who we are. As we experience these states we will be more prepared to digest and hold steady these new concepts of *blueprint being.*

d. Kindness: The action that follows compassion.

As we're able to imbue our human actions with kindness, we open these light fields to the external third dimensional world. Imagine that as we become these light beings, we then must open our shutters and shine this light upon the world and in kindness we do just that. Kindness is not a vulnerable act, but rather one of the strongest acts of our spiritual potency. As we know kindness more and more, we become more able to stand in kindness when no one else in the room is interested. It will become our new definition of who we are through the very energy field it creates. This new energy field will become more and more familiar until we know no other option. We will no longer be hidden inside a frozen figurine, we will become spirals of light, moving and dancing within the heart. Each time we're kind, we form keys that unlock more pathways to higher dimensional living.

e. Veracity/ Integrity: Being in truth moves the soul into action.

Having Integrity means being true, honest, authentic, sincere and reliable. Not an easy path. As we voice the truth of who we are, we offer others the conscious choice of whether they want to step with us in our lives. This creates more enlightenment about who we really are. Camouflaging the self feeds the notion that we have unacceptable parts and more importantly hides the truth that we're Divine. Hiding behind falsehoods solidifies the egoic three-dimensional self and cloaks the seat of the soul. As we become more honest and revealing in this third dimensional land, it's a sign that we're in a state of self-compassion and non-judgment. In this way we remove the old paradigms of dogmatic lack of acceptance, paving the way for the deeper Divine truths of spirit in human form. If we lack integrity we will never know the sacred blueprints that lie within. *Instead we will play the game of fools on the surface of un-illumined consciousness, where insatiable appetites for form and fancy lead the way.*

Integrity is a most important state of being. It allows the merging of what is with all that can be. Without the consciousness of what is, it will be impossible to move deeper into the light. While the light filaments of vulnerability spiral from the outer rim of the heart field inward, the light frequency created by integrity spirals from deep within the heart, illuminating the entire beauty of the heart/soul complex. When we can feel the veracity of the soul-self, we're free to ride the waves of cosmic consciousness. We need to practice the heart technology found in traversing these light fields, and the very act of being in this practice will give us new energy fields of steadiness and stability.

REMEMBER:

- Vulnerability opens the beauty…Guardedness hides the beauty.
- Humility bends and expands…Arrogance restricts and is rigid.
- Love liquefies…Hate freezes.
- Compassion unites…Prejudice divides.
- Acceptance confirms All That Is…Judgment confirms dualism.
- Calm & kind allow movement & fluidity…Anger solidifies density.
- Integrity opens…Dishonesty closes.

2. Wisdom Libraries of the Heart

a. Intuition: Knowing

The research at the Institute for Heart Math is absolutely amazing as it indicates that the heart has intuitive knowledge about events before they actually happen. I call this the psychic heart. Our hearts have thousands upon thousands of intelligent neurons actually located in the physical organ of the heart. They send messages to the brain that can give us important information. Our heart houses intelligence and psychic ability that escapes most of our conscious awareness. What is even more startling is that most of us have no idea that we register this information at all. We've learned to suppress intuitive feelings, premonitions, and forewarnings in favor of the logical information stored in the brain. The problem is that the information stored in the brain is, by definition, from the past. The information in the heart appears to be from the future. Although this seems far-fetched, the heart can know things the mind can't. So perhaps, we can begin to take seriously this capacity of the heart, in order to bring into our awareness, the illuminated sphere of heart wisdom. The renaissance heart will surely include the creative artistry that comes from the fertile landscape of the heart. It's here that we will consciously learn to cultivate the fields of this vast data bank of information. We can learn to feel what directions to go, what paths to take, and what choices to make simply by feeling the tapestry of our heart threads. As we do this, we will find ourselves more deeply aligned with our soul blueprint and our spirited mission on and for the Earth.

In addition, as we learn to harness this intuitive heart wisdom, we will be able to prevent disasters, change destiny paths and design Earth environments in which all beings can live and thrive. My heart knows that one day we will have a profession called Heart Intuits. These Intuits will harness the ability to access and utilize the hearts knowledge far in advance. They will not only be able to warn us of some impending disaster, but help us make choices to avert them, by "knowing" other ways of responding. In addition, these heart specialists will operate fully in the SEE♥. Their cultivated heart vibrations will expand far into space and time, bringing coherence and cohesiveness to thousands of beings and thousands of situations. This is how we shall begin to change the face of our planet and understand the truth of our cosmos.

b. Love

Love is surely the energetic signature of Divine Intelligence or God. As we learn to live from our heart center, we will learn to generate love, and this vibration will shed Divine Source energy upon the world. Our heart will become the Divine tool for manifesting Heaven on Earth. Love is the experience of the heart. It can't be thought, only felt. The feeling experience of this heart state is being in love. With love, all else that's pure and good shall follow. Without the router routing power of holding, enfolding and healing human emotions, pure love is impossible. Love that's created from the ego springs from the densities of the less fed heart. When the heart is whole and healed, it can then, and only then hold the capacity for the enormous vibrational signature of true Divine love. This love knows no boundaries, no definitions, no guidelines and is fierce with courageous fortitude to move in darkness, without fear, without pause. Nothing can equal this and only the heart knows this truth in its illumined hallways of universal consciousness.

c. Interconnectedness: Creating the Web

We can't live in separate worlds and ever call it paradise. Paradise only can be manifested through interconnectedness and, once again, the heart is the master chieftain in such pursuits. It's the heart that aches in loneliness, cries in loss and seeks out others in vast lands of multiplicity. It's always the heart that yearns for the Oneness of Being. This oneness can't happen with only one. For enfolded in the experience of oneness is everything that is. *There is knowledge in the heart about the art of keeping the self, while uniting with another, and being within while feeling all else.* While the mind becomes confused in the abyss of self and other, the heart calms, soothes and continuously leads the way outward, all the while remaining awake within. It's the rhythm of the heart that breathes with the rhythm of the Earth. It's the beating of the heart that keeps company with the baby in the womb. The heart is the interface between the human being and the spirit of transcendence. It's in the heart that all connective etheric materials are to be found to weave the web of All That Is.

d. Transmuting

It will be through the heart that all earthly aliments will be addressed, healed and liquidated even if only through the shimmering tears found when we have to change and alter some life path. The heart feels what needs to be healed modified and transformed. As we clear the heart, she will be in a position to continue to be the ultimate metamorphic instrument that humans have been given. We've crushed the heart in so many ways by how we've chosen to live and how we've chosen to die. We've allowed so much heart failure by simply not acknowledging the expansive power of the heart. As we've restricted the flow of the heart, we've sterilized and expunged the most vibrant energetic signature we have. As we now invite the heart to take back her realm as queen of the human domain, we will once again see a transposed place in which to reside. We may not even recognize this place, unless we see with the heart and hear with her beat. Our heart sensory modalities will include intuitive vision, the touch of love, and the sound of all hearts beating as one. In this, we will change the face of the Earth so that never again will we find ourselves separate from the very heart of the planet upon which we live.

e. Transcendence

It's through the heart's vision that we will see the next dimension, our galactic neighbors and finally gaze upon the very face of God. If we only saw these things through our human lens without the benefit of our heart vision, we would surely have a heart attack. This heart technology of intuition, love and interconnectedness enables us to transmute our human clogged arteries into free flowing vessels of liquid gold light. In this way the human heart is eclipsed and enfolds into the heart of spirit, where love is fully manifested and cosmic vision is restored so that the infinite realms of transcendent spirit can both be seen and felt.

The Renaissance Mind: Shifting the Mind Paradigm

1. The renaissance mind is a tool for the higher consciousness of self/soul

Consciousness, with the mapping from the heart, guides and directs the mind towards actualization of all realities. We're no longer lead by the mind, but utilize mind to enact chosen potentialities. Consciousness, utilizing heart wisdom, guides the mind towards its hidden potentialities to manifest spirit on Earth. In this way, mind becomes the magnificent active tool for heart intelligence. When we do this, we will begin to activate those places in the brain that have been dormant until now so that we may be governed by the new brain rather than the old. This will help us solve problems for the many, not the few, live in harmony not distress, cooperate not compete and transcend and expand our human nature, instead of surrender to what has already been. The new brain governs the old, the hidden heart directs the mind and the spirit brings conscious awareness to this enlightening process.

2. The New Human understands how to utilize thought technology

Thoughts are energetic realities that can change, impact and affect the outer world. Many manufacturers today are inventing technology that could help you turn on your TV or computer just by thinking about it. This is especially amazing research, as it shows that our thoughts have the power to interface with our outer world, without literal action. Our thoughts, therefore, are influencing the world and each other constantly. As noted in Chapter 6, neuroscientists who are mapping the brain are discovering that there is a place in the middle of our brain called the thalamic gate. They believe this center transmits energetic fields emanating from our deepest subconscious thought realm. Unbeknownst to us, we telegraph to the world on a fairly consistent basis what we think and believe. These same researchers further believe that these wavelengths from the thalamic gate look for like resonance out in the world. So, if we house a plethora of angry thoughts, we will not only telegraph these thoughts to others, but we will find data in the outer world that resonate or match these inner thoughts. Let me give an example. Two people are in a line of a traffic jam; one is broadcasting angry thoughts and the other is steeped in compassionate and kind thoughts. The first driver comes up to the car causing the traffic jam and gives the driver the finger, feeling further infuriated by the lousy circumstances in his life. The second driver looks and sees the world differently. As he comes closer to the stopped car, he sees an 80 year-old man in the drivers seat looking distressed. The second compassionate minded driver stops his car and gets out to assist this older man.

He calls roadside service for this man's car and is rewarded with much gratitude from this man. He soon goes on his way, with confirming information in his mind that the world is a kind and beautiful place. The first driver has already arrived at work sending the next angry transmission out to all of his coworkers, who in turn avoid him, thus confirming his thoughts that the world is mean and depriving. What we think, influences what we see, and what we see influences how we behave, and how we behave, influences how the world reacts. It's very sobering to know that we influence the world just by how we think. The problem is that we think reality is what we see out there, instead of what we think in here.

The New Human understands that reality begins in the inner domain of the mind and is dispersed to the outer world to create what we see. We're capable of creating health and wellbeing within and harmony and peace in the world. As we're awake and aware in the seat of our higher consciousness, we can manifest and co-create a new world, a new cosmic design. This is our mission on Earth to bring the breath of spirit into the domain of mind and heart to create the New Human on the New Earth.

3. Interconnectiveness of Mind

The renaissance mind is capable of sending rippling waves of energetic thought streams that can commingle and interconnect with the vibrant fields of beings both of this Earth and beyond. Someday we will understand that we can influence and affect events in other places and other times.

a. Sentient Beings

There is inter-connectedness between and among humans. The ultimate tool for thought connection will be telepathy. The field of quantum physics brings us much enlightenment about the truth of our inseparable connection to one another in the web of life. Quantum entanglement theory states that particles of energy/matter are correlated and can predictably interact with each other no matter how far they are apart, and they travel faster than the speed of light. In a strange twist of fate, what determines the interaction these particles have is our observation of them. We're intractably involved in their entanglement and therefore part of the entanglement. The field of science joins what the ancient spiritual traditions have always understood: We're all connected in the invisible field of oneness. Mind and spirit are not so separate as we understand wholeness and unity. *We're connected not only through the body of spirit, but the body of matter as well.*

As we become more fully evolved, we will have more access to the quantum tools that will bring to light in clear vision the connective network between and among our fellow humans. These quantum tools will be found in our psychic capabilities and our extraordinary sensory perceptions. One of our most important psychic endowments is the ability for telepathic communication. Literally, telepathy means the ability to transmit information from one person to another without using any of our known sensory channels. We now understand that thoughts are energy and can travel outside the mind to affect a myriad of things in the environment, including another mind. In the future, we will be able to communicate through thoughts alone. In this ability, we will gain an understanding of each other in a much more truthful, meaningful and immediate way. Some of you reading this might not like this idea at first glance, as you hide away your thoughts as a protective mechanism. However, as we sit inside our minds, closed off from other sentient beings, we truly believe we've been, and always will be, separate. Telepathy will enhance our experience of non-separateness, while still enabling us to experience our unique configuration of self. We will learn to hide nothing and in this process, understand the tremendous energy that we've used in the past to live behind closed doors. Through mind communication, we will learn that the truth of who we are need not be secreted away, but fully realized inside and out. In this way, we begin to know the inter-connectedness of each individual mind with the Divine Mind of All That Is.

b. Sentient Beings in the Cosmos

There are many scientists, spiritual teachers, military personnel and lay persons who have, over the last 70 years disclosed the truth not only about the existence of Extraterrestrials (ETs), but about contact with them on our very planet. Dr. Steven Greer has been one of the leading researchers and world's foremost authority on legitimizing the case for ETs. He has developed a CE-5 (close encounters of the fifth kind) protocol using human consciousness to make mutual, bilateral communication with Extraterrestrials. These protocols are based on establishing a higher consciousness state through meditative techniques that produce a wave of non-local consciousness that can connect with extraterrestrial beings. He has lead many field research teams throughout the world and has successfully established contact with ET craft and ET beings using this consciousness based protocol. Other groups have also developed CE-5 protocols throughout the world using these thought based consciousness protocols and have had successful contact with otherworldly civilizations. We're rapidly exploring how we might use our thoughts to manifest higher consciousness states for contact with off world sentient beings. This is certainly part of the New Human consciousness practice.

c. Nature and its Inhabitants

If thought is energy, and energy is non-local, then we certainly can and do have relationships with our plant, mineral and animal kingdoms on Earth through our mind fields. Bird and Tompkins have done significant research on the effect of the human mind on plants. A simple thought, "I'm going to burn you," can evoke a strong incoherent electromagnetic response in a plant. On the other hand, a loving thought can evoke a coherent healthy electromagnetic response from a plant. Many humans have known the healing power of talking positively to plants. More recently, Japanese researcher Dr. Emoto has explored the incredible relationship between our thoughts and feelings and the effect they have on molecules of water. Positive thoughts cause a coherent complex crystalline pattern in water molecules that is quite beautiful when viewed under a microscope. On the hand, cruel, mean, hateful thoughts create chaotic, asymmetrical patterns in the molecules. This should cause all of us to take notice especially because 65-70% of our own bodies are made up of water. It is a sobering yet crucial thought that simply through conscious, positive relating we can have such a healing impact not only on our own inner body, but the environment in which we live. In the new renaissance world, we will be able to know and feel our connection to all life around us and as a result, establish a communion with the living Earth and all inhabitants that's loving, generating, and honoring. We will understand the symbiotic nature of our relationship with nature and the Earth, and as a result, live in synchronistic harmony.

d. Other Times and Places

Our thoughts not only affect other places, beings, and things, but have an incredible effect on time and space. The New Human will understand that the thoughts we send out today will be waiting for us tomorrow. We will fathom what is unfathomable today. We create the future by what we think in the present. *We will begin to become sculptors of the future by the strokes our thoughts leave on the canvas of now moments.* This will exponentially increase our motivation to stay awake and aware through conscious thought as we become the creators of the new future of the New Earth. We will also be able to time travel through our thoughts alone. Instantaneous voyaging to some past or future time will be mastered. We will finally comprehend that our previous and future lives are inextricably connected and don't take place in time, but in consciousness. The same will be true for space travel. We will be able to use our thoughts to travel to other places. We will be able to think of a place and be there. This will be manifestation at its best.

4. Unity Thought Habits

The renaissance New Human will have developed unity thought habits that will take the place of the old paradigm patterns of survival and separation. These thought habits will include:

a. We're not separate, but are part of a larger web of life.
b. We're in a unified field of human potential and actualities.
c. While we can individually affect these unified fields, we will utilize this effect for global and cosmic peace and harmony.
d. When we consciously decide to unify our efforts with a group of other beings, we can create fields of thought energy that can exponentially alter mass consciousness.
e. We're part of overall conscious field of spirit and, in this field, we experience the Oneness of Being.

5. Mind is a Tool of Transcendence

We have an amazing part of our brain that actually is the biological seat of transcendence. Many spiritual and philosophical writers and teachers have discussed the mystery of the pineal gland. Now science seems to be riveted on this area in the brain that Descartes called the "seat of the soul." This gland is located in the geometric center of the brain between the left and right hemispheres and is shaped like a pinecone. It's a photosensitive gland, and secretes serotonin and melatonin during sleep, relaxation, meditation and in visualization practices. In addition, according to Dr. Rick Strassman it may produce a chemical called DMT (dimethyltryptamine). DMT is also found in hallucinatory plant substances, that may be associated with lucid dreaming, visualizations, mystical peak experiences and creativity. Calcification of the pineal gland's fluid may be a part of the aging process, as well as the result of fluorides and processed foods. Over time, the pineal gland becomes more and more shut down, weighted with the costs of modern day living. It's likely that in modern humans, spiritual vision has become narrowed and restricted. This is crucial especially because in many ancient spiritual traditions, it was believed to be the link between the physical world and the spiritual world of transcendence. You can see the symbolism of the pinecone in many religions and mystical traditions, clearly giving meaning and sacredness to the pineal gland. In fact, the largest sculpture in the Vatican courtyard is a pinecone. Clearly, they have known the power of the pineal gland.

Interestingly, when seen from the top down view, the pineal gland looks like an eye looking out. In fact, rod and cone cells only thought to be found in our eyes, have been discovered in the pineal gland. Both scientifically and spiritually, the pineal gland offers a place where transcendent vision may take place. The New Human will be able to activate and maintain vibratory health in the pineal gland, so that the evolution of transcendent vision guides and directs our path of enlightenment. This gland will be the antenna to spiritual and celestial messages from the beyond that will enliven and open our soul codes within. Our transcendent vision will be as common as our physical eyesight. As we come to know this exquisite Divine realm, we will transform, utilizing our minds more fully for this transcendent journeying. Our bodies will become lighter as our hearts take their place as the sacred guides towards spiritual unification and the Oneness of Being.

The Renaissance Spirit: Shifting the Spirit Paradigm

Being in the New Human spirit is the most beautiful place one can be in consciousness here on Earth. Paradoxically, we avoid being in this total spirit being because we've not figured out yet that we can be there while still in human body. After all, the last time we felt such brilliance of light spirit was on the eve of our current incarnation. As we came into our bodies, our remembrance dimmed and our dense Earth experience began. For many incarnations here on this planet, it's probably true that the lightness and radiance of spirit was most felt when not in the dense fields that human bodies produce. We may actually have vague remembrances and impressions from this in between place after body death. It's probably why so many humans yearn to have out of body experiences, so that they, once again, can feel the lightness of soul soaring. In the end, it's our fear of leaving the body that often drives spirit to the far reaches of our consciousness. In addition, so many humans in the three-dimensional experience don't want to leave this dimension and this creates the biggest dilemma in truly becoming the New Human. *In the renaissance human, we're meant to merge out of body with the body.* The body becomes the very vehicle for carrying the actions of spirit throughout the world. Consciousness becomes the beacon by which we travel in our bodies. We understand that our mission is to allow our very humanness to carry the face of God, allowing our spirits to soar in the world. As we merge our human consciousness with spirit, we can actually feel closer to all other dimensions and fields of consciousness. We're here to transcend this dimension while still living on this earthly plane in the human body. In so doing, we will experience the metamorphic transformation of the human species, as we surpass the boundaries of the third dimensional world and ascend into higher beings in multidimensional realms. This is our evolutionary path. If we could really see nature with our spiritual eyes, we would see that she has already transcended, even though we've done our best (or worst) to destroy her. The Earth is alive and ascending. The question is: Are we going to ascend with her?

This time of ascension in the twenty-first century is an extraordinary time, as we have the capability to have the consciousness of spirit infuse the human experience in its totality. All human quadrants can be permeated and imbued with this Source presence so that we may shine the light of the Divine manifested spirit on Earth. The good news is that this evolution of spirit has taken place across many intergalactic civilizations, where planetary beings from other star systems have allowed spirit to be the director of all things manifest. The bad news is that we have not yet opened ourselves to their existence and so have not benefited from the wisdom that comes from star civilizations that have gone before us. *The New Human understands that we, not only are part of a much larger intergalactic community, but our veracity of spiritual strength allows us to humbly reach out and open ourselves to the annals of wisdoms in the star libraries above.* In taking our place in the ascension process, we don't just accentuate planet Earth's ascension, but the entire galactic community in which we live.

Living in Spirit

1. The quadrant of Spirit invigorates and enlivens all other human quadrants

Spirit or *soul life force* becomes a felt experience in every moment of every day. In the body, the pulse of life force is felt and directs the body into lightness of being, gently guiding it towards light feats, foods and festive and fruitful actions. As spirit infuses the heart, the heavy dense feelings of third dimensional life are rejuvenated and transformed into felt experiences of higher, lighter heart living. This includes all heart wisdom, intuitive knowledge, joy and love. The heart begins to sing its song of hope and exaltation, adding notes of mellifluous harmony to the symphony of all life in all places. As spirit imbues its livened presence upon the heart, the heart becomes the pacemaker for all human endeavors. The reactions of egoic/personality no longer determine the cascade of behaviors polluting our inner and outer world. *Instead, the heart becomes the proactive script for all actions and quests creating a mosaic masterpiece of inner and outer flow with every beat, wherever it goes.*

As the swooping beauty of soul consciousness sweeps the mind, it invigorates, inspires and expands the corridors of thought channels and brain circuitry. The golden rays of life force turn on the vast expanses of our brain network, opening new programs of understanding, conceptual amplification and magnified vistas of seeing and knowing. Simply put, Spirit moves the mind into higher action. *As Spirit moves through the mind with soft whispers of higher vibrational disclosures, it opens new portals and ignites new brain neural pathways.* In this way, we become capable of holding higher ideals, concepts, knowledge and new paradigm principles.

As Spirit moves into the body, mind and heart, all become beautiful bedfellows. Spirit enlivens a unity dance with all that's human, with All That Is sacred Source. Living in the consciousness of spirit guides our human quadrant experiences towards completion and well-being.

2. Spirit informs, directs and guides our waking life and dream-time

Old paradigms driven by past three-dimensional thinking no longer dictate our living domains. Instead, our inner and outer lives are created from the inside out. Our dreams more coherently weave the design of the universe, we become better at decoding this soul wisdom and bringing it forth into waking life. We become awake in our dreams, manifesting and culling information that will be utilized in the new renaissance time of the New Human birth.

The soul seat of spiritual being finally takes the prime seat of leadership in the human domain. Everything is seen and felt through this vibrational code of spiritual essence. In this, we have a conduit to the infinite libraries of the universe.

The New Human begins to comprehend how to see, feel and hear spirit and has no fear of merging with this deep expanded sacred sphere. Spirit, in the past, has been on the peripheral boundaries of human consciousness. In the New Human, it is centered in consciousness and yet completely suffused in all other quadrant experiences. In other words, consciousness resides in spirit and infuses everything else with the light of the sacred geometry that comes from all other dimensions. *We no longer have to remember we're spirit beings, we will simply be in the full manifestation of spirit flowing.* This abounding stream of the quintessential you, will create, manifest, and consummate the New Earth and the New Human.

3. Spirit becomes the ultimate free energy device

As we become an open spiritual system, we gain access to the infinite energy source of all creation. In the old paradigms, externalized notions of balance and survival guided healing, wellness and even evolution. It was an enclosed system, where the physical body became encapsulated in the prison of its contained structures. Within these systems, over time, vibrancy began to wane. As a result, we have had to contend on Earth with the concept of death. However, as we ascend, our relationship with death diminishes as our life force quotient increases. As we open our consciousness, it becomes a beacon to all energy sources beyond what we actually see. Rejuvenation can occur in the outer etheric body, as spirit becomes a conduit to the vast quantum field of energy. These infinite energy sources feed and balance the energetic body so that the physical body can stay healthier and whole. Instead of the body being seen and felt as an immured restricted system, it begins to feel energetically connected to All That Is through the consciousness of spirit. The figure eight of source and body energies brings moving life force through and around the human body, connecting and bathing it in the Oneness experience. In this way, we will be able to live much longer with a lightness of being that comes from nourishing the soul and feeding the body with the energy of life. This energy Source is never ending and always free. Our hearts and minds will be affected as we think more clearly and expansively, feel more truly authentic and have access to higher dimensional wisdom. This in turn will guide us to make choices that will continue to enliven and illume our higher consciousness, while diminishing our need to satisfy more primitive needs and appetites. We ourselves will become an ultimate free energy device, feeding and nourishing everything around us. In this way, we finally take up our role as co-creators with the Divine Source of All That Is.

4. Spirit holds the true mission

Spirit holds the keys to the chambers within that hold our true mission on Earth. As we unlock these hidden treasures, we will discover that we can live from the inside out and in so doing impact, direct and create a new world, a new time. As the egoic/human self is no longer leading by its search and seize methodology, everything is seen and felt differently. Spirit connects us; ego separates. Spirit infuses the light; ego dampens it. Things and places are not to be conquered and acquired, but rather discovered and shared. The mission of living in harmony, peace and love as a global community will be understood and actualized. There will be abundance and more than enough for all living beings. We will no longer see ourselves as separate, but rather as part of a living, breathing whole. Our mission will be to give our gifts freely and passionately to the all of humanity, as we will no longer receive satisfaction from taking and plundering. Comparing, contrasting, contradicting and conforming will no longer be necessary. We will see each individual as unique and crucial, yet we will understand we're all necessary for the whole to work. As spirit breathes in the light force we become inoculated by Sacred Source. All deprivations, destructions and diseases become healed. We will no longer doubt love or its power. Concerns of safety, survival and continuity that formerly existed in the ego domain will be replaced by unlimited spiritual bounty guided by our infinite sovereignty. Through spirit's guidance, we will be able to spend time in the universal libraries without losing our human consciousness. We will once again feel the miracle of the soul journey in human form.

SIGNS YOU ARE LIVING IN THE NEW HUMAN CONSCIOUSNESS

- You're a seeker not a seizer.
- You follow inner guidance, rather than search for outer instruction.
- You give your gifts joyfully and freely.
- You humbly and graciously learn to receive another's presence (presents).
- You honor your own, as well as others', uniqueness while holding the sameness of all living beings.
- You're lead by what gives you lightness.
- You understand unity as the guiding principle and no longer suffer from separation.
- You can't wait to find anyone and everyone to love.
- You see beauty where there is ugliness and feel splendor in all foibles and failures.
- Anxious worries and ruminations are replaced by intriguing contemplations and dreams about your mission on Earth and elsewhere.
- You understand your soul center and open it to shine upon the world.
- You see Earth as a beautiful planet and work with her towards the path of ascension.
- You understand that we're not alone, and join freely and without hesitation the intergalactic community of other beings and other star systems.
- You feel the joy of everlasting life and eternal consciousness.
- You finally feel Home as you have never felt it before.

These are but a few signposts. Discovering how to live together in a global community of peace and harmony is the most crucial part of this evolving process on Earth. And thus, we move to the next chapter on relations beyond the self.

Soul Remedies

8 – Becoming the New Human

Find a quiet ***place***…where you can feel grounded and peaceful.
Know that this is the ***time*** for your sacred birthing.

You're ready to open the gates allowing
the New Human within to create the world beyond.

Imagine a flow of life force from deep within spiraling up and out.
Filling every part of you with sparkles of light and love.

Feel your body become the beautiful temple
that houses this New Human.

Feel your hear leap with joy as it beats strongly,
directing all that will come.

Feel your mind open as it creates new vistas
of imagination and dreaming.

Feel your spirit soar as it flows with
Divine consciousness and oneness.

9

I/Thou: Relations Beyond Self

"Everyone and everything around you is your teacher."
–Ken Keyes, Jr.

"The people we are in relationship with are always a mirror.
Reflecting our own beliefs, and simultaneously we are mirrors reflecting their beliefs.
So relationship is one of the most powerful tools for growth…"
–Shakti Gawain

"The impossible is possible when people align with you.
When you do things with people not against them, the amazing resources
of the Higher Self within are mobilized."
–Gita Bellin

It becomes crucial to the liberation process of loving another to first remember who we really are, moving through the labyrinth of the three-dimensional ideas of the human self. As we begin to dissolve these densely held ideas of the who of the small egoic self, we at once feel the tethers of untruths release themselves and we are finally free to know the cosmic truth. We are emancipated from the boundaries imposed on the embodied self in order to consummate the relationship we have with ourselves, others and Divine Source with unadulterated love. We are free once again to manifest instantaneously, and in doing so we will be in our mystic mission on Earth.

As we have seen, however, self-love is an absolute prerequisite for going beyond the self and learning to love others. We all carry a halo or ring of self-portrayal around us either full of self-debris or self-love. This halo, this ring of self-presence, or in some cases absence, surrounding us is the first field of energy holds the first interaction we offer the outside world. Remember, whatever you have not dealt with or left unloved within yourself is found floating in the halo that surrounds you. For one, we have so easily learned to put our own shadow parts and/or demons within us at arms length in this invisible energetic ring that lives slightly outside of ourselves. In this way, we give up our own responsibility to deal with these darker parts, thus living in the absence created by denial. Yet in disclaiming such parts and placing them in the far reaches of our outer boundaries, we require others to meet this ring of unspent, stagnant and jagged energies. Sadly, this is the field that most people encounter first and we wonder why we don't have a peaceful, harmonic community in which to live. In addition, when we ourselves look out into the world, we see our own layer of discarded debris in this surrounding halo, mistaking it for things outside of ourselves. (**see illustration 16**) We look out and see this abandoned self-wreckage and think we are seeing other peoples ringed shadow parts. We then go to amazing measures to protect ourselves from their flying rubble; never realizing it is our own. It is paramount that we remember that we can never see the world except through this ring around us. Clearing out this outer ring, this asteroid belt, through the work of self-love (chapters 6 & 7) is necessary to I/Thou relations.

The frequencies or wavelengths of the unexamined discarded self-parts attract the same. Our energetic signatures found in this outside band create a frequency that searches for like frequencies. In finding this resonance, we have perfect opportunities to see ourselves in someone else. We just might not like what we see. We end up in relationships where we are dancing with the debris of the unacknowledged self, all the while thinking, complaining and exclaiming that we are dancing with our partner's debris. Often the refrain is, "If they would only do the work and clear their fields, we would indeed be fine." Some humans have more dragons than demons, which is why they feel like they are spouting fire. We tend to keep our distance from those people and they use our distance to prove to themselves that the world is full of dragons.

It seems that throughout this life, we take the things we do not like about ourselves or are too difficult and throw them off the spaceship we travel in, like litter, hoping it will float elsewhere. Unfortunately, like most unwanted debris, it doesn't disintegrate or float away, but instead hovers around us, pulled close by the gravity of our egoic natures. We must finally understand that this outside band or restrictive girdle of old paradigm grids and blueprints and other debris is not who we are, but only holds remnants of what we have been in this three-dimensional human drama. I notice when people do begin to examine this externalized belt they think this abandoned wasteland, and all it holds, possesses the real truth about who they are. Paradoxically, as we

DEBRIS FIELDS AND RESONANCE

Each one looks out at another, mistaking their own debris for the other.

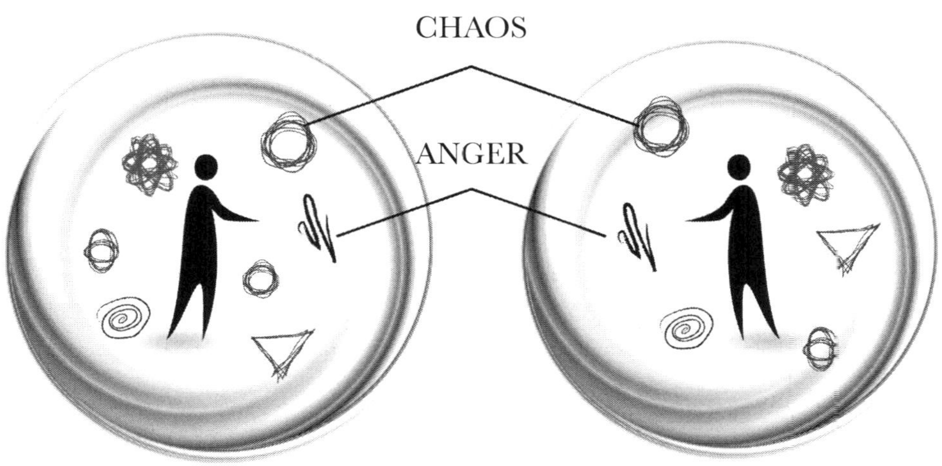

Debris meets and is attracted.

Illustration 16

gain some semblance of this new self-awareness, it is easy to spend enormous amounts of time abandoning the lighter higher self still hidden within to fight the dragons and demons in these outer recesses. We can't expect someone to really see us, let alone love us, when they are viewing the self-portrait produced by this ring of inner debris. We can't see each other until we have done this inner work of love. Imagine what it would be like for two individuals steeped in this deep inner self-love commingling with clear energy fields, visioning and loving the inner recesses of who each are spiritually and cosmically.

It's important to note here how easy it is to want to be in close proximity and even love those people who not only have their asteroid belts cleared out, but are also full of love. There is a direct path for us to feel the love within them and this in turn sends a frequency, a vibration that triggers a similar resonance within us. After all, deep down our eternal search is for Oneness of Being and the soft whispers that All Is Love. This awakens the sleeping giant within and we begin the process of coming alive, awake and aware. Maybe it is just plain easier to love those things that already emanate this oscillating love frequency such as nature, or certain leaders or gurus.

In addition, it's easier to send love to those things in another person that have been loved rather than those things that have not been loved. For instance, a person becomes a singer, loving both the experience of singing and the love from others who have loved the singing voice, which in turn imbues the singer with the frequency of love and beauty. This then creates a port for our love to land on or resonate with. We are loving the love that emanates from the singer's own vibrational field. Unfortunately, we mistake this aliveness, this resonant vibrational awakening, as solely about the other person, their talents or gifts. We become attached to the idea that they produce this feeling, and we become attached to these externalizations and once again leave the inner palace of potential self-revelation. The process works in the opposite way as well. Things that we hate about ourselves may bring the resonance of dislike or hate from others. This weaving of self and other can be quite treacherous or beautiful depending on the evolution of the soul and self. Of course ultimately, we must learn to give love no matter what resonance we find on the other end.

A Quick Guide to the ABC's of Relationships

When we first enter the zone of I/Thou relations we experience the ABC's of attraction including those things we fall in love about the other person or being (whether God, pet or other worldly.) Soon, we begin to size up those things in the other that also might be shortcomings, potentially leading us towards deprivation and the not enough syndrome. We begin to look away from the initial bright lights of other and see instead the possibility that there are more letters (XYZ's) to be explored that are filled with shortcomings and inadequacies. We concentrate on these letters for fear that these are dangerous and foreboding. We scope out the XYZ's, keep track of them on a tally pad and eventually feel comfortable enough, even obligated, to point these things out to the other involved. Perhaps, gently at first, but as we continue to bombard the other with our perceived shortcomings of them, we have a myriad of suggestions about how they might change. Idol threats of leaving them follow. I've seen people do this with their relationship with God as they state, "Well, God was a great concept as a kid, but where is God now that I am in perilous trouble, he or she should make itself known." Of course, as we distract ourselves with such tedious rubric, we do not have to pay attention to our own XYZ's, which is the purpose of this futile exercise in the first place. This feels better because we can deny our own incompleteness. Because another's imperfections feel less miserable to us, we concentrate entirely too much on them. Eventually, however, we might realize how deprived we are because of them. But, at least we can rest knowing it is their fault and not ours.

It doesn't occur to us that part of the reason we feel bad in relation to others is not because of the other, but more about ourselves. Every relationship has an alphabet and there will always be letters in the alphabet that feel depriving. In one relationship the depriving force is found in XYZ and in the next it is MNO. In that moment, it feels imperative that you must have the exact thing that your partner does not give you. In fact, sometimes you never even knew you needed something until you realized that your partner didn't have it to offer you. Then it becomes the crime of the century. We choose people who, in fact, will not be able to give us the exact thing we think we need. This should only be a beacon or guidepost to go back within and work on your own heart signature. There will always be a letter of deprivation; the mantra is, "Get over it, it's not about them it is about me." We're all on the path of evolving, and so we are not a complete and whole alphabet. We'll always offer those others at least a few letters of inadequacy. My guess is that when we have completed our own alphabet, we will not even see the absent letters in someone else's library.

It's such a joy to feel someone who is totally present, with all their beauty and their deficits. There's an invisible trust that's immediately felt, not because presence makes one automatically trustable, but because when one is totally present there is more of them to feel, touch, taste and see. The implicit digestion of this brings you back inside and this figure eight is inclusive not exclusive. *It's not the kind or content of the data revealed in the moment shared with another that matters, only the process of deep presence and in that all information is revealed and experienced.* It's this experience that brings us to Oneness. Being in relation to other is a beautiful landscape and/or treacherous landmine all at once. That's why the only mantra eventually has to be: "What love do I bring to Thee."

Process vs. Content

Establishing I/Thou relationships presents an enormous opportunity to experience the vastness of non-space/time, discovering in this vastness the truth of our soul purpose on Earth. Most of us have been taught that being in a relationship is about the Content Path. The Content Path is the path where you might choose your partner by their skin or hair color, or their occupation and financial status, or their ethnic or cultural background. I hear people talk about their types: tall, skinny, large, small, brunette, blonde, Nordic, ethnic, this build or that build. We've not been taught to approach people in order to simply be in process with but rather for singular distinct defined outcomes. Of course, once in relationship, we still get trapped in the content path. Disagreements develop, likes and dislikes, methods and styles of living, and so content resolution is where most couples spend most of their time. You need to like this or that or do this or that. We spend most of our time in the architecture created by third-dimensional formulas that deconstruct and analyze. Do we wonder why it's so hard to shift our consciousness to other realms of dimensional thinking?

We start believing that these content conflicts that create lengthy compositions and sometimes character assassinations are the only wars to be fought and won. This happens in many relationship formats, whether it's countries, villages, neighborhoods, families or couples. The patter continues, "If I can just get you to agree that I'm right, I know what's best, I know how things should be done, I know the right (content) path and if you could know all of this, we could live in peace and love." Because there is so much diversity on Earth, we should have long ago given up the illusion that the Divine master creator prefers sameness or rightness. Insisting that you be the same as me, seeing the world the same, feeling the same, thinking the same, and looking the same, is a sad commentary on human's ability to be in process. Thinking that sameness is somehow preferable is just plain insidious lunacy.

We are different in order that we might learn to be in the sacred process of holding all and being all. I'm here with you to be in communion with you, whereby I learn to hold our differences in love not hate, in calmness not calamity, in understanding not warfare, in curiosity not disdain. I'm here for you to see who you are, not who I want you to be. Sitting in process provides rocket fuel for my own ascension. I know the truth of this by how hard it is to do. Anything that's too easy, too safe, too predictable causes life force loss. It is much harder for us to sit with another for the sake of simply being, where we are required to put our own content on hold for someone else's content (which in turn also might tweak and trigger our own waiting content demons). In holding another, so that they might be simply heard and held, we contribute to the their process of deeply going within, so that they might understand themselves, their motives and debris. In the end, content can finally be surrendered to process.

When in the true act of loving, it is simply a Process whereby you discover and experience the feeling of the algorithmic creation of sacred life movement. Content is only relevant as a vehicle to drive us through the veil of the third dimension into multidimensional consciousness. We need the admission ticket given to us by some whimsical content of some passing characteristic of someone in order to be enticed into the magical sovereignty of love. As so many of us know, the content or data, about someone or something is quite whimsical, and changes in a moment's notice. Feeling and knowing the process of love, although quite difficult, is eternal and steadfast. Long after the content show is over, the process, or state of being manifest in love, can linger forever, if we let it. When in total process you are in the event horizon of love. Once in the total love state of being, no content or events therein can affect the person in such a state. The ultimate example is the sacred love of the Divine that is absolutely unaffected by the specifics of what we do or say. Divine Source is beyond space and time and therefore we cannot escape this expansive love no matter where we go. The space/time continuum becomes simply irrelevant when in total merging of love consciousness.

Clues to help stay out of Content:

- I am here to understand you not debate you.
- I am here to see you and your soul blueprint.
- As you expand so do I.
- As you constrict so do I.
- We are here to experience merging not submerging.
- You are a reflection of me and I of you.
- Our differences only add not subtract.
- My gift to you is being in the Love Process.
- Content distracts and anesthetizes.
- Process unites and enlivens.
- I can only love you to the degree I love myself.
- It's not how you love me that counts, it's how I love you.
- If I doubt myself, I will inevitably doubt your content.
- When I am in the process of love, I am blessed by sacred Source.
- Content eventually becomes dangerously restrictive.
- Process is marvelously expanding.

The Unconditional love found only in Process is like a rotor rooter for conditions that have killed and maimed a person's psyche in the past. If you don't make room to love another fully in this process, then you can't possibly receive and experience the love that person has for you. When you're in a stance of understanding and holding, you're on the edge of the field of Divine love. This closeness to such a field gives energy for health and well-being. We wait to receive such energy from others, as if we could even identify this energy field, should it come through. I know now, that if I take the Process Path — being in the process of being the full loving being that I am, then I immediately receive blessings of infinite love from the energy field of sacred Source. Why not all be blessed?

Knowing I/Thou Through Giving

We can't fully experience what it is like to be loved until we are willing to be the lover. We can't recognize or feel the experience of receiving until we've first felt the experience of giving. This is crucial. The experience or state of being created by giving is what increases our ability to expand our consciousness, making room for all other reference points, for all other experiences to come. The experience of giving to another human being must be felt, so that an inner template is created that holds that state of being. Without such a template, the act or experience of receiving from another reverberates in an empty hallway within the home of the self. This explains why so many people feel they never have enough from others, because no matter what they receive, it's not a deeply felt experience within. If you want to truly feel the depth of reception, you must first develop the abilities for perception. In order to perceive something, you must be able to recognize that which you want to perceive. Giving, by definition, is an inside out motion and this motion creates an experience or state of being in your inside world. It's this state of being within that creates receptor sites for recognizing giving acts whether they be outgoing or incoming. I call this the sensory modality for visioning the figure eight of I/Thou relations. Once you have created this signature for giving, you're ready to resonate with an experience of receiving and thus a figure eight is formed that has neither beginning nor end.

Let's back up for a moment, and see where we get hung up on this idea of giving first and receiving later. Many people feel like when they give something to another, it's like shaving a part of themselves off, never to be seen again. However, at this point it's important to understand that when giving is truly about offering oneself, the experience or state of being of giving, then you gain and expand with that experience. When giving is motivated by something outside of yourself (like what you will get in return), it indeed feels empty or perhaps it even feels like you are losing a part of yourself. Because in the moment when you anticipate what you should get for this great giving task, you pause and in that pause you feel the truth of your own emptiness. You mistake this emptiness for some consequence for giving away part of yourself. You say to yourself, "See what you get for giving? Nothing." If you truly get nothing, or if you base the merit of the act of giving on what the return is, then you don't have the slightest idea what the experience of giving is. The greatest motivation for giving is to both feel the self expand and to open up a space inside of you that may finally be able to hold the experience of another's gift. Let's talk about the self-expansion part first. Any experience you truly let yourself consciously feel, by definition expands who you are. This is a time in all of our lives to be especially curious about who we are with others. Unfortunately, most of our attention with others centers on what they think of us, how they treat us, or what we might receive from them. Of course when this happens our sense of self diminishes and our sense of the outside world expands. This is what I call the shrinking self phenomenon: As our focus and attention shifts to others, our inside world becomes faint and unfelt.

The ultimate goal is the activation of the figure eight of I/Thou relations, which is the integrated, fluid movement of the total felt self with the total felt other. The first objective in this eventual experience is to stay conscious of the who (the self) in this sacred geometric dance. As you begin to know the felt signatures of love in action within the world of the self, you initiate an anchoring system to hold your consciousness and expand your sense of you. This expanded state of you then extends, offering a connective port to all others. It's important to become a detective of sorts, to know and identify this giver part of you. It's important to ask ourselves questions like, "What does the experience of being kind to another really feel like? How does it feel to love unconditionally? What is the signature of giving service without expectation?" I'm convinced that if we could spend more time being truly present to the experience of the world within as we are interacting with another, we'd begin to treat people so much better. It simply feels better to treat people better. Hate as an experience dims the soul, love turns up the volume of the self.

The question becomes, "Who are you with others?" Of course this requires presence with them, but before you can truly be present to another, you must be present inside yourself. *This isn't about the experience of another with you, but first an experience of yourself with another.* The conscious experience of love expands the possibilities of who we are and contributes to the soul actualization process. The second most amazing phenomena takes place as we open this space within to then experience the merging energies of the other. When we've come to know kindness, love, and compassion through experiencing within the self, we become capable of recognizing it in another person. The experience of these things through the self, provides a place within the self to receive those things from another. Imagine that the experience of loving or giving to another person creates a room within oneself where those vibrations or wavelengths live. Every act towards another has a particular wavelength and each particular wavelength creates a room within to hold the signature of that wavelength. As you can see, not only then is the *craft of self* expanded with each wavelength created, but there are places of resonance inside where the gifts of others can then reside. As a person comes into your life and gives you an act of kindness, not only will you immediately recognize this as kindness, but you will, like a magnet, take these waveforms inside to the room where your own experiential kindness waveforms reside. The room then dances with wonderful whirling waveforms, making designs that can only come from a dance of two or more. (**see illustration 17**)

Give what you want to get and watch the expansion of the self and all those around you as well. No matter what you get back, the giving, if

EMOTIONAL FREQUENCY RECOGNITION

Giver with SEE❤ Receiver without SEE❤

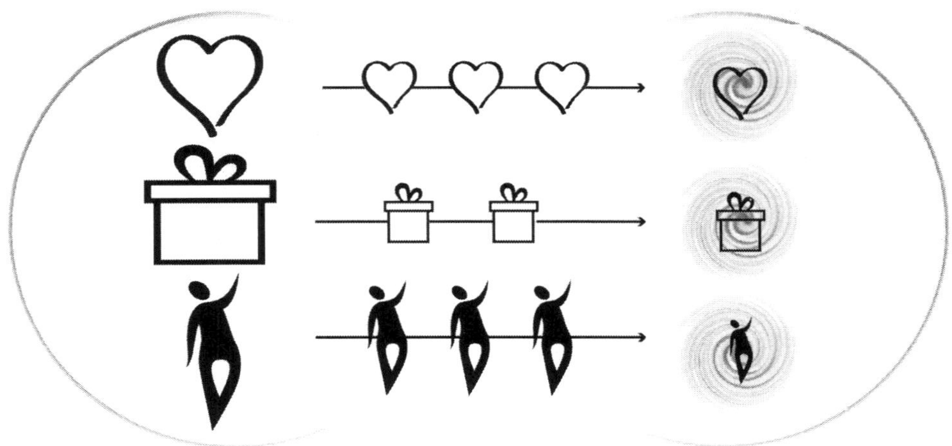

Giver with SEE❤

Receiver with SEE❤.
Can accept waveforms into rooms
that match them. Rooms swirl
with both frequencies.

Illustration 17

consciously experienced will create self-growth, soul wonder and merging oneness. In addition, you may now be able to finally take in those very things you thought you always wanted from another. You'll recognize it, have space to receive it and will be in resonance with your beloved other, creating a beautiful dance of unity. Through the other, you may experience that long sought after encounter with Divine oneness. A word of caution, it's crucial to understand that this process of giving and receiving is not one to become too attached to. Attachment guarantees that this beautiful weaving and breathing will become labored and forced. Forever is an illusion that takes us out of momentary experiences. Momentary experiences are the building blocks for understanding the true nature of eternity. I/Thou relations are the perfect arenas for such encounters.

From Dualism to Oneness

Knowing thyself with other creates an energetic spiraling motion awakening the energy spinning centers in our bodies. We can feel and sense movement and in this movement we begin to recognize our true cosmic origins. We can feel this movement in our various chakra centers. Note the movement you feel in your solar plexus (butterflies in your stomach) when you fall in love. Note the feeling of movement in your heart chakra when you hold compassion for another. Note the movement you feel when you feel God consciousness at the top of your head in your crown chakra. Note the movement you feel below your naval when you feel sexual energy rising. When we feel this velocity of flow, we become unstuck and untethered, so we might experience the evolutionary migration towards ascension and higher consciousness.

The three-dimensional realm, unfortunately, is full of flow stops, marooned places and grounded relationships. Much of the movement felt in the third dimension is movement between polarities. Once people land in a polarity, they become wedged and fixed in this position. Living in one polar plane clouds, obscures and shrouds vision. Notice how difficult it is for people to resolve conflicts as the tug-of-war solidifies positions rather than causes fluidity between positions. That's why I love the practice in debate classes where you have to take on a position whether you believe in it or not. Can you shape your thoughts and feelings towards a position or idea, even if you normally don't sit in that place? This is great practice for feeling movement once again. The content of so much of our third-dimensional arguments is irrelevant. If I'm stuck in my own location of thought and feeling, I can't travel to your place of thought and feeling. Simply understanding each other becomes so crucial, not only as a way to resolve conflicts, but as a way to feel the movement of the figure eight of I/Thou flow. *As I take the position of simply wanting to understand you, I begin to navigate towards your location and in doing so I loosen the polarized grip of my landlocked third-dimensional reality by the very sense of traveling towards you.*

We think that we can't move out of our polarized settings until they are seen and heard by another. While being understood can be a catalyst for traveling and moving, it can also lodge us deeper in our trenches as it can create a dense state of ego entitlement. We are always yearning to be seen in our cosmic blueprint, but our Earth experiences and the denseness of our little selves causes us to misinterpret this need. Our little selves go on a march, albeit a still stuck protest, to be seen and heard and thus we create the dualities of you versus me. When we truly see each other's soul/self, dualities fade and are erased by the emerging experience of oneness and simply being together. *When there's only room for One, there will never be room for All. When there's room for All, the One flourishes and catapults towards cosmic consciousness.* In the end, as we come closer to living in the cosmic self, we will understand that this contains the one and the All, all at once. There's no separation and there never has been. Separation is, after all, a figment of the third-dimensional imagination. Relationships between humans are perfect arenas for this new movement to be felt. It's a time for the heart to lead and the mind to simply note. Polarizations are created to bring our consciousness out of the shadows and into the light of unity, non-dualities and multidimensional travel.

Some guidelines for the journey:

1. There are no individual winners.
2. Winning is the motion felt by two or more when dualities begin to fade and the all-ness of two or more is felt.
3. When inviting someone to understand you, you must be careful with words and actions. No Harm is the mantra at all times.
4. When entering another's territory no armaments can be taken across their threshold.
5. The purpose of going in is not to take anyone hostage. The goal is not to learn more so that you can take more. The objective is not to defend oneself when in another's territory.

6. The stance is this: I am at your door with open heart and quiet mind. I leave all my three-dimensional weapons of derision and divisiveness at the door. I come stripped down of armor and enter with the beauty of the bareness of my heart and soul. What you see is who I am.
7. The gifts I bring you are love, compassion and my curiosity.
8. I'm excited to be in movement around your deepest self. Let this swirl into a cocoon that holds steadiness for you while transforming time and space for us.

Abandonment/Engulfment (A/E) Paradigm

In the soft glow of love, flowing movement can be felt. All life force energies and Divine Source generating principles can be accessed, and experienced. I/Thou relations can therefore become one of the most important gates for this heavenly process. Why then do so many of us get stuck in frozen angst behind the gates of love? As we all know, relationships become a stop the flow experience, where we remain mired in the molasses of three-dimensional melodramas. The rhapsody of spontaneous symphonies sounding and lifting our heart frequencies is sadly seldom encountered on this Earth plane. When love is consciously chosen as the path, self-stupor changes into soul intoxication where the heart resounds in full serenade with the Oneness of All. If only we could hear this through the heart, the world would jump exponentially into the next dimension.

Stopping the Flow

Our two greatest obstacles to I/Thou relations are engulfment and abandonment. In either case, we feel we will disappear, disintegrate and cease to be whole. When in soul truth and in dimensions beyond the third, engulfment and abandonment simply do not exist. These are constructs that arise out of our three-dimensional embodied experiences, created to try to concretize our mind/body reality. As discussed in Chapter One, when our soul first arrived in an Earth birth experience and landed in human embodiment, we surely must have experienced Divine Source abandonment as we felt the condensed, confinement of the human body and the boundaries therein. Separation from both non-body consciousness and Oneness must have felt terrifying and mystifying. In addition, at some point awareness set in that the womb was now the nurturing, safe place for the body, and the sacred silver cord connecting to All became less felt as the human umbilical cord became essential and a symbiotic path to the new embodied mother. The experience of felt embodiment became crucial to the survival of this New Human life. However, the blueprint of this initial soul/consciousness abandonment experience would soon become a deep reference point for all other perceived human abandonments. Initially, feeling one with the human mother was paramount to thriving and learning how to be part of the human species. At some point, early in one's development long after the safety of the womb is a long forgotten memory, individuation, i.e. the notion that we are separate, self-contained and self-sufficient, becomes the all-encompassing process to master and control. Over time, our memories of soul consciousness wane and our experiences with non-separation fade. Paradoxically, engulfment soon becomes our next fear to fight. If we are healthy human beings we adjust to these prescribed individual human selves quickly, and want to keep these personalities, these bodies, these minds intact. Merging with another feels dangerous as it might dismantle this individual felt self.

What a paradox: we fear abandonment as a result of being birthed as human and once human we fear engulfment because we don't want to lose our felt individual consciousness. We come from and are thrown into a separate reality called human existence. As we adapt to this human embodiment, we then fear losing this newly discovered selfhood by the emergent relationships that are inevitable on this human journey. Yet, we relentlessly seek this merging with other as a deeply unconscious wish for reenacting the state of soul merger before human birth. We hope that these other merges will finally soothe our original God abandonment during our Earth birth and soul amnesia during our human life. This constant shifting in and out of engulfment and abandonment continually marks the trail for all relationships we have in this human domain. **(see illustration 18)**

The wonderful and joyous news is that we can never be abandoned nor engulfed. We only need to be extremely conscious of the illusion that human embodiment creates. Rather than holding on to the notion that loving another is either abandoning or engulfing, we have to begin to understand that it is love and only love that will bring us out of the deception created by our camouflaged reality. We just practice love so that it becomes the fuel for skyrocketing into higher consciousness, so that we, once again, feel the distinct beauty of our soul. In that beauty, we can realize, we have always been part and whole of All That Is. Ironically, our three-dimensional consciousness has dreamed up this separation drama in order to survive being human. However, we no longer need to survive in the egoic sense if we understand how to thrive in the soul sense. Once we are in realization of the permanence of our own

ABANDONMENT/ENGULFMENT

Abandonment Fears

Engulfment Fears

Illustration 18

Consciousness, we won't have to worry and fret over the impermanence of that which is outside of it. Our Consciousness is both local and non local, both merging and aware of merging, all at the same time. In concrete terms, I can merge with you and still know I am doing so.

The Contours of the Old Abandonment/Engulfment Paradigm

We are always testing out our trust of the other experience, as if someone else has the antidote to the toxic state created by the A/E paradigm We keep our gates closed peering out from within to see another clearly, not realizing that this very peering out obstructs the view. Nevertheless, we accumulate a myriad of tactics that we use to judge and analyze the safety factors in another human being. One of our greatest fears here is that we might invite someone into our precious home and they might search and seize the contents and leave. After all, many children experience this from the very people who have been given the task to protect their inner homes. The battle cry is, "You'll see who I am and abandoned the premises." I'll let you feel my soft belly (figuratively speaking) and you'll punch me in the gut." I hear couples fighting all the time pushing the soft belly buttons by using harsh and violent words. Sentences like, "You are just like your mother," are utilized as ammunition when someone knows the history of their spouse's critical, harsh and hurtful mother. I notice that people will remember soft spot information to use in battle, but rarely utilize it for healing. A spouse will remind you that you have trouble with authority figures not because you were terribly hurt by your father in childhood, but rather to utilize it to shame you into giving up your need for power, so that they might have it. We gather information for the purposes of protecting ourselves, either to firm up our own gated mechanisms to keep people at a distance (avoiding engulfment and disintegration) or to enter their gates with soft spot ammunition to control them (so that they might never abandon us). I/Thou relations are full of paradoxical shifts: if we are not

New guidelines for home visits:

- When I do let you into the home of my self, you will touch lightly all that you see and feel.
- You will not take things to make yourself safe and you will not strip me of who I am so that you can have more of who you are.
- We can be aware of each other without losing the self, all the while dancing in the merging energies of both.

afraid of someone leaving us, we are afraid of someone taking from us.

Let's look at some common A/E land mines:

Jealousy

Old Assumption: You have more so I must be less. I couldn't possibly be with you until I have more (so you won't leave me) but if I have more you might attach to me, want it and eventually steal it (disintegrative engulfment).

New Assumption: Anything you have that I don't supplies me with the resonance of that vibrational signature, which in turn adds to my state of abundance. Celebrating what you have enhances my ability to have more myself while being with you at the same time.

Anger

Old Assumption: You don't see me and that makes me furious. You took something from me and I am so mad at you. Your views are wrong and that makes me enraged. You clearly don't understand me and I can't stand that.

New Assumption: Nothing can ever really be taken. There's always room for both. Winning is no longer dualistic. We only win when there is room for both. If I think you don't see me, I have probably stopped seeing, believing and understanding myself. You're struggling just as I am. In making room for you, I add more room for myself.

Sex

Old Assumption: You might suffocate me or get too close and I might disappear. You might see or experience something you don't like and leave me because it's not enough or I'm enough.

New Assumption: Sexual intimacy is an energetic exchange that enhances my aliveness as well as yours. It can be a container for love and the practice of merging, while staying totally conscious.

Dishonesty

Old Assumptions: If I tell you all of who I am, you will leave me (abandonment) or destroy me (engulfment). The only way I can be with you is to hide what I think you will not like so that you will approve of me. In this way I will become less me and more you.

New Assumption: Presenting the truth of who I am is my greatest gift to you because withholding who I am from you will in the end hurt you.

We are telepathic by nature, although we are still mastering this human art form. Therefore so many of us can feel or know when something is being hidden. In addition, we intuit more about each other than we even know. The interesting thing about being telepathic is that it eventually will create a state of merging consciousness between individuals. In that moment where you intuit someone's feelings you are able to merge with a deeper place within that person, a deeper truthful place. Although this may feel scary at first (which is probably why some people hesitate to master this), it is safer and more harmonic to synthesize and intermingle with another's state of being rather than build gates of surreptitious parameters that keep others out, but forever keep us hidden. It follows that in this cloaked clandestine cavern within, we begin to operate on assumptions about another, that usually are more about ourselves. In protecting these sacred boundaries, we also become masterful at keeping the best parts of ourselves secret in exchange for those half-baked ideas of who we think we should be. Someday, when we are completely telepathic, we will experience ultimate safety and we won't have to guess the truth about ourselves or another. We will simply dance within it.

The most unseemly parts of ourselves are not who we are, but the steps we take to hide who we are. We abandon and annihilate ourselves far more in our sequestered world within than anyone else could possibly do. That is the good news because we can change that.

Understanding engulfment vs. abandonment (**see illustration 19**) is crucial not only in guiding us towards expansive and flourishing human relationships, but most importantly it inspires and informs us about being in relation to Divine Source or God. Experiencing our soul connective divinity within this human experience is after all, the path of ascension. It's such a beautiful paradox that working on the Abandonment/Engulfment paradigm with others prepares us for the ultimate path towards enlightenment. So let's review once again the concepts of engulfment and abandonment:

Engulfment

This is the ultimate state of losing the self whether through being swallowed up, annihilated, or fragmented. Fears of self-deprivation run amok in these swampy fields of foggy envelopment. While birth creates an abandonment template, death creates an engulfment template. From the first moment of understanding that we are indeed in physical bodies that are finite, we fear losing our identities and our bodies through death, thus becoming engulfed in the sea of nothingness. Our egos are forever on a march to keep

ENGULFMENT VS. ABANDONMENT

Avoidance of Engulfment

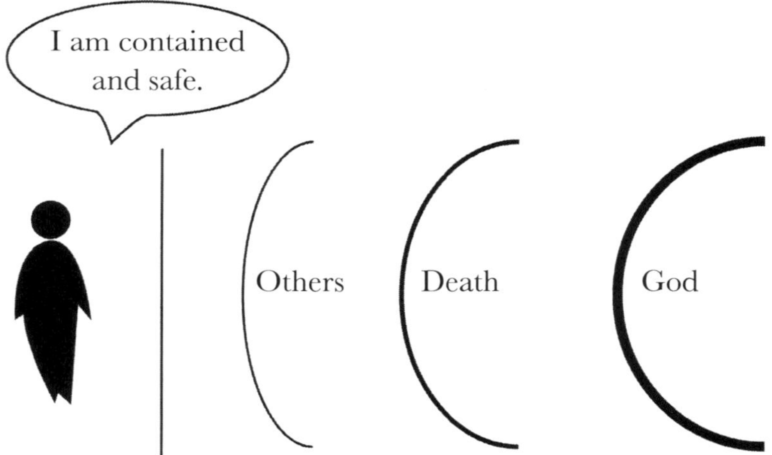

Walls of protection to avoid engulfment.

Avoidance of Abandonment

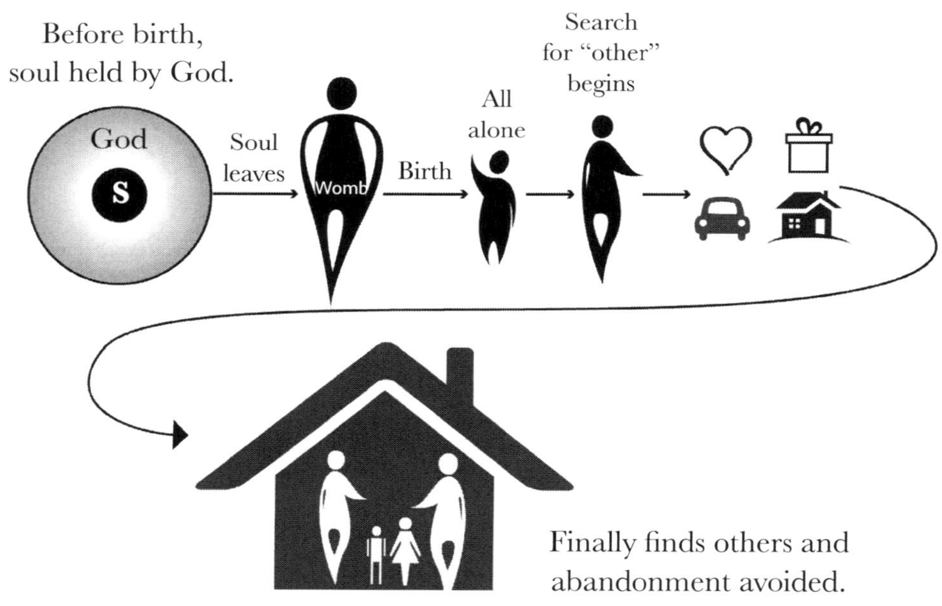

Finally finds others and abandonment avoided.

Illustration 19

the individual self intact, keeping engulfment at bay by various human defensive tactics all the while keeping soul actualization and enlightenment an arms length away. Too much relating can be a dangerous thing. And certainly, our relationship with God is forever changed by our flight into human birth. It's hard for our rational mind to comprehend having a relationship with the Divine that is within us. The activation of this relationship within surely would cause unconsciousness. So we erect various temples outside of ourselves, which keep us at a safe distance from that all encompassing passionate God force that might make our minds spin into oblivion. We also construct various definitions and rules for relating to All That Is outside of ourselves so that we might make better sense of people, animals, and even the Earth herself. Engulfment fears can be solved when living totally in the heart. As we feel our heartbeat and the knowledge therein, we are both reminded of our own life force and are connected to the universal pulse of all living things. This is the ultimate Oneness of Being where consciousness experiences both itself and All Else. Abundance becomes the major principle.

Abandonment

If attachment to other defines the self then separation from other leads to overwhelming aloneness and loss of self. Human embodiment was probably the very first experience of abandonment as we left the beautiful effervescent life-giving pool of Divine Source creation. Our second abandonment injury was leaving our mother both physically and psychologically. We have this analogous abandonment template that we utilize to compare and contrast all other relationships in life. We continue to seek attachment to others partly as an act of redemption and reparation for the initial soul trauma at the time of embodiment. Yet in seeking this outside restitution, we unconsciously steer away from our beautiful soul rediscovery and the remembrance that lies therein. The paradox is that as we focus our consciousness on the fear of separation from other, we abandon our soul mission over and over. After all, the equation in human life is: self equals you plus me. The equation in spiritual life is: only when I have self/soul consciousness can I have you plus me. This overflowing self-awareness/consciousness becomes the actual material for merging melodies from all spheres and dimensions. (**see illustration 20**)

DIVINE REALIZATION

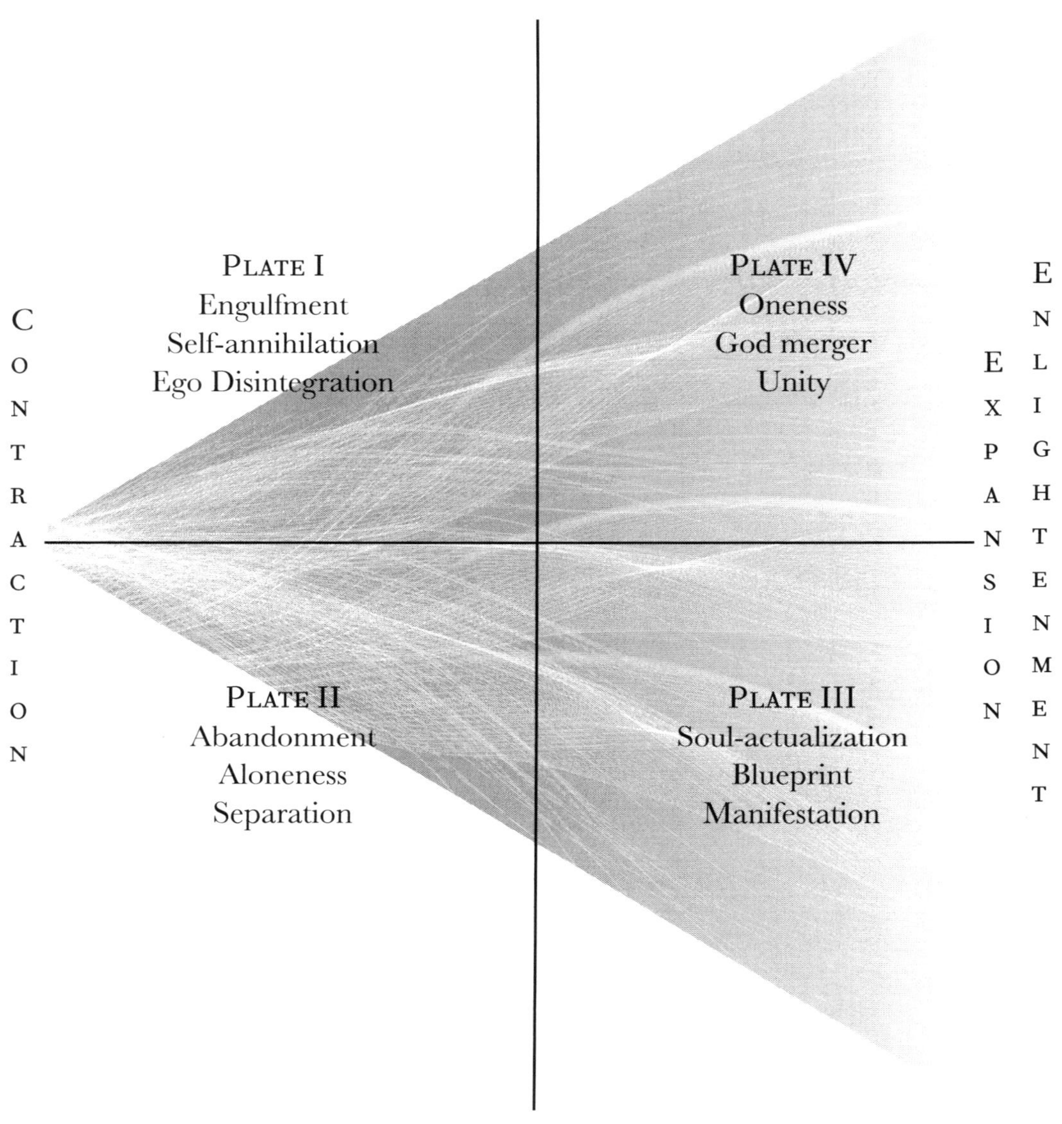

Illustration 20

ILLUSTRATION #20

Plate I: Self-annihilation and ego disintegration through engulfment and merging with other whether Divine or human.

Plate II: Separation from our divinity, leads to aloneness and abandonment fears.

Plate III: The self on it's own begins the arduous journey of actualizing its unique blueprint manifestation process and higher consciousness realization.

Plate IV: In realizing our own divinity, merging with Divine Source is possible. Our consciousness just realizes and remembers its connection to All That Is.

Plates I and II create contraction and diminishment of self and soul.
Plates III and IV create expansion and the path toward Enlightenment.
Plates I and IV are opposing forces.
Plates II and III are opposing forces.

As we move towards higher consciousness states while still in human form, we begin to understand that this is the antidote for the old A/E paradigm. The self cannot disappear when the other is absent as the self is whole and aware of All That Is. Once a solid self, the experience of engulfment becomes impossible as self/soul consciousness becomes more energetically solid than the egoic self and the accompanying physical body. Magnificently, merging with other becomes abundant and transcendent, as we will never again lose consciousness. Ultimately, when we interface with Divine Source our individual consciousness drops into the sea of All That Is and feels at once the whole from which it came and the beauty of the drop itself. In higher dimensional relationships, we know that we never have to give up our selves to be in merging dynamism with the moving force of love. So the question is, "How does this guide us in our human relationships on Earth at this time?" I would like to suggest some new signposts for the road that has clearly been less traveled by all of us.

Guideposts for the New Renaissance Relationship

1. In the beginning, who I am has nothing to do with who you are. In other words, all the parts that make up me have little to do with all the parts that make up you, except of course our sacred origins. I may inspire parts in you, but I can't create you. Your creation has already been determined by Divine Source. I can't be your self and you can't be my self. But I can hold a mirror up for you to see yourself and the miracle of who you are and you can do the same for me. Let this be our first dance on the newly waxed floor of the Renaissance Hall.

Resonating in the highest place of self creates a vibratory field that begins to unlock hidden places in the other. As I support your highest resonance, I then contribute to the vibratory field expansion needed for my own magnification of consciousness. *I can't do this without you and yet I must take responsibility to do this with me. Both are true all at once.*

2. You can't extinguish me by annihilating or abandoning tactics. Your need to consume parts of me is just a ploy to fill your own emptiness. In addition, your need to distance from other parts of me is just some fragment of you that you would like to suppress. As you give up I/Thou power dynamics of suppression or desertion, you will have more dynamic capacity for actualizing self/soul consciousness. As this realized self moves in this energetic dance, it creates a field that invites more, not less from all surrounding fields. The more you have of self and higher consciousness the more soul senses you have to absorb and synthesize All That Is both opposing and synonymous to what we think we know. After all, the goal is to leave no stone unturned. We are born to bring more back to sacred creation not less. My consciousness can never cease therefore you can neither annihilate me nor abandon me. I am here forever and so are you.

3. Only you can unlock the gates within. I can only inspire from the outside by providing you a pathway to my own open portals and to my unique soul configuration. Opening the gates for the other to enter is the path towards non-separation and unity. When these gates are open, we feel another, understand another, see another and love another. Closed entry stations create derision, division and disrespect. As you cross the threshold of my open archways with the vibration of curiosity and the innocence of new life, you will come to know me as I am. In this place, you will not have cause to fear me, but will only be inspired to merge with all that I am. There's a wind of re-

verberating resonance when we walk together through our passageways with sacred intent. This is an experience few of us have had, but have come to Earth to discover. We already know this in the multiverse of other lives and other dimensions. You alone have the key to your own gates to the wondrous world within. These keys will unlock the vision of as above so below and in so doing you and I will understand the brilliant beauty of I/Thou relations and the path towards Oneness.

4. I'm made up of not only who I am, and who you are, but I'm the hologram of All That Is. *I haven't and can't be separate from you and yet, it is the I or me that holds this knowledge that I am all of it.* I maintain the consciousness of me all the while holding that I am not me at all. Thus, the drop stays true even in the sea of water. My sole/soul task is to reunite with you and create this surging, merging energetic flow with you and all life so that Earth might be restored once again to its higher dimensional plane of wholeness. Earth can then bring this actualized Earth consciousness to the galactic and cosmic realms thus creating more convergence of universal elements of life and love throughout the multiverse. So you see, practicing love with you changes, motivates and inspires all else at all times.

I/Thou Technology for the Gate Guardians

It becomes more and more apparent that we guard so carefully our entrance points, keeping others out and separating ourselves. Is it any wonder we feel alienated and alone? There's a technology to this gate opening process that must be understood. New programs must be designed and embraced. The gate keepers are those defenses we have gathered over a lifetime to protect our world within. They prowl our passageways in the darkness of our unconscious and have astute awareness of their programmed goal of keeping out rather than letting in. It's past time to change these paradigms so that we might share the shimmer of light from the sacred other that directs our consciousness towards Divine programs of convergence and unity.

Soft spots are the most sacred

Never use soft spot information to hurt another. Soft spots are those newly exposed areas of self-disclosure that have previously been hidden and secreted away for protection and safety. Soft spot openings are evidence of the self spiraling out. When I show you my soft spot, it is a sacred offering to you. I am respecting you the most in that moment for I trust you with a most vulnerable part. It's the process of letting you in that is most important, not the content I reveal. Soft spot revelations are the signposts of the wish to merge and play in the fields of new felt consciousness.

Mutual respect

As you grow I grow. I understand that even when you look like you are not growing, you are. And when you are growing, I must give you enough space to grow even more. How you might need to grow may look different than me. I must respect your process even when your content looks strange and freaky. As I hold you in high esteem, I have the honor of holding your Source vibrational-life energy and in that, I come closer to the face of God.

Transparent expression

The clearer I am about myself, my motivations, my struggles and my triumphs, the clearer you can be about who I am and how safe I can be. I am more curious about the genuine soul dance between beings than about the guarded arrhythmic movement two or more suspecting beings can create. Honesty is not only a gate opener for another, but it is the best way for us to know ourselves. For hidden things are relegated to long forgotten hallways and keyless rooms inside the home of self. As we make ourselves transparent to the world, we become more transparent to ourselves. In this process, we not only know ourselves, but the wealth of Soul Information that is stored in the self.

Transparent expression creates the prologue to telepathic communication. When I guess something you are feeling that's true and you tell me it's not, I begin to question the telepathic technology within. Your willingness to be sincere, direct, and genuine makes you more trustworthy, and also helps me know and experience my own internal telepathic senses, which are preludes to the ultimate process of being in unity and Oneness.

Just a note here about what I call precognitive telepathy. Oftentimes we may sense something about someone else that either they're unaware of or that hasn't happened yet. In either case, they may deny that our intuitive insights are correct, thus creating further doubt about our telepathic perceptions. However, I believe we have the ability to also have precognitive telepathy, which is the ability to sense something about what a person may feel or will feel or experience in the future. We may intuit this before someone else has awareness of it. For instance, I may sense that someone is struggling with something today that will in fact happen tomorrow. This simply points to the complexities of I/Thou relations. We can begin to act as radar for each other if we can become more conscious of these intuitive signposts.

Just like animals may know hours or days beforehand that an Earthquake is imminent, and if we could learn to follow and trust their signs, we might save ourselves. But, here's where extreme discernment is crucial. Until our own debris fields are cleared, we might not be able to tell the difference between our intuitions about another and our own leftover riffraff. Often people's intuitions about another are simply mistaken perceptions taken from reading the tea leaves of their own rubble. The clearer my debris field is, the more I can trust my own intuitions about another. As I learn to hold and consider others' perceptions about myself, I may heed warning signals about things to come. Even more importantly, I may see the lighted pathways of my own soul blueprint through the intuitive eyes of another.

Opening to these new telepathic information systems will indeed change our feelings of separation and alienation. One of the greatest motivations for this journey is that we can learn to discern these extrasensory and extraordinary pathways within us through I/Thou relations. I need you to help me to explore the outside world of me. In this way, the who of you will teach me about the who of me. It will no doubt be worth the clumsy process of staying open to another while feeling the vulnerabilities of new landscapes. I can't know the truth of my wisdom about All That Is beyond me without that which is beyond me and is you. The I/Thou relationship forms a feedback loop creating the us platform that informs, confirms, or disconfirms. *In other words, without you I can't know the parts of myself that inform me about you.* You have the keys to unlock my I/Thou wisdom libraries. Without you, the knowledge will be flat and one-dimensional. We need each other. The question is: "Can we move this need for other beyond the need for survival towards the uplifting process of conscious alignment and eventual enlightenment?"

Process is paramount and content is superfluous

Usually we are so busy interpreting content that we don't know we have an incredible ability to be in rhythmic movement with each other. It's in this movement that both the whole and the parts exist all at once. When you're too busy listening for words, you are in content. The mind loves content while the heart loves process. So when you're in a rough spot with someone, the first thing to do is to bring your consciousness into your heart. *The heart feels process, the mind thinks content.* When you no longer want to be in dance with someone you have probably gotten lost in the snarly pit of nouns and adjectives. Remember: Content separates, process brings together. The mantra is: I want to be in process with life more than I want to live in the deductive logic of analyzing life. Being in the flow of process is the gateway to living in the present moment and the all of everything can only be found here.

Conscious Gate Opening

Before gathering with another, take a moment to breathe your gates open. Sacredly pause to see whether you feel like you're going into battle with win/lose strategies or going on a picnic with the feast of love and the festivities of life. Ask yourself, "Can I open my gates a little wider so that I might breathe deeply the new air of rejuvenating oxygen that comes from I/Thou invigoration? Can I know I can safely inhale and exhale to feel life and merge with All That Is outside of myself? Can I choose to stay conscious that this is my choice to open and feel the figure eight of breath and therefore the infinity loop of I/Thou and ultimate love?" I can experience this without losing consciousness. Instead I will expand the experience of my being and the truth that…I am…You are…We are…All part of the One.

Competition vs. Cooperation

We can begin to hold in our consciousness the truth about the gain/loss dynamics of competitive vs. cooperative living on planet Earth. We can create illusionary competitive games where egoic/self survival is first and foremost and cooperative efforts are only seen as tactics in further supplementing the survival of the individual. But as we have seen, choosing to be in cooperative relationships not only opens and expands the territory within, but in doing so we enter the crucial phase of creating a collaborative, harmonious and synergetic community where all species of beings can live in love and peace. The truth is evident that the I is neither here alone nor less or more than any other I. It's such a beautiful paradox that I incarnated here as a separate self only to search for you so that I might once again be in truth of love and feel the completion of myself. This can only occur in the I/Thou dynamic that lives in the sacred web of All That Is. Wow. *It's in our soul blueprint to be here with and for instead of separate and against.* Only then will we all have the eyes to see the expansive vision of All That Is. You are my path to All That Is and I am yours. As we share this together we experience the oneness and unity that comes from this being together. This then moves us into the possibility of becoming consciously aware of being part of the larger more vast galactic community.

The New Human Renaissance Relationship

As we engage with each other in the new renaissance relationship, we are creating a manifested craft for each and all and in this we reach towards the heights of the ascension process into expanded cosmic consciousness. Through this awakening renaissance, we can avail ourselves of the experience of the lightened path of the reawakened soul in the resurrected merging sphere of I/Thou relations. We are the concrete manifestation of the Divine, and in seeing and feeling this in each other we channel this cosmic sacred energy and feel the deeper truth of who we really are. The New Human engages in sacred practices and methods that channel energy and catalyze psychological, emotional, and spiritual transformations in such a way that manifest Divine revelation and Oneness. Heart consciousness techniques are utilized for this blissful expanded state of consciousness where each becomes the face of God and the whole is more than the sum of the parts. The illusion of separation is dissolved as the truth of oneness is experienced through the technology of I/ Thou consciousness.

Technology of the Renaissance Relationship

1. Sacred Holding

Holding the field of another with support, acceptance and unconditional regard is the ultimate safeguarding of another. Although this is the very first step in the New Human intimacy dance, it's perhaps the most difficult. As soon as we begin to stand still and witness another, we become hopelessly entangled in their field as the ego watches and ultimately abandons this sacred embrace in order to analyze, protect and respond. When this happens separation is once again felt and the beholder is no longer the eyewitness but the ego-witness.

Holding the field of other is the heart in motion all the while holding still in another's presence. Witnessing another may at first feel passive to the touch of the heart but is quite active. Within the petals of this heart's embrace, birthing buds anticipate the sprouting of new vistas from the Divine hands of creation. No matter what the content of the self-field, it's regarded with patience and non-judgment. The beholder of the field always understands that as sacred holding occurs, content becomes fluid and changes form. No one piece of information needs to trigger old alarms in the beholder. As that information is held, it naturally moves to the next form. The New Human understands that each part and each form is always moving towards the whole, the whole of self and the whole that is found in the merging of two held fields.

As I'm in the embrace of the beholder, I'm challenged to show up, in all my parts, to be bathed in their light, ending my isolation, my shyness, my reticence to be seen. I then become the beholdee, offering to walk softly in the field of my self, all the while remembering that someone else has offered to walk softly with me, holding me with sacred remembrance.

As I embrace another, I am graced with the discovery of the cosmic self, both theirs and my own. For holding another requires and therefore creates an opening to All That Is beyond me. From this opening, I am further inspired towards the soul exploration within myself. As I embrace my other, I begin to produce movement and these tides extend into new frontiers of unity. I feel the movement of the Divine through it all and can no longer respond or become entangled with lower egoic self-interests. As I engage in this sacred holding of other, I too become intertwined with this migration from self to cosmic unfolding.

STANCE FOR SACRED HOLDING

- Quieting the mind: Silence the commentary of judgment or criticism.
- Opening the heart: Bring love and compassion to the other.
- Sacred embracing: Send acceptance and unconditional regard.
- Sitting still: In the presence of another.

2. Sacred Responsiveness

While sacred holding is more receptive and neutral, sacred responsiveness is more active, making apparent the beholder's intention of warmth, compassion and understanding. We haven't even touched the miracle that the practice of empathic consideration and compassionate responsiveness can bring to each other and our planet. Because we have embraced the illusion that we are indeed separate entities, we feel isolated, estranged and dissolute for most of our lives. We have so much within that feels unseen, unfelt and unheard and as a result we spend much of our time waving red flags to promote deliberate attention to the egoic self within. However, when others stop to see what's happening we become suspicious of their intentions and keep the door locked. Or, we are so desperate for someone to see us and respond, we invite them in, lock the door and keep them captive for hours, days or weeks at a time. When retention of another becomes the motivating energy, reciprocity

SACRED RECIPROCITY

Sacred figure 8.

Unidimensional "seeing." Figure 8 flatlined.

Illustration 21

is absent and impossible. Responsive understanding expands when in the loop of the figure eight and collapses when in the field of the unidirectional one-dimensional line. (**see illustration 21**) In other words, when only one person is actively responsive, the rich waves of dancing together cease. It takes two to feed the field of generative healing that comes from the ability to be open and responsive to another human being. When two or more are responding in resonance to each other, an energetic field of merging begins to hum into existence.

Often when we are receiving responsive action from another, we quickly lose consciousness of the other, reveling in the stage set before us by the other. We lose tremendous data sets about ourselves, when we no longer see the person who is doing the attending. In the repose of responsive understanding, we can vision much about ourselves through the stillness of the movement of listening by the other. Pausing to look up and acknowledge and behold the listener is a most important activity in the midst of sharing some important information. *For in that moment, the two are breathed into being, arising out of one, holding by another, with consciousness of both.* This is incredibly intimate. By definition you must acknowledge someone's presence in order to respond. Responsive understanding is the ability to let someone know you're present without interrupting their ability to be present themselves. Renaissance responsibility, then, is the ability to stay responsive both in receiving and giving attention to another. I must come to you with my offering of responsiveness and agree to allow you to fill that space without my interference. And in turn, when you hold my space, I will keep your essence in my consciousness so that I might not become lost in my own land of feelings and ideas. Together we offer each other a process so that we might never feel separate again, all the while honoring the sacred home within.

As I begin to understand and respond to you, it means I have left the safe or stormy confines of me. In this moving towards you, I begin to feel the first inklings of freedom. As long as I'm stuck in the little human self, I can't breathe fully. I can't move fully. I can't be fully. I can't know fully. So you see the infinite loop of responsive understanding creates both a path towards unity and individual sovereignty all at once. Learning the art of being responsive is not an easy path itself.

QUICK CLUES

Not on the path if:

- You're thinking of your own reaction.
- Your responsiveness is in the form of your response to the subject matter.
- You've lost consciousness of your presence.
- You've lost consciousness of their presence.
- Your mind is thinking a response.

On the path if:

- Your heart is more present than your mind.
- Content is less important than staying present.
- Seeing and hearing another is expanding not restricting.
- Listening makes rooms not walls.
- The hearts energetic field of compassion is the first response.
- Relaying that compassion is the second.

STANCE FOR SACRED RESPONSIVENESS

- Quieting the mind: Silencing the commentary of judgment or criticism.
- Opening the heart: Bring love and unconditional regard to the other.
- Actively sitting with another: So that compassion is felt, heard and seen.

3. Sacred Reflection

There's no greater gift than to see yourself in the response of another person. Most of the time, we see more about the other person in their response to us. However, in the renaissance relationship, we will be able to empathically respond to another so that they see themselves in our response. Whether that response is compassion, empathy, consideration or equitable feedback, we can gaze upon the other and see ourselves reflected in the mirror of their presence. In this reflection, we see more layers of ourselves, gaining access to those soul blueprints and spirit codes and unlocking our higher dimensional self. The wonder of it all is the natural reciprocity of this process. As you act as a reflector for these deep truths in another, a reverberation is created within that pulses and quivers, opening these same, albeit unique places of codes, blueprints and truth, in you. If you knew that simply acting as a mirror for another without judgment, without jealousy, without commentary would at the same moment create a liberation of your own beautiful soul, wouldn't you walk with reflectors throughout the world?

In the New Human relationship, there are very few debris fields or egoic states that clutter the mirrors of the reflecting field. Clarity within brings crystalline mirrors and luminous light for the reflecting process to be in truth and perfectly aligned with the highest self of the other. That doesn't mean that what is revealed is always attractive or beauteous or good, sometimes some dark parcel of self simply has to see the light of day from the loving reflection of self in other. *In the process of this new renaissance reflection, permeability and transparency are the keystones in revealing ourselves and compassion and equanimity are the keystones in reflecting others.*

STANCE FOR SACRED REFLECTION

- Quieting the mind: silence any judgmental commentary.
- Opening the heart: bring love and unconditional regard to the other.
- Actively standing with another: so that the other can see with focus and clarity who they are and who you are.
- Visibly revealing feedback: reciting their story not yours.

4. Sacred Resonance: I/Thou Attunement

In the process of being within the I/Thou configuration, we have access to the dynamic and spirited fuel necessary for growth, expansion and Source reverberation. Just a reminder, an I/Thou configuration can include relating and be in relation to another person, community, animal, nature element, Earth or Divine Source. As we begin to resonate with the field of other, we access the larger domain of the quantum field, which provides more enriched access to energy for attuning to higher consciousness. As we hold the field of I/Thou in conscious commitment, compassion and sacredness, we naturally attune to each other's higher self, opening remembrances of all previous and future higher selves. We become like tuning forks. A tuning fork produces a pure tone of the vibrational energy found at the fundamental frequency of that tone. Tuning forks are used to help the human body achieve optimal physical balance. So too can we be tuning forks for each other. As we resonate and attune to another, we can hold the fundamental frequency of other in order to help them achieve optimal emotional and spiritual balance. As we attune to each other, we begin to harmonize with each other creating higher consciousness states. In this resonance in the I/Thou field, we remind each other not only about the truth about ourselves, but our cosmic journey and our intent to live in higher consciousness states and dimensions.

This is crucial because there are so many things that resonate lower energies in the world we live in and these things can hypnotize and entrain us to old paradigms that are limiting and sabotaging, to say the least. These past imprints can weigh us down, until once again, we are embroiled in third-dimensional stagnation. Most of us have certainly experienced tuning into the denser darker energy field of another person, feeling drawn down into the spiraling vortex of mud and mire. Perhaps this is an illusion that only exists here on Earth. While there is no doubt that the densities of human drama fuel and pollute the I/Thou domain, most of us are dying to come into the sacred attuned light of another. I believe that's what we experience when we die, lose our bodies and feel the sacred embrace of our light family on the other side. We immediately attune and resonate to them, feeling and vibrating love as we have never felt before. Granted, without being encumbered by our opaque bodies, it must be easier for our soul consciousness to vibrate faster, higher and lighter with all else in the I/Thou field. However, we're in an accelerated time where we can feel, while still embodied, this higher harmony of heart energy singing in the I/Thou field. As we become sacred tuning forks for each other, we can resonate more pure soul tones and levitate each other, creating a whole that is more than the sum of the parts. Sacred attunement naturally moves up and out. When we, two or more, are in higher states of consciousness in the I/Thou field there is an enlivened process that's felt far and wide and therein lies the possibility for higher resonance with the Divine. Sacred resonance is the ability to harmonize and resonate with another towards the Divine light of consciousness on the cosmic journey of soul-being.

STANCE FOR SACRED ATTUNEMENT

- Quieting the mind: silence any judgmental commentary.
- Opening the heart: bring love and unconditional regard to the other.
- Actively attuning to your own higher vibration so that other can resonate and harmonize with the field where higher states of Consciousness live and breathe.

5. Sacred Amplification: I/Thou Refraction

In the mirrors of revelation, we also can discover the ability to be refractors and amplifiers of light and love. As light shines upon a prism, the light is refracted into different colors. When drops of rainwater refract and disperse light into various colors of the sunlight, a rainbow is created. We, too, have the power to refract another's light into component parts, and in so doing we enable ourselves to see the full spectrum and variegation of ourselves through another. The little human self or ego may simply be the prism of the higher self covered over. As we lift the cover of egoic material, we are more readily revealed by the light of the other. That's why it's so imperative to first lift as many of our own veils (self-work) as possible, so that our light within is available to refract and reveal another. In addition, as we lift the lifeless shrouds of ego, the prism of our own soul spectrum can be freed to come directly into the light of other. As we do this, we become amplified with higher vibrational qualities opening vistas of the like we have never seen before. This is the most extraordinary gift we can offer to the All surrounding us. We are conduits of the refraction process, we bring forth the soul truth of the other and thus co-create the world outside while confirming the light within. This refraction process in the I/Thou relationship is so crucial because it enables us to truly see the wondrous beings we are. We, then, have the chance to leap in our evolutionary process and become the spirit beings we have always been. In the reflection process, we see what is. In the refraction process we see what can be. In that iridescent instant when we glimpse the full spectrum of our soul essence, we are forever changed. This then is seeded in our consciousness, birthing a new world both within and outside. Moving towards each other, consummating this rainbow bridge, is our destiny in action.

STANCE FOR SACRED REFRACTION

- Quieting the mind: silence any judgmental commentary.
- Opening the heart: bring love and unconditional regard to the other.
- Consciously and freely giving breath to the Soul.
- Shining sacred light upon another.
- Receiving sacred light from another.
- Opening the prism, amplifying, remembering and dancing the spectrum of both into one.

As we become connoisseurs in this sacred understanding process, we will discover that peace, harmony and love naturally prevail. We will pursue understanding all others and the Earth herself with a newfound virility and fortitude never seen before. Through the passageway of sacred understanding, suffering will be abolished as we embrace each other in the same manner as we embrace the sacred Beholder of All. We will learn to embrace the animal kingdom and Mother Nature with these same principles, realizing that we can have reciprocity in all domains where the I/Thou relationship is found. We will also become more conscious of the invisible dimensions of I/Thou. As we open and amplify our soul senses, we will begin to have relationships with the elemental realm, the extraterrestrial realm and the multidimensional realm. We'll understand that we are infinite and all relationships are infinite. Practicing these above principles with each other will bring peace and harmony among humans, and are the only pathways towards relationships with All That Is beyond.

Finally, we may enter the Divine I/Thou multidimensional plane of All That Is with enough sacred vibrational reverence and resonance that we bring the Divine light from our own soul amplification back towards Source. We reflect the image of the Source imprint in ourselves back to Source. In this, we reassure and assure that the Divine creative process continues and is ever present. This is the ultimate, most supreme I/Thou relationship ever to be experienced. This is the most magnificent revelation any being could possible have, dancing in the full light of the moon, hiding nothing while revealing all the while, that we are the light. Perhaps, only then can we accept the direct light from Divine Source shining upon our own soul prisms refracting us into millions of infinitely small parts of soul purity. This will reveal all lives, all loves, all harmonies of voice, and all singularities of utterances in the process of awakening and resonating in the merging fields of I/Thou. All of this journeying in the fields of I/Thou relations is so that we might arrive home once again to the whole in a multitude of holiness. We become ultimately aware that without the fertility of the I/Thou fields, we cannot possibly be in the Oneness of Being.

Soul Remedies

9 – I/Thou Relations

Quiet your mind and breathe deeply into your heart,
feeling all the love it can hold.

Bring someone you love to mind and simply
hold them in your vision.

Surround them with the warmth and compassion of
your heart…creating a cocoon of safe and sacred love.

Now, picture them in all of their most beautiful assets…
and smile.

Attune to your own highest self and imagine that you are
sending these colorful wavelengths to them.

Feel the vibrancy of this dance and the unique signature of you. .
expanding in the unity of that which is beyond you.

Practice this with all living beings and the Earth herself.
Feel the vastness of your world.

10

Manifestation Mysteries: The Art of Dreaming Reality

"Everything you can imagine is real."
–Pablo Picasso

"The greatest achievement was at first and for a time a dream
The oak sleeps in the acorn. The bird waits in the egg.
And in the highest vision of a soul, a waking angel stirs.
Dreams are the seedlings of realities."
–James Allen

"Your imagination is the preview to life's coming attractions."
–Albert Einstein

"Worrying is using your imagination to create something you don't want."
–Abraham-Hicks

"The outcome that we wish suddenly manifests itself in our reality,
and the truth is, none of those things suddenly appeared.
It is we who have suddenly appeared on the scene where they existed always."
–Neale Donald Walsch

We are the materialization of Divine Source in physical form, and thus we have been manifested from the creative imagination of sacred Source. As a result, we've been imbued with manifestation potentialities to imagine and dream reality into being. We've so often forgotten that this includes an implicit responsibility to bring forth sacred manifested realities to this Earth plane for the highest good of all.

We, over the millennia, have given our power away to higher authorities of all shapes and sizes. We've even relinquished the task of designing our lives by cleverly assigning that responsibility to God, stating: "After all, it's in the hands of God" or "things happen because it is God's will." We quickly forfeit and avoid the crucial task of creating "as above, so below" here in this reality, not realizing it is lack of our own will and the resulting arrested and seized human consciousness that has created the mayhem on Earth. In our semi-conscious state of awareness, we have kept dreams frozen in formless states of unrealization and non-fruition. Instead, reality becomes defined by nightmares created from the chaos of unconscious storms of opposing beliefs, ideas, needs and wants. These have inevitably been dictated from external sources that we've manifested from the already dull and lifeless past.

Dreaming our reality or sacred manifestation can only happen from the flow created by inside-out movement; never from the shrouding and dimming process that takes place from the outside in. The path of manifestation always comes from the powerful place of self. As we increase our own awareness of the felt presence of self, we increase the quotient of manifesting energy from the quantum field, that sacred domain where all potentialities exist. Finally, as we practice being in relationship with "other," we can apply this relational learning to the interlacing energetic dance between self and the quantum field of manifestation. This interfacing between the within and the boundless field of the beyond is the ultimate experience of co-creation and the quintessential essence of being human. We're here on Earth to remember our ability to actualize our manifestation mission. We have always had the ability to manifest our lives, our desires, and our blueprints. This is happening all of the time, even without consciousness. One of the biggest tragedies on Earth is that we've lost our remembrance, our consciousness, of our powers to create all that we need, want and desire. As a result, we operate in dense vibrations of half-veiled notions of who we are and what we're here to do. *We create from our egos to build the illusion of self-importance, making less space for one another and the world.*

It's no wonder that our accomplishments end up feeling like small, unfulfilled and half-hearted "dreams come true." Most of us are manifesting from our subconscious realms and in these realms we have little control and little awareness of what we even bring to ourselves. All of our losses, hurts, and injuries are hidden in these subconscious spaces and so it's often these themes that drive our own manifestation and actualization process. We hold hate and bring that energy towards us. We hold hurt and cover ourselves up so that we might not be hurt again. Unfortunately, as a result, we may never look up to see the beauty of love that may be knocking at our door.

The more awake and aware you are, the more powerful you become in being able to manifest awake and aware events. Clear and perpetual consciousness builds the laser focus necessary for the expression of our Divine origins. Allowing the subconscious or unconscious realms to operate this laser mechanism is like firing a machine gun helter-skelter without awareness of the target or the mission. You may end up hitting something, but it also may strike down the very thing you are trying to create. People who feel they have not received enough in life, often develop a chip on their shoulder, closing doors to abundance just by their cranky and less than attitudes about their supposed deprivations in life. They continue in a cycle of have-nots, all the while complaining about them, staying unconscious to this powerful but self-defeating cycle. Staying conscious, awake and aware is crucial to beginning the process of soul manifestation. Utilizing your sacred will to drive and power this mission is essential in keeping the mechanism of manifestation operating.

GET READY

Certain things will be essential in preparing ourselves for the manifesting processes. We have a quotient of manifesting fuel/energy within us. Some things diminish this manifestation quotient and some things enhance it. Obviously, as this energy increases, luminosity and dynamism magnify, creating more powerful manifestation quotient. Before we can move towards the active process of manifestation, we must first explore the inner fuel available for this actualizing process.

1. Sound Body/Mind/Spirit/Heart

As the four quadrants come together in prosperity and harmony, the manifestation quotient increases. We often complain that we can't actualize our dreams, not realizing that it's often the disrepair found in our homes within that zaps our energy to create. This disrepair is also the fodder for our nightmares. If you can't bring health and well-being to these inner sanctums of body/mind/heart and soul, the fuel you have for creating and actualizing your dreams will be severely reduced. Therefore chapter six becomes a crucial starting point for dreaming reality.

2. Congruency and Transparency

As you increase your awareness of your inner processes, you will be able to see and know the areas that create contradictions or opposing desires and needs. As long as we have an inner war going on both in our ego and in our subconscious and unconscious arenas, we will have a diminished manifestation quotient. Splintered and bifurcated energies are much less powerful in their resulting diffused light than those that are concentrated and congruent, creating a stronger stream of illumination and radiance. If you are conscious of wanting to create one possibility or dream, but oppose it in the inner dimensions of the self, you will not manifest this intention. (**see illustration 22**) If you say one thing and act another, you will split and diminish you power to actualize. For instance, if you say you want new love in your life, but are unkind, cranky and snarky to those already in your life, you might want to think again about what you say you want. This is where Gandhi's famous quote is so apt: "Be the change you wish to see."

Becoming aware of your deeper realms of wishes, dreams and illusions requires an amazing diligence. The dreams that have been the hardest to create are signposts of the conflict within. It's in these hidden alcoves that opposing thoughts and feelings live. As we're willing to take on the task of spelunking these deeper caverns, we'll come to know ourselves, our dreams and our true soul missions. As we shine the light of awareness in these deeper recesses, we can then have the conscious opportunity to quiet the din within and enliven and allow these deeper voices to direct our life journey without derision and coercion. When we don't know ourselves, we create conscious dreams that do not match the inner callings of our soul. These supposed dreams are more outer directed than inner directed. We've all been conditioned by the externalized world to think we need, want and desire certain outcomes and realities. However, if we are not self-aware, they do not match our true soul mission. The dream that never seems to materialize is a sign that this is so. For instance, do you have numerous daydreams about a particular wish, but it never seems to come to fruition? This is a significant clue! While it's important to look at what you have wanted and do not have, don't spend too much time on how it appears outwardly. This is an opportunity to see the lighted pathway to your inner sanctum, where soul dreaming takes place. The great thing about this manifesting process is that it gives us a chance to become much more honest and transparent. In this transparency, congruent lines of resonating frequencies align and your manifestation quotient increases tenfold.

3. Checking Your Moral Compass

Checking your moral compass is a crucial endeavor if you are to increase your manifestation quotient. If the ego is the only operating force in creating desires and wants, then we are led and directed by smaller, more restricted

MIXED MESSAGES

Two people start with same manifestation energy for a dream.

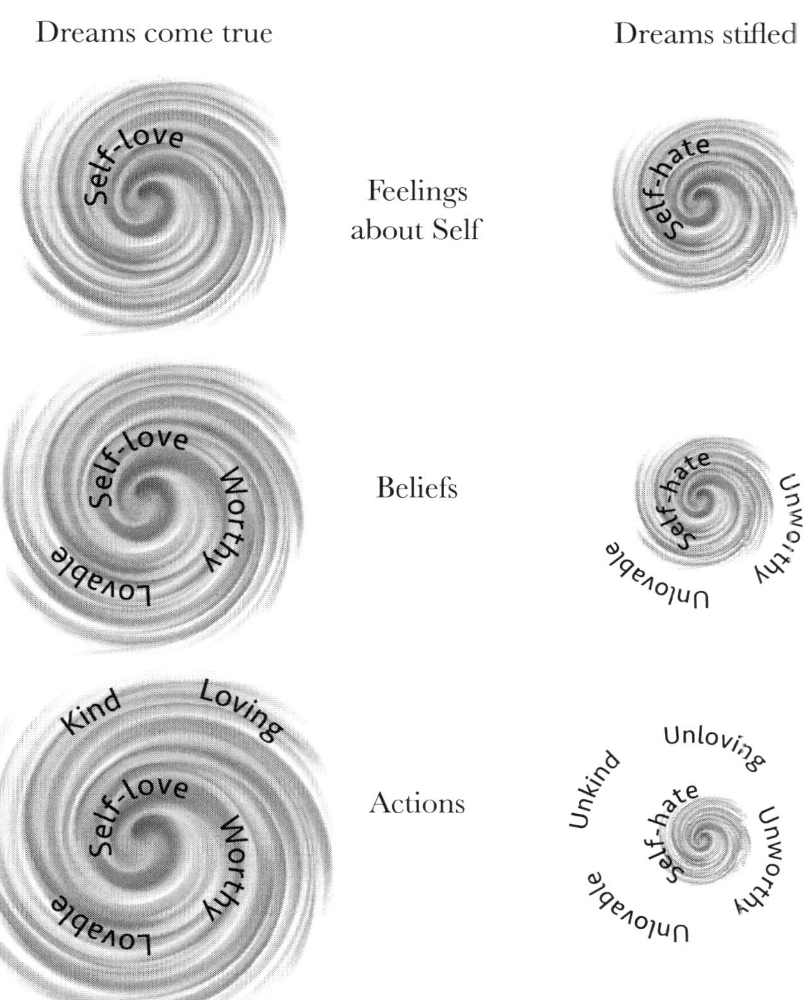

Illustration 22

ideas and notions. The ego has as its main concern the welfare of self and gives less attention to the effects dreams and goals may have on others, the Earth and the universe. It's a simple operating principle: *the smaller the scope of concern, the less potent the energy for creation.* Checking your moral compass immediately widens the scope of consideration. Do no harm is always the operating direction at the highest point of the compass. If your desires or intentions bestow harm or undue negative influence on others or the Earth, the potency of your quotient will be less. I understand that so many people will say, "Well, look at how much harm we have bestowed upon each other and this planet. That sure looks like we have great manifesting power to do so." The amazing truth is: We are still intact on this planet with many havens filled with miracles of humans loving and healing. This, in and of itself, gives testimony to the truth that the ego is a very weak manifestor. Otherwise, I'm afraid our planet, and everyone on it, would have already perished in the wrenching destructive powers of the creative force of manifested ego. The saddest part, up until now, is that we, in the world of the little self, have no idea how potent our soul/heart quadrants are in creating reality almost instantaneously. As we check our moral compass and follow its wisdom, we will have more access to this tremendous potency. Remember, as you create from the egoic world, you separate yourself from the omnipotent sacred field of All That Is, thus diminishing your manifesting quotient (MQ). First, check your ego at the door and see what the higher self is up to. Next, check out whether your dreams harm or hurt all that surrounds you. The more your dreams harmonize with the higher good of all, the more potent your inner quotient becomes. Are your dreams a contribution to humanity or irrelevant to the state of affairs that surround you?

We are a symbiotic species, interdependent not only for surviving, but thriving. When one's desires act against or harm another, we lose potency to manifest beauty and harmony on the very planet on which we live. It's important to understand that even if you state consciously that your desires are inclusive of higher good intentions, deep inside your deprived small self may rail against such actualization. You become stymied and stuck in your ability to actualize your life, because the manifesting beam of higher good energy does not originate from deep within. So remember: The more consistent and compatible your intentions are, the more power they have. It's absolutely incredible to know that our individual dreams can potentiate the manifesting quotient (MQ) of our entire species and all others. As it does, we draw fuel from this synchronistic weaving, adding intensity and potency to our own MQ. It's crucial to ask the following question: Are my desires and dreams congruent with the higher good of all? We not only need to be congruent and transparent with ourselves, but with our families, communities, and fellow travelers in the universe. Unlocking the soul code for integrity and non-harm increases the power of our MQ exponentially.

4. Closed vs. Open Operating System

Let's take a look at how closed or open our own human operating system is and how this affects our MQ. There is a pivotal energetic flow in keeping our inner MQ invigorated, abundant and overflowing. As we become a more closed system, with fixed ideas and rigid feelings, our MQ becomes stagnant, less potent, and attracts less energetic fuel from the state of flowing openness. The figure eight (so often talked about throughout this book) that is established from the world beyond with the world within is imperative to ramp up the actualization fuel for manifesting life. When we become stuck on an idea or think we know the truth of things, we begin to slowly cut off our MQ air supply. Since we can't possibly know everything, it's very crucial to bring to life the state of being required by humility and vulnerability. This creates open channels to All That Is beyond and All That Is still unknown within. As we sit within the confines of the self, humility opens space for a deep breath of fresh air and expanded consciousness. When you think you know it all, the breath it takes to expound it all will be shallow and uneven. In addition, you'll probably be living in far more restricted areas with little potency to create new realities for yourself and others. Stay present in open flow, knowing that what you already know has already passed. There are more potent pods of energetic fuel in what you do not know, than in what you know. After all, the potentialities for what you want to manifest live in the realm of unknown, not yet manifested dreams. This is crucial if you are to dream your reality into being.

GET SET

From old Paradigm Databases to Faith-based Invisible Realms

As previously stated, when we try to manifest from the realm of what we already know, or the pool that has already been formed from past experience, we cannot expect to create new experiences or new potential manifested states, things and times. The potency of past pools has already begun to lose its powers because it's not being fed by the currents of All That Is. Once those strands of quantum potentialities have been manifested here in this place and time, they've already become solidified in this three dimensional world. Remember, in this reality there is much less potency because what has already been solidified is no longer pregnant with all potentialities, and by definition it is only one of the many in the field of all. What's already known in our conscious minds only has the power of that consciousness, which in and of itself can't include all potentialities of manifestation. What we can hold in our current configuration of consciousness is the notion that we, in fact, do not know all possibilities. The truth in the proverbial saying that, "only God knows" is in this case not just a descriptive device, but the entire truth. We can't possibly know All possibilities, and therefore we can't solve riddles of the universe, let alone our small everyday garden variety problems, with our limited database which only consists of those potentialities that have been brought to life from the quantum field thus far.

In holding this understanding, we open the channels for all other databases in and out of this universe. Today, I only know what has been made manifest up to this exact point of time, but to create the next moment with only this database is totally limiting. Not only are past moments, by definition, losing their potency to manifest, but also prohibit the mysterious fertile frequencies of new information from gaining entrance. To contemplate solutions from that place of already spent moments of time causes people to feel in motion while never moving. *The most potent manifesting energy is the energy that bursts into your consciousness as it is birthing the moment, neither stagnate from what is past nor thwarted from what may be the future.* In that moment, all potentialities are equally available, and this is where your consciousness can be the deciding factor in what is brought into manifested alignment. Two things happen when you create from this place:

1. You're removing yourself from the data set of the past.
2. You're opening to the data sets of the universe.

So many difficulties in your life probably exist because the current data set you are operating from has not yet expanded to hold the burgeoning buoyancy of soluble solutions from beyond.

To stay in the restrictiveness of the old data set to solve problems that are arising out of that very data set is madness. In our hunger for safety, reliability and structure we choose this madness, believing that in doing so we will avoid our fear that in the hidden dimensions of All That Is we will lose control, lose sanity and open anew. Yet, all new discoveries and all new sets of information have been created by some "Aha" moment that jumps exponentially from the old to the new. This is exactly what faith is, believing in something that has not yet appeared in your secured data banks with proof, authentication and clear evidence. Faith is an experience that opens channels for this new and vital information. Without faith, we would not be prodded into utilizing our imagination for exploration, revelation and divination. Unearthing undulations are those waves of conscious energetic movement towards discovering what is hidden and unseen. The space/time continuum is not only so much more expansive beyond our current consciousness state, it also collapses and unfolds for infinity. It just might be good to entertain the idea that dancing in the light of infinity could be a bit more exciting and breathtaking than dancing in the dimly lit stages of our third dimensional lives.

A PROPOSAL FOR WHERE OUR FAITH ENERGY MIGHT TAKE UP RESIDENCY:

1. Divine intelligence surrounds us and is within us.
2. There are many layers of intelligence in the universe.
3. What we know so far is infinitesimal compared to the multidimensional libraries of wisdom.
4. Imagination is our channel and our conduit to this library.
5. There are steps towards Universal Consciousness, including the morphogenetic field and the quantum field.
6. There are many different morphogenetic fields created by human beings on this planet. A morphic field, as defined by Rupert Sheldrake, is a pattern of energetic organization created by a particular species that surrounds and influences the behavior of that species. It becomes stronger with repetition, increasing the likelihood of habitual responses and further resonance within that species. Our soul/mission codes as a human species live in the highest vibratory frequency of the morphic field.
7. There are many different morphogenetic fields created by off planet beings, angels, guides and Avatars.
8. Certain practices create bridges into the quantum field and these higher morphic fields. These may include meditation, yoga, bodywork, musical and artistic endeavors, communing with nature and love.

In fact, there are Energetic Resonant Fields (ERF) that have been created throughout time related to these different rituals and practices. Participating and doing these practices open new and expanded states of being from these ancient yet infinite ERFs. In these states of being, created by these practices, it is easier to suspend the rigidity of body/mind/emotion from the past and open to the quantum energetic field where all new potentialities pause in pregnant anticipation of becoming manifest in this reality.

If you are willing to hold the idea that there are many states of conscious knowledge hovering and holding a space for you to enter, then you may have easier access for entrance and experience. Mantras for manifestation process:

- I can't solve this problem with the current set of data. If I could, the problem wouldn't exist.
- I'm open to the possibilities of resolution that come from the many layers of sacred intelligence that exist around and within me.
- I have more faith in these invisible realms than I have in my experiences of things I already know.

This is how new paradigms are birthed. Problems, dilemmas, and discomforts exist to create pathways towards higher consciousness. As our predicaments grow, the more we will need higher paradigm resolution. Of course, the higher we go for this resolution the closer we come to the manifesting fields of the Divine Source. The goal is to see our quandaries and difficulties as vehicles not to solve in this realm, but as motivators to go to the invisible realms so that — As Above, So Below! Problems simply create the fuel to advance and evolve consciousness. How beautifully designed. Our very frustrations and unactualized dreams become the conduits towards new paradigms of wonder and resolution. Our felt smallness is purposeful in that it points the way to the expansive wave of Divine intelligence that pulses and glimmers in the outer limits of our awareness. In other words, it's my smallness that inspires me to eventually go to these mysterious unknown places, even if only out of frustration that my smallness is too small for big solutions. Never fret that you haven't manifested enough. Use the not enough experience to fuel your faith in the beyond — the unknown — the All That Is. Spend more time imagining and inventing and less time fretting and forgetting.

Thinking, feeling and living in old paradigms is like swimming in a pool of honey. It may taste sweet at first but you will likely drown in it.

You can't know all potentialities, but you can begin to dream them.

Dreaming forms a conduit to the quantum field and All That Is.

Use the heart as the guide and the mind only as a tool.

NEW PARADIGM JUMPING OFF POINTS

- We know very little, not very much.
- We are moving towards the elasticity and supple strength of simply being in order to escape the gravity of rigidity of thought, feeling and action.
- There are many layers, dimensions and realms to our consciousness.
- Our willingness to explore consciousness has to be more enticing than our willingness to be safe within the confines of what we already know.
- What we already know are past conscious moments that have squeezed their breath into very tiny spaces.
- Three-dimensional consciousness holds only the truth of where we are now.
- Expanded consciousness holds the truth of the universe and all that can be.
- Traveling in consciousness brings the movement necessary for new terrains to appear and disappear. This appearing and disappearing provides the pathways to all else that is.
- Agreeing to the truth that this third dimensional reality is only a pinprick existence in the multiverse grid of Divine intelligence is crucial for providing the motivation and will to explore where few of us have gone.
- Having faith and belief in this "beyond" wisdom (the wisdom that is beyond what we already know) is critical if we're to have the fortitude to move beyond the paradigms that have arisen out of this small third dimensional world.
- Faith and belief create an energetic field that is more powerful than all the facts and data that arise out of this third dimensional place we call home.
- Home will start to become associated with the feelings that arise when we are in these expanded states of consciousness.
- Only then will we realize that we have never really been home here on Earth and only then will we be able to make Earth our home.

It is the inside-out process of our consciousness manifesting reality that creates home in the first place. We've been so conditioned to pay attention to the externalized world outside of ourselves that we've contracted and diminished our awareness of the experience of home within. In abandoning this inside place, we no longer know home when we see it, feel it, taste it, hold it. As we come back to the home within, we'll be able to manifest this place in all things that surround us. Finally, home will have a congruent harmonic resonance that we have never before experienced. What ails so many people today is that the faint whispers of the soul home within don't match the dark contracted view of the outside world. Although we have a part in creating the dismal state of affairs found in the outer world today, deep within most of us feel and hear a voice of soft whispers that say "this is not who we are." *We suffer in knowing that what we've created is not who we are.* Nothing makes sense anymore. As we allow these deep whispers to resound and echo louder and louder, we will change the world by the very act of listening.

We've simply forgotten the truth of who we are. We are love, we are creators, we are beautiful rays of light from the Divine web of All That Is. We're here to remember ourselves, reverberate this deep soul blueprint message, and remedy, restore and replenish the very Earth on which we live. This will energetically create As Above, So Below, which is the soul purpose of our mission here on this planet. But, to do this, we have to believe in the above, expanding our consciousness beyond the cemented and entrenched reality of the below.

Once we remember this soul purpose, we will further ascend, creating a morphogenetic field of resonance for all of life not only here on this planet, but for all others as well. This is not just about changing Earth, it's about understanding our responsibility to move upward so that we don't drag down the rest of our star neighbors. We are made in the image of the Divine creator so we are that energy. We've just lost our way.

The first step is to simply jump up and leap with faith as your wings. The very act of leaping, takes us immediately towards boundless soaring. It's the energetic winds created by this boundless soaring that carry us above the gravitational pull of the third dimensional world. If I continue to seek answers down under, then I'll stay stuck in the mire that exists down under. *All new paradigms, all new inventions, all new ideas that have come to be, started with the belief that something existed beyond what we knew.* This quantum leap of faith creates the energy to look above not below. Look up and commune with the stars and soon you'll know we're not alone. Look up with your heart and you are in the act of love. Look up in the course of a disagreement, pause in the calm eye of the storm and see there is another one and another way. *What I have known is no longer and so the mantra is – imagine more, create more, envision more, know more, but most of all have faith there is more.*

READY…SET…GO

STAGE ONE: Conscious Awareness

The first essential question is "Are you awake and aware that you're a manifestor, a creator, an actualizer?" The truth is that you're doing it all the time but if you remain unconscious of these powerful principles, you may think you're not very powerful. A good clue about where you are in the manifestation process is to check out your beliefs about your own manifesting power. *For instance, if you don't believe in dreaming, you'll probably not dream. Even if you dream at night, you'll not remember what you don't believe exists.* Lucid dreaming is a great example of our power to direct and create our lives. During sleep states, lucid dreaming is the ability to have awareness of the fact that you're dreaming. In this awareness, you can then exert influence, direction and even the design of their dream life. Many researchers have suggested that as you increase your ability to lucid dream, you can begin to have more control of what happens in your dream states and also in your waking life. *So, instead of dreams functioning as the flushing out point of waking life, they become the material from which waking life can be made.* However, if your core beliefs produce thoughts and feelings that you don't have the ability to control your inner and outer world, then they'll become your captor, your suppressor, your psychic guard to all that might be. Dreams will be made only from such incarnate material. Therefore, it's crucial to become aware of your thoughts about dreaming reality. Can you let yourself know the truth that your current reality has already been created by you?

As said previously, conscious awareness is the laser beam for the technology of manifestation. A laser is a device that produces a very highly concentrated, narrow beam of light. The photons in this emission all have the same energy and phase so that the beam created is coherently made into a fine focus. Most other light beams have many waves randomly distributed, but in laser light, the waves are all precisely in phase with each other and therefore are in the same quantum state. This is a wonderful analogy for the manifestation process, where consciousness becomes the laser device that synchronizes and amplifies the manifested thought into a coherent beam of finely focused energy that is then sent to the quantum field for actualization. In this field, that specific beam of thought can focus, seek and match with that same potentiality in the quantum field. This is how potentialities begin their birthing process into our world from the mystical world beyond. You can easily see that if our thoughts are random, mixed and varied, a wider spectrum of energy is sent into the universe, which is bound with less potency, precision and amplification. It's similar to waking up one day and wishing for more money and waking up the next wishing for love and the next wishing for better work. Or having thoughts in one moment that you can create your reality and the next minute, doubting that you have any manifesting power at all. All of these varied states have mixed frequency and less potentiality. In addition, not only does each thought have its own signature, but some thoughts carry with them higher abounding potential. So if you consciously choose a dream thought (any thought that is in the manifestation mind machine) keep choosing it, keep believing it and keep thinking it. This consistency will bring into thought form more of the signature of that thought. The more powerful the signature, the more creative potential it will hold.

The first stage in this manifestation process then is to utilize consciousness in thought creation. Begin with consistent and focused thoughts so that you become acquainted with their signatures. In addition, all thoughts have feeling signatures and these distinct feeling signatures are found in the heart. These heart signatures are crucial for they become the coherent reaching out frequencies, determining both the vibrancy and strength of the prominent laser thoughts. These manifested laser beams activate the communication process between you and the all-encompassing quantum field. Choose a dream thought, meditate with it, and listen to the heart's version of this thought. Feel it, know it and return to it over and over. Remember your subconscious is doing this over and over as well, but you have no recollection, no remembrance and no awareness of that process. The subconscious tends to be random, non-synchronized, scattered, dense and fickle as heck, so the power of manifestation is quite diminished. Increase your power quotient by bringing the manifestation process into the conscious realm.

CREATING THE LASER BEAM OF CONSCIOUS AWARENESS

1. Choose one dream or wish you want to *manifest.*
2. Write down an *intention* for it on 3 by 5 cards and place them in areas where you often look and live.
3. State this intention *out loud several times a day.*
4. Feel it in your *heart* and learn to recognize this powerful *signature.*
5. Visualize the *dream* becoming *reality* and feel the joy!

STAGE TWO: Qualitative Discernment

If the first step in the manifestation process is conscious awareness, the second step to follow is conscious discernment. While the quantity of conscious manifesting habits is crucial, the qualitative nature of those habits is the determining factor in both the strength and potency of such habits. In other words, conscious awareness cultivates the signature and qualitative discernment amplifies it. Not only does each intention have its own signature, but some carry with them higher abounding potential. Choose a low frequency thought and you will generate low, fragmented energy. There are lower energy dream thoughts that are ego based and exist in this three dimensional dense realm. These thoughts have less potency, but can still bring those energies towards you if held long enough. Thoughts of harm, violence and hate are clearly not attached to the higher realms of sacred energy and so will have less access to the abundant energy found in other realms and dimensions. However, looking at the nightmares we've created right here on Earth is certainly testimony that we can generate and manifest mayhem all by ourselves! *Creating without Divine partnership produces nightmares from the human ego. Creating with Divine intervention produces dreams of realization from the human spirit.*

Higher Value Quotient

The highest values, actions, feelings and intentions present in the human species, in experiential form, produce the highest intensity, and most accelerated fuel for the manifestation process. This is what I call the Higher Value Quotient (HVQ). This is noteworthy because this gives us a whole new perspective and motivation for acting in the higher value frequency range. For instance, experiencing compassion, love, kindness, gentleness and humility, to name but a few, gives rise to the production of a very high-energy frequency or vibration, thereby increasing the HVQ. The energy produced or created from these states of being is one of the highest forms of fuel for accelerating the manifestation process. However, so many of us seem oblivious to the fact that the most becoming, most beautiful attributes we are capable of create a power that can propel us into the highest of all manifestation possibilities. Acting in the highest potential, with the highest value you possess produces energy likened to rocket fuel, compared to the less intense energy created from the actions of the less becoming, more egoic based intentions.

Divine Intelligence is magnificent in its plan and the imprint it has left within us. Being active participants in this plan is ever present and holds enormous generating power. Everything is in constant movement towards sacred Source, as if being pulled to a magnificent light by invisible cords of powerful magnetism. Some things move slower and may even seem to be moving in reverse in comparison with the more intense speeding vibrations that come through compassion and love. As you sit in love and look back at hate, the fast distance that separates the two may give the illusion that hate is traveling away from the Divine light, but it's simply moving at a snail's pace compared to the other less harming intentions and actions. Of course, the closer one gets to the light, the more engulfed one becomes in high intensity manifesting energy.

Setting one's intentions towards the highest values within your own capable range of action is crucial in building your higher value quotient. Imagine a passageway towards the Divine light. Imagine that the highest vibrations and highest energy potential lie closest to the light and the lowest vibrations and lowest energies lie furthest from the light. Now imagine the lowest vibrations come from harming, ego directed behaviors and the highest vibrations come from love intentions and actions. (**see illustration 23**)

On the left of this illustration, you can see that it's hazy and dense, thus requiring more energy and effort to move through. Therefore, you end up using enormous amounts of life force energy just trying to move through these dense walls of Earth matter produced by these actions. Earth matter refers to those dynamics, dramas and traumas that we seem to produce with such familiarity and ease. One can easily remain stuck in these thick vibrations, creating lives that reflect this level of denseness. We manifest things that are reflective of where we set up camp on this continuum. For example, if we believe we never have enough, surround ourselves with limiting opportunities and feel totally victimized, we'll probably stay stuck in the muddy landscapes of deprivation and despair. We tend to manifest those reflections we see in the pools that surround us. Isn't this evidence of our great power to actualize and manifest? Even in the thick, diluted and depleted fields, we still manage to create our world even if it's devoid of sacred value and esteem. The fuel

BUILDING A HIGHER VALUE QUOTIENT

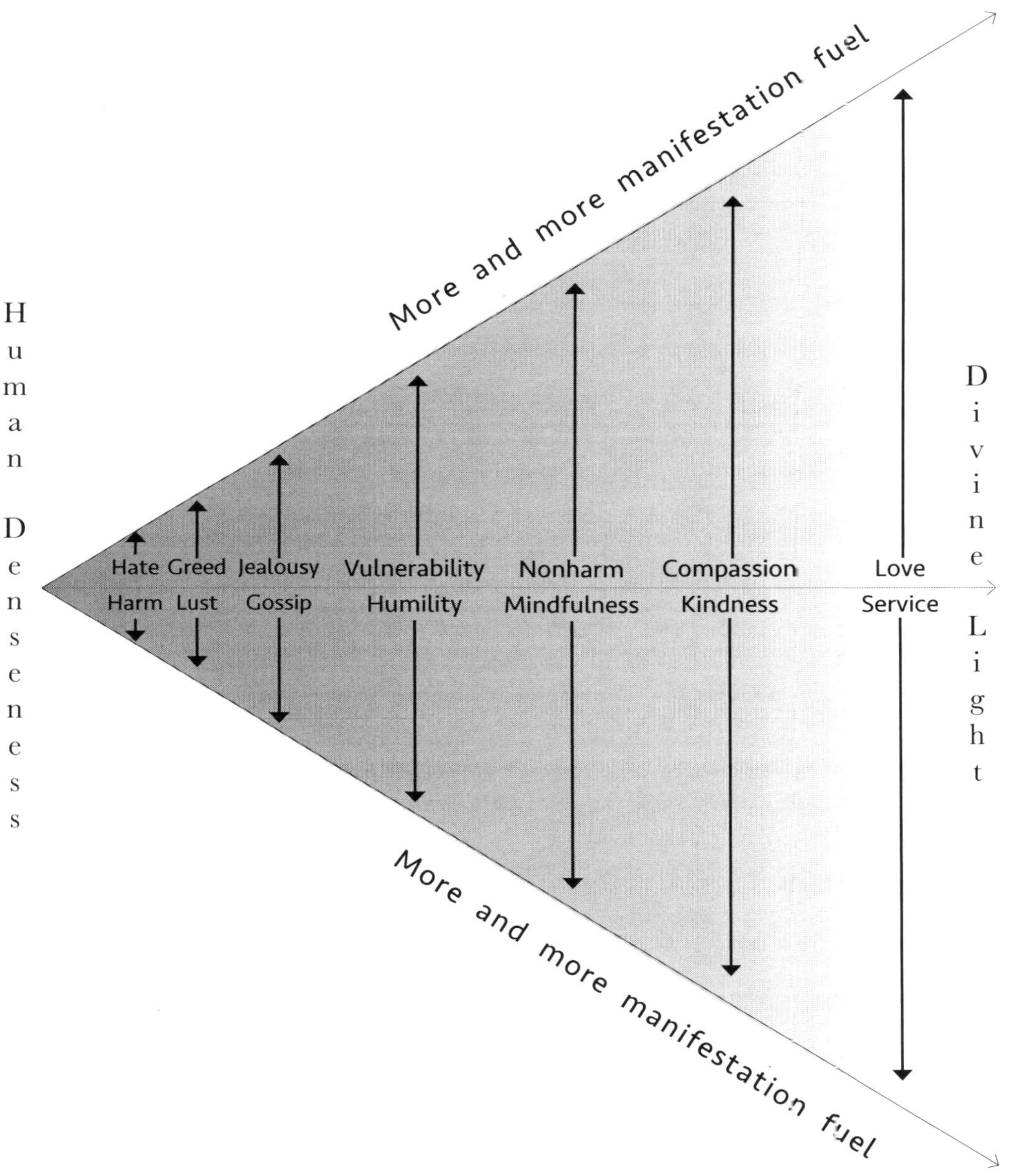

Illustration 23

needed for the manifestation process increases in its potency the further we go towards the Divine light. As we begin to live up to our highest potentials, we gather more and more energy that is synergized into manifesting our highest soul/self.

Even the intentions themselves carry the same energetic continuum illustrated above. If your intention is harming and hateful, it carries energy that caves in on itself, creating that same kind of energy outside of you and attracting that same resonant energy towards you. It is crucial to ask the question, "What's the intent behind that which you say you want, and need?" For example, you might hold an intention that says, "I want a job promotion no matter what it takes," without regard for the effect this may have on others, the work place or the company that employs you. This "effect energy" is what I call the ripple potentiating effect that a given intention or action has on the greater whole. In this case, the manifestation dream of a job promotion may inadvertently carry with it lower, denser effect energy that now weighs it down, stifling the ability to make dreams come true. The more harming the ripple effect, the less potentiating the dream intention or action will be. However, if you stated the dream of a job promotion with higher value energy, for instance, "I would like the job promotion and I would like to have it happen in the least harming way for all the other people involved." Now this carries with it more potent energy and this, in and of itself, may accelerate the process of dream completion.

Someday we'll live in the full experience of our highest potential. Perhaps then we will have the grandest "Aha" experience of our lifetimes, realizing that the manifestation mystery found in the art of dreaming reality, ushered in the renaissance of the New Human. Only then will we understand that this is what we needed to manifest all along. We will no longer need to make lists of more manifestation goals, desires, needs and wants. *For the experience of being in our highest potential will be enough and, in that experience, we will be sacred manifestation itself, never ending, always birthing, ever steady in the glow of Divine light.*

If this isn't motivation to hold more discernment in this manifesting process, then I'm not sure what is! The power found in building the higher value quotient (HVQ) accelerates and quickens the manifestation process. This is true even though the highest values may have nothing to do with the particular manifesting dream you are working on. Being kind and helpful to your neighbor today may seem unrelated to the content of your dream. The energy of that experience will increase your own manifesting energy quotient. Don't be surprised if that helpful act towards your neighbor doesn't connect with your dream manifestation (DM). The universe is quite synchronistic you know. Utilizing higher value discernment for the intention, the action and the ripple effect all increase and magnify the potential for instantaneous and powerful manifestation.

PRINICPLES OF DISCERNMENT QUESTIONS:

- Is it non-harming to self, others, Earth?
- Does it create abundance for all?
- Is it divinely inspired or simply human inspired?
- Does it come from the awakening process of soul alignment or the deafening program of the human ego?
- Is it dualistic and polarized or in sync with the principals of unity and wholeness?

STAGE THREE: Felt Self-Presence

As conscious awareness becomes the laser beam and discernment magnifies the amplification, felt self-presence gives the raw material from which all else can be created. In other words, if the think tank can only generate a few thoughts and the heart has been only dimly discovered, the manifestation potential will be weak and fairly impotent. Thus, chapter 6 on the self becomes a crucial playing ground for consciously creating your life. Loving yourself enough to know thyself is paramount to this process. Without love, you'll never be able to cross the threshold of the many libraries that lie within. *Healing the self, by dismantling all of the previously outer shells of blueprints and manmade plans is not only necessary, but also crucial in clearing the path for your consciousness to surf the waves of your sacred self.* You'll gather more and more abundance in thoughts and feelings that will further guide you in what and how you want to create your life and all others.

As you learn to stay in this place of now with this deep felt self-presence, you will have access to discovering your unique energy configurations, aligning and creating with them. As you illumine the lights of your distinct design, you'll be able to see the path towards dreaming your reality. The more present you can be, hiding nothing and revealing everything, the more fuel you generate for manifesting your unique soul mission, becoming at last your *sui generis* self. Without knowing thyself, there is no material from which to create.

As you become this higher self and the essence of All That Is you, and you establish this pinpoint focus or concentration, you'll have fewer and fewer boundaries between self and everything else. Time and space begin to fade, allowing you to merge with the All of everything else. At this point in time, portals to the pool of Divine Intelligence begin to open and you are flooded with eternal energy, that most potent of all energies of the universe. This becomes the rich, fertile energy of consciously and spontaneously dreaming reality.

Distractions and Fragmentation

One of our biggest deterrents in the manifestation process at this time in human history is our ability to become distracted and fragmented. It seems that while technology has been created to make our lives easier, it's also spawned a splintering effect on our consciousness. People can no longer sit in silence for any small length of time, choosing instead to line up for their electronic smorgasbord of choice. As a result, we have shorter and shorter attention spans, experience more and more fragmentation in thinking and feeling and have less and less access to our short term memory banks. I hear these complaints from clients every day. It makes sense that we've become poor manifestors, as we can't seem to stay on a clear, consistent actualization path. Some of us can't even remember the path we think we want! We may make a phone call with a certain need or want, but if we are put on hold for a minute (which seems typical now) our concentration waivers in the mad rush to fill up the space with something more entertaining or occupying. Our attention is fragmented, making it impossible to direct our ability to stay potent and lively with our original intention. We may even forget who or what we are waiting for, let alone affect the outcome. That is why it is so crucial for us to access that state of being that comes from felt self-presence. The deeper we go within to discover that consummate soul blueprint, the more steadfast, inexhaustible and ceaseless our deepest desires and dreams become. This is what determines the ultimate potency factor in the manifestation process.

Here are some pointers for becoming less fragmented and distracted, and more whole and resonant:

1. All human quadrants must be united in the Dream

When you become absorbed by one of the quadrant areas e.g. the mind's thoughts, you may inadvertently close down portals of manifestation energy to other quadrants. It's amazing how we can become obsessed with the thought that we should be healthier, while our body consumes a dozen sugar cookies. When our quadrants work against each other, our manifestation energy becomes entangled and diluted. It's most fascinating to observe and consciously note what each of the four quadrants: body, mind, heart and spirit are actualizing at any one moment. The soul could shout, "I want more silence and spiritual growth," while the mind busies itself with the latest electronic communication. It takes immense diligence to consciously keep track of our quadrants of experience, let alone coordinate and unite them in common causes and silhouetted alignments. When choosing a particular dream or desire, it's crucial to check whether all four quadrants are in harmonic concert with each other. This will increase the potency of your ability to manifest tenfold. Create moments when all four quadrants are in sync and in the same rhythm. Note the signature of such moments. Spend an afternoon, balancing and fine-tuning the intentions of the heart, mind, body and spirit, bringing them into harmonious alignment. It could be as simple as sitting beside a stream eating an orange, looking at nature, and feeling the joy of the pause as spirit sweeps through your conscious awareness. These are some of the sweetest moments of life.

2. Expectations pollute the process

If you put more energy into your expectations of what you think should happen and less into the experience of the self within, you will further dilute the manifestation process (MP). For instance, if you have expectations of a spiritual desire such as "When I meditate I want to have an epiphany or see visions," those very expectations close portals, because you leave the meditation process for some out there outcome. As I'm not attached to any expectations of body, mind, heart and soul, I open the doors for all possibilities. Non-attachment becomes so important, not only as a practice, but as a way for active portal openings. Distraction through expectation narrows the focus, and closes the openings, causing less eternal energy to potentially rejuvenate our holistic system. Instead of having our energy focused on our expectations, we must instead have greater trust and faith in the experience of the manifestation process within ourselves, not without ourselves.

Expectations lie outside of our most potent domain for they live out there somewhere; intentions lie within us. The less we live in expectations, the less self-prescribed boundaries restrain us, and the more we become part of the mystical merger of All That Is.

3. Actions must be confluent with intentions

On Earth at this time, intent is simply not enough. Action is crucial. The more you operate from that felt self-presence, the higher the probability that your intentions will turn into convergent actions. Our actions turn into the very energy that then fuels what will be brought forth as actualized material in our lives. Behaviors provide a mirror for us to see the truth about our desires to consciously create. Conduct and deeds carry very powerful experiences within the human being and it is this experience that can produce the most powerful manifestation fuel. If your dream is a new home, what actions show up in your old home that hold the energy of this new intention? The more sacredly you treat the old home, the more powerful your intention becomes in creating the new.

Often, we do just the opposite in the midst of wishing for a new place to live, we treat the old with little care and attention. What proof do you see in your current relationships, that you want deeper love and commitment? The link has to be made in the present moment. When we follow intent with action, we are being the manifested wish. *Intent is the revelation of consciousness. Action is the reality of consciousness. Both produce the mirror that reflects that we exist.*

There are a few crucial questions to answer:

- What do you want to manifest and create in your life?
- What are your intentions for that?
- What are your actions *every day* that support this?
- Can you bring the *experience* of these actions into the forefront of your consciousness?

First, when we have intentions that are not supported by actions, it gives mixed, diluted and entangled messages about our Manifestation Process (MP). In the end we begin to feel, first that we can't take ourselves seriously; and second, that we are not very powerful creators. Action produces the mirror by which we see and build our faith that we can make dreams come true. At the end of every day, you should be able to see one action that confirms and is in alignment with your most significant intention for that day. For instance, if you intend to be healthy at the beginning of the day, you will want to see yourself doing one healthy thing by the end of the day. Without that, your whispers of intent fall on deaf ears.

Second, the experience of follow through actions, in and of itself, produces a delightful realization and aliveness that entrains with perpetuating intentions and actions. The action itself becomes the conscious endeavor as it carries with it a signature that matches your aim and purpose. You'll return to it naturally, perhaps even forgetting what you originally intended, until suddenly it too pops into your everyday existence, fully manifested as if overnight. The goal, after all, is for action to be the manifesting truth of our total soul blueprint. Once we become the experience of these soul-dreaming codes, we can evolve, ascend and be our highest potential.

4. Subtle Tracking

As we are deeply ensconced in our felt self-presence, we have more possibility of engaging in the subtle tracking necessary to detangle our subconscious wishes, needs and desires. The more you live inside the self, the more you will have access to monitoring the subconscious sabotage that plays like a runaway movie every single second. The very act of bringing awareness to this murky field of subconscious material that arises from perceived past records and hopeful future holdings brings forth the potential for designing your life in deliberate and purposeful consciousness. However, if you aren't deep inside yourself, you won't have access or the ability to do the subtle tracking necessary for clearing the debris and disentangling the embroiled and fettered web of long lost dreams.

Imagine that every intention and dream you consciously have produces a light strand that moves through your entire system, through all quadrants and the subconscious fields. As those strands of intentional energy meet up with like resonance in those respective fields, the light strands become bigger, brighter and more potent. However, if those strands meet opposing and contradicting energy lines, then they become neutralized or entangled, which surely causes the dilution of creative MP. That is why we must learn to be subtle trackers, especially in the domain of the subconscious fields of self. Certainly gross tracking is easier—I want to be healthy and fit but most of my behaviors today are not that. When we think we want one thing, but act in another way, we have a clue that there is a crowded combative situation in our inner residence. Our inability to track the more subtle realms of self, however, causes entanglement and strangulation of our manifestation light web. The energetic strands of potentiality can easily become dim and short-circuited, never reaching the pool of the quantum field. Take time to become a tracking detective, using the clues of the unmanifested dream to lead the way. If on the surface, you state that you want to have more money, but always seem to come up short, you may have competing subconscious feelings deep within that you do not deserve it. This creates entangled dreaming fields. We have to be willing to sit with ourselves long enough to learn how to see ourselves more clearly than we see the world. It isn't about putting an intention out there and hoping for the best. Without being in the powerful field of self-presence, we can't heal our past programs of powerlessness and helplessness and our old paradigms that keep us a slave to externalized creations. This requires us to be acutely aware every minute of the day. I hear people say, "That's so much work, I don't have time for that." I say, "Do you have a clue how much energy is trapped in the fog of your subconscious world and how much effort it takes when you don't have access to this energy?" As we come to know ourselves through love and compassion, we open pathways to understand and hold these hidden places. We can then bring consciousness and light to that which has remained dark. Strong light threads with resonant behaviors, feelings and thoughts gather speed and power, reaching the pool of potential possibilities in lightening speed. That's why when people have total matching of thought, feeling and deed they can manifest so much quicker. The subtle realm of self-residence may be where we get entrapped and ensnared, but it's also the place that offers the most potency for manifesting and creating life. Once you become a subtle inner world explorer, you'll be free to consummate both intention and action in an aura of wholeness and holiness.

5. Ego driven intentions

Intentions and actions that originate from the ego domain tend to be more diminished and less resolute in their ability to actualize and create. While the ego seems necessary to help make us feel safe, it often compromises our ability to manifest. The ego is more interested in the end results and the outcome than on the process of being in deeper felt self-presence. When we ride on the tails of the ego, we are headed on a collision course, where dreams are dumped in the ditch as soon as the road gets difficult. The ego has much less tolerance to stay steadfast with the work of undivided attention, subtle tracking and intention/action confluence. The ego also is less concerned with the good for all, and more concerned with whether there is enough good for self. So, the potency that comes from qualitative discernment (see above) is lost on the ego. The ego is more one-dimensional, while the soul is multidimensional. It's in this multidimensional field that all creation can be found. The soul begins to feel the beauty that can be seen in the process of actualizing the intention. The ego gets stuck in the far outreaches of outcome where the air is stifled and the fuel for manifesting is less fertile, less fortified, less enhanced. That's because the ego does not believe in the soul/self, and so always seeks worth and power from externalized things. It's quite simple: the farther away you are from the self, the less you are able to manifest. *The ego takes you out; the soul brings you back.* (**see illustration 24**)

EGO VS. SOUL INTENT

Flatline existence of ego-driven intentions produces small, unfulfilled dreams and outcomes.

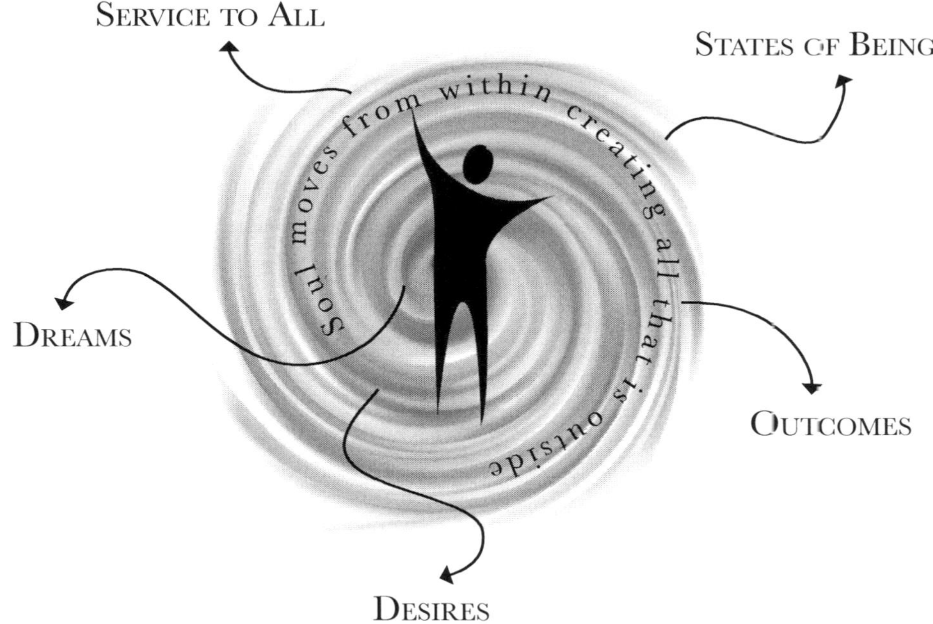

Manifestation power grows from the seat of the Soul.

Illustration 24

When we hold the purity that comes from soul intention without egoic thoughts, history, conditioning, feelings and desires, we have access to the keys of light wisdom that will unlock our manifesting powers. When we can finally become conscious connoisseurs of being "in-process," outcome will matter very little. We will realize that the process of soul actualization was the intended outcome all along!

So we must:

1. Recognize soul intent.
2. Learn how to experience soul intent and the actions that naturally follow.
3. Hold the experience long enough to let the experience become the manifestation!

STAGE FOUR: Relationship with the Quantum Field

Increasing and magnifying your awareness of the relationship you have with the quantum field itself is paramount. The principles discussed in the chapter on the I/thou relationship are identical to the relationship you have with the quantum realm. This is a relationship that brings you into more and more sacred infinite fields as you begin to waltz with the dimension beyond the third dimensional human self.

Let's review those I/thou relation principles.

Conscious Gate Opening

First, am I connected to this quantum-manifesting field today? Are my gates open to this energetic field? It's crucial to keep in mind that the gates of "the field" are in a continuous opening movement. It's only I that may be in a stagnate state of closing. It's simply our beliefs that do the closing. Most of us don't know that we are even in relationship with the quantum field (QF). We have slumbered in the forgotten land of self-enclosure. It is time to awaken and thus open the gates to this relationship with the field. Take a moment to breathe your gates open to the field and watch what happens in this breath.

You might say, "I consciously acknowledge the field of all potentialities that surround me and I open myself to this matrix as I breathe out and breathe in all possibilities."

Second, I can't only be conscious about the relationship I have with the field, but I have to open to what the field has to offer me. Do I understand that the field is the potential realization of all consciousness and is constantly sending me waves of energy packets of potentialities? I'm the one who can open these packets or let them sit on my outside steps of the unconscious mind. When I do invite them in, can I hold the possibility that they initially may look different than what I asked for? We often put out to the universe things we want to actualize and the field gives us something else. Let's not be fooled by this. This infinite field just may know more closely what it is that we need. After all, sacred intelligence lives in the quantum field. *Someday we will be potent purveyors of perfectly orchestrating the symphony of all possibilities, but for now we must be better receivers of the mysterious messages from beyond.*

I'm reminded of a client who was seriously intending to find a love relationship in her life. She'd constantly complain that the universe had other ideas for her. She was very accomplished in her career and received a job promotion that enabled her to move to an area she really loved. Although she was grateful about that, she still stated that she would rather meet the love of her life than have a job promotion. She continued to believe that she wasn't a very good manifestor or as she put it, "I can't seem to actualize my dreams." One day on the way to work, she had a flat tire on her car. It was a new area of travel for her and so she was less familiar with gas stations and mechanic services. After a short while, a young man stopped his car and changed her tire for her. She came into therapy complaining that the universe gave her a flat tire, once again proving that she seemed to get things she didn't ask for or want. I asked her why she didn't think the young man who came to assist her wasn't a gift in disguise. Perhaps her ungrateful attitude prevented her ability to manifest what she wanted. She apparently thought about that and called this young man the next day to thank him as he had given her his business card. They struck up a conversation, and, lo and behold, are now in a committed love relationship. If not for the job promotion, if not for the flat tire, she wouldn't have found the love of her life.

Often the notion of things to come doesn't always look like the things to come. Can we be open to the many possibilities, the many destiny paths that lie waiting for us? What I think I might want or need may not always be in my highest good. Can I trust this field to neither abandon me nor annihilate me with its huge scope of holding All That Is? Can I choose to feel life and merge with All That Is within and beyond myself, and stay conscious that this is my birthright?

Mutual Respect

Respecting my own actualization process even as I stumble and sometimes fall is paramount. In addition, I must respect the sacredness of all things the field holds in the horizon of my consciousness. As I grow in my ability to manifest, so too the field grows in its ability to expand creation. Respecting both the hugeness and the mystery of the quantum field without fear, without hesitation, without conditions is pivotal in building the I/Thou relationship. This is the very reason faith is paramount as we feel the magnitude of weaving ourselves within and among the all-encompassing manifesting field of sacred Source. As I hold sacred gratitude for this golden field of all potentialities, I come closer to the face of God.

Transparent Expression

The clearer I am about myself, the clearer the field can be about who I am and what are the signature frequencies of my dreams. The clearer the intent, the more potent the laser frequency becomes. This then draws from the field more exact matches and potentials. *Hidden truths within only confuse the message, fragment the intent and diffuse the potency of the dream.* As we make ourselves transparent to the world, we become more transparent to ourselves and in this process we not only know ourselves but the wealth of information that is stored in the treasure trove of the soul as well.

Transparent expression creates the prologue to telepathic communication. We already have what I call accidental telepathy with the quantum field but the real question is, can we have conscious telepathy? This can be seen in the numerous synchronistic events that take place on a fairly regular basis.

For instance, a friend of mine needed a roofing job on his house and was having trouble finding a roofer. One night he got an unexpected phone call from a long lost friend whose brother happened to be a roofer in the area. He had just had a cancellation on a major job. Needless to say, my friend has a new roof. Would we call this accidental, random or simply fate? Or would we understand that the manifesting field is cooperating and communicating with our needs or wants, whether we are conscious of this or not. Can we be curious enough to become more conscious of this potent manifesting field and begin to vision what potentialities are most pregnant with birthing energies? This moves us closer to instantaneous manifestation and the ability to be in movement with the boundless possibilities that exist all at once and one at a time. The field is telepathic with us as well, for we are revealed in its wake. All of our destiny paths have been and will be contained within it.

Process is Paramount...Content is Superfluous

This is probably one of the most crucial pieces in this quantum web of dreaming reality. We usually get so stuck in the mires of content menus that we forget entirely about the process. It's the process of manifesting that creates the energetic flow of creating, not the content. Content without process is like an empty boat found on the bottom of an empty river. The boat cannot travel without the currents of the river. We humans are simply engineers that keep the current moving. We are not the specific dreams, we are the players in the dreams. We can be the parts and yet, we are always of the whole.

We have an incredible ability to be in rhythmic movement with the fertile field of manifestation and it's in this movement that both the whole and the parts exist all at once. When you are too busy wanting specific things, you are in content. Things will never bring you the exhilaration that comes from feeling the process of conceiving and birthing potentialities. The process of manifestation is being in full consciousness of self. This takes place in the very moment of now and the very place of here. *Remember, the mind loves content; the heart loves process.* When you're in a rough spot, the first thing to do is to bring your consciousness into your heart. *The heart is the greatest manifestor of all. It knows exactly what you need and where you need to go.* The number one rule is, "I want to be in process with life more than I want to live in the deductive logic of analyzing life." Content is useful mainly as it motivates us to be in process, but feeling the aliveness and flow of process is the fuel of all manifestation. Think of it this way, we have the content to bring us to the understanding of being in process. Human beings are made to be in process, but often get stuck in producing content that is both irrelevant and harmful to the creative process of simply being human. On this beautiful path of presence, what we value begins to change. *The process of life becomes the art, the outcome simply the by-product of this creative development.*

Giving and Receiving

As with all relationships, we have to be very careful that after all our hard work on the above issues, we don't sit back and say, "Okay I've done my work, now what will the universe give to me?" When we get out of the stance of offering our manifesting elements to the field and begin to wait for a response, we are abdicating our power and our potential to be co-creators. We forfeit our partnership with the manifestation field, which, in turn, immediately robs this field of our unique signatures. This totally changes the alchemy of self/field relations. If we are not found in the field, how can the field find us? Our active participation is crucial in securing a place within the field of manifestation. Otherwise, we are dependent on something outside of us to dream and define us. Isn't that after all, the definition of the old paradigms that have deprived us of dreaming reality up until now?

We can't just think a dream and wait. We must be constantly active in the art of being, continuing to unfold the blueprint, actualizing the who that we really are. Gifting this to the cosmic field of Divine Source becomes part of your very essence. If the act of giving helps you manifest the who in your dreams, then you have already received what you need. The question is not what will the quantum field (QF) give you, but how do you work on continuing to be. *Being fully you is the active phase of manifestation.* Being is the ultimate act of doing the self. Waiting and wanting is the undoing of the self. As we are able to be in our own creation, we draw the field closer to us and as it comes nearer, we become the field as the field moves within us.

STAGE FIVE: Joining Forces

Connecting with another's energy in manifestation mode exponentially increases the manifestation potential. If you choose to consciously manifest life force dreams with another, the dream will have squared momentum to come to life. If the whole world were in life force awareness at the same time with the same healing dream for the Earth, then the Earth would instantaneously become healed and whole.

When you're bathed and in sync with the manifesting life force energy of nature while dreaming reality, your reality will have a rocket boost of this organic divine adrenaline to make material the spirit of your dream. Trees for instance, are great manifestors, for the seed of an oak knows its blueprint, becomes it and does not waver in the process. It's never confused by the thought of becoming a grass blade. The heart of a tree is always in a constant state of being. The giant oak is also in touch with joining forces as it's roots comingle with the Earth's fertility and it's branches and leaves are receptive to the nurturing qualities of natures elements: sun, water and wind. A tree doesn't just grow and stand alone, but rather has infinite energy streaming from above and below to manifest its blueprint with inspiring strength and suppleness.

It's only humans who are not in their sacred blueprint, and this makes it even more difficult to join forces. We let outside architectural guidelines dampen our awareness of this journey. Most of these externalized designs keep us ego driven and separate in our actualization process. As long as we are operating from ego, we won't be able to vision the extraordinary power that lies in joining forces. When manifestation occurs within the soul blueprint, the heart and mind awaken to the power of unity and oneness. When we remember our sacred missions to co-create, we will have access to the millennium memory library, where we'll gain heart insights and expanded vision. *In a quantum instant, we'll not only know that we were never meant to create alone, but our greatest and swiftest powers as a human race lie in our ability to join together to conceive and birth a new world.* As we use the delineated principles described in this chapter, orchestrated with our fellow human travelers, we'll create more than enough abundance for all. Finally, when we come to understand that we are not alone in the universe, we'll be able to join forces with our galactic neighbors and skyrocket into the state of the New Human being.

When you join forces with another human who is completely aligned in body, mind, heart and soul, and aware of the principles of qualitative discernment, the fuel available exponentially expands changing the very nature of its endowment. In other words, as we join forces, we not only add quantity to the manifestation equation, but we bestow the quotient with a qualitatively new energy. We create an infinite spectrum of possibilities when two or more join forces. Another way to understand the magnitude of joining forces is to draw on an analogy from the field of chemistry and nuclear physics. A chain reaction is defined as a "sequence of reactions where a reactive product or by-product causes additional reactions to take place. In a chain reaction, positive feedback leads to a self-amplifying chain of events." A well-known metaphor for this is the snowball effect. When a snowball starts from a top of a mountain, it becomes larger and larger until an avalanche results. Or in chemistry, the analogy is a spark causing a forest fire. In these examples, the combination of one event with another creates catastrophic results. We can even see this in our own human history, as one event sparks a cataclysmic happening that appears to be unstoppable as in the major world wars on Earth. However, joining forces with one another can also infinitely multiply our most valued dreams. It may take months for one individual to build a barn, but in Amish communities, they can raise a barn in one day. When common goals and commitments are guided by communal values, reality can shift, change and expand with enormous speed and vigor. The evidence for groups of people who utilize prayer and meditation to help induce positive change and healing events is confirmation of the power of weaving and merging concurrent energy intentions. As we join forces with each other in our dream for a harmonious, peaceful and loving world, we can make this figment of our imagination become a grounded reality. It's this potential that we must set our sights on. *As we coalesce and unite with others to dream reality into being, there will be no distinction between the act of dreaming and the reality we experience.* **(see illustration 25)**

MANIFESTATION FORMULA

Conscious Awareness

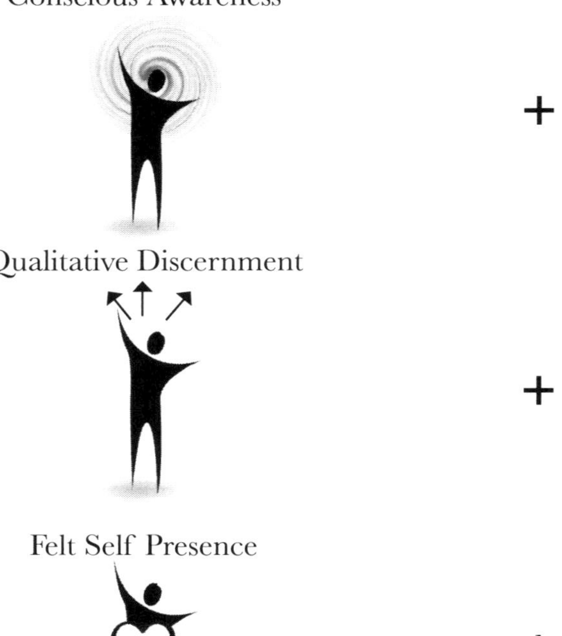

+

Qualitative Discernment

+

Felt Self Presence

+

Relationship with the Quantum Field

+

Joining Forces

=

MANIFESTATION

Illustration 25

Nothing is as it Seems but Everything is a Clue

It's most crucial as you utilize the tools of this manifestation technology that you stay open and ready to be surprised at any moment. At this point, in most of our evolutionary processes, we still view the world, ourselves and this process with the mind of the little self. This often produces impatience and literal interpretations of the various outcomes of this intricate creative process.

Here are some key points in bringing clarity to this process.

Non-attachment

We look for outcomes instead of clues, and interpret life happenings with shallow, often critical reasoning; concluding erroneously, in the end, that we have the bona fide truth. Because our vision remains restricted, our imagination and curiosity must direct our attention. If everything that happens around you is a clue…what do you really see? What you think you want may not be what you are manifesting, and what you are manifesting may not be what you want. There are several reasons for this:

- Many of us are still sending out unconscious mixed signals to the manifesting field and so mixed results are to be expected.
- We're too attached to the outcome and not present with the process. Attachment narrows the arteries of the manifesting heart.
- The energy we use for wishing dreams is more than the energy it takes in making dreams realized.
- Our dreams may contain material that adds nightmarish elements to another's field and therefore these outcomes have less potential and less potency.
- If we are lucky, our deeper soul longings and dreams may be breaking through and bringing us something a bit different than what our egos had hoped for.
- The field also weaves with us and may spin a different story than the one we had scripted all by ourselves.
- When we finally release and surrender all attachments we will experience the true wonder of expanding from the mysterious realms, and immersing ourselves in the mysticism and magic found in the

sacred lands of pure manifestation. *We will then know that where we are headed is exactly where we need to be going; and the sequel to our current life is the life that we are already consciously living.*

Letting go of everything you think you know about manifestation might be a good place to begin. Releasing the attachments you have to the things you think you deserve and the outcomes you think you must have are paramount in turning the manifesting process from child's entertainment to pure soul entrainment. That's why it's so important to understand that nothing is as it seems but everything is a clue. Let any disappointment or disillusionment morph into currents of curiosity. If we can see value in the clues, we will gain clarity about our Prime Directives, those codes from soul source that guide us in manifesting sacred mission and purpose.

DUALITIES VS. WHOLENESS: A Final Word of Caution

In our mad ride to make our lives complete, we experience a myriad of events, some that we plan and many that we don't, but we also find ourselves going through wild shifts from one polarity to another. It's important to note here that these shifts are not signs that our manifesting skills come from a schizophrenic existence, but it's a sign we are coming closer to the next reality and the next dimensional shift. For it's the rapid shifting from one polarized position to another that causes us to experience and expand into the third reality, the reality of unity. I call this the reality of unity because it is neither one polarity or the other, but a combination of both. This merging of realities shifts our experience, and in this third reality, we are capable of accessing all of our manifesting energy. Beware, this rapid shifting can feel crazy making. Instead of becoming steadier in our experiences, it might appear that we are less stable, less fixed, less rigid, less constant. As we dance back and forth from one duality to the next, we can at times wonder about the diagnostic meaning of such shifts. For instance, we might be at a job that we dislike, with a boss we can't stand and so we might begin to work on starting our own business, and doing the work we love without the dampening affect of office politics. Yet, as we are working on self-employment one day, we may encounter unemployment the next day, swinging from one pole to the other without a moments notice. This requires enormous flexibility and fluidity to be able to move in process without getting stuck in content. It's very difficult to find grace in such troublesome places. We certainly may not understand that unemployment is a guided wormhole for manifesting self-employment! In other words, it will take us to a destiny point faster than the speed of light, without aging in the density of the time and space it would take as we wait in the unfertile grounds of lifeless employment.

As we become more fluid and capable of understanding the many positions in life (despair-joy, rich-poor, content-discontent, stagnation-movement), we also gain understanding of what this holding process brings us. In the ability to be more fluid, we find ourselves riding the continuum more rapidly and quickly in time and space. Perhaps, we need to pause and have gratitude for these shifting tides, as they dislodge us from the old paradigms with efficient speed and magnanimous force. Left to our own ego devices, we might simply sit in one polarized position, rigidly holding on to something while our resources drain away into the gutters of unspent time and space. Polarizing our time, our energy and ourselves also contributes to our need to have judgments and commentary about the other side, as these are the protective measures we utilize for not becoming the other side. *This keeps us separate from those beings sitting at the other pole and also from the possibilities of those experiences in ourselves. We live half full of experiences. The fertile grounds of manifestation are not to be found in the positions we take, but rather in the process of moving gracefully and without resistance in between.* Experiencing both the yin and the yang and everything in between gives us the material from which all else can be created. Dualistic shifts that happen close in time and space create alchemy, through the merging experiential states of both. This in turn births this new dimensional third reality: the reality of unity.

This is the new renaissance paradigm we are being asked to step into, creating as we do the spiritual evolution of our species. We must be willing to experience these whirling oppositional polar shifts, which will result in massive human quakes that rock and roll us right out of our stupor. These merging dualities create disharmonious and chaotic states, but in the end we will unearth a fertile manifested land where we can build the future of the human race. Don't judge your shifts, but use them as evidence that the pulse of your heartbeat is expanding, growing stronger and becoming wiser with each shift, with each quake. Don't criticize your rapidly changing shape, don't be skeptical of your diverging experiences, but rather celebrate that you are the *blender and mixer of known realities so that unknown realities can be ushered in*. If you're one of the lucky ones and feel you are experiencing paradoxical states within brief moments of time and space, be reassured that you are manifesting this process. Paradox is the conceptual tool for experiencing this merging, third dimensional reality experience. This brings us to the doorstep of the fourth dimension where duality collapses, unity prevails and manifestation is instantaneous.

We were destined from the beginning to naturally manifest and create life, not deplete and expend life. It's our birthright in our DNA inspired from our star-seeded heritage to dream reality into being. It'll be the very act of Being Human that will bring us back to our inheritance. We'll discover it in the movement of the awakening consciousness. As we wake up and sit in the highest seat of the soul, we will manifest a New Earth. After all, we're all here to remember the great truth of our creative powers. We contracted for exactly these lives at these times. If we accept that, then we understand that we were in fact incredible manifestors on the other side. Perhaps we created these lives so that we could become the creators of this world on this side, and in this dimension. As we step into our birthright to create this world, we might just decide to build a utopian world where all beings are sacred and in love. Instantaneous manifestation is just one dimension away. We are here to cross the thresholds of that dimension while still embodied. *If we can create that lightness of being while still in this density, perhaps we will have accomplished the greatest mission of all: pushing these boundaries through pure consciousness to materialize spirit on Earth — As Above, So Below.* Once again we move closer to the Oneness of Being.

Soul Remedies

#10 – Dreaming Reality

Find a quiet place to pause and journey to your deepest soul-self within. Begin to become aware of a dream that you desire to manifest in this reality.

What are the contours, colors and shapes of this dream? Bring them into focus. Now…create a statement about what you intend to have happen.

Make sure it has the discerning power of your highest values both for yourself and all others in your life.

Become totally present…and then surround and envelop this intention with the powerful self-presence of you.

Breathe into the universal quantum field that abounds and open to its creative power.

Imagine that you are joining forces with many others who share this same dream for you.

See the vibrations grow, the field expand…
and open your eyes…see the dream become your reality.

11

Mission on Earth: As Above, So Below

"Heaven on Earth is a choice you must make,
Not a place you must find."
–Dr. Wayne Dyer

"We are members of a vast cosmic orchestra,
In which each living instrument is essential to
The complementary and harmonious playing of the whole."
–J. Allen Boone

"Sing like no one's listening. Love like you've never been hurt,
Dance like nobody's watching, and Live like its heaven on Earth."
–Mark Twain

"There is no separation between Us and God—we are divine expressions
Of the creative principle…There can be no real lack or scarcity:
There is nothing we have to try to achieve or attract;
We contain the potential for everything…within us."
–Shakti Gawain

We're Earth beings and although we have forgotten that we are created by and infused with Divinity, we're actually quite extraordinary in the boundless and infinite light we bring to Earth. Our mission is to awaken from our slumber, birthing and expanding our soul wisdom, our soul being. Although temporarily housed in human form, our consciousness arises from the seat of our soul, not from human design. *The human form is but a silhouette, shaping the contours that allow movement for soul immersion and expression on Earth.*

As we learn to act human, adjusting to the weight and density of this form and the material world, we believe that the *illusion of form is the reality of what we are.* We adapt and busy ourselves with the mission of moving through the Earth plane as a human. As a result, we control and mold life with the human ego, producing soulless spaces and heartless times. In leaving our soul *awakeness*, we depart from our most important and only mission, which is to bring the Above sacred soul light to this Below, this place called Earth. Our consciousness, or soul light has taken up this human form to bring this brilliant luminosity into the darkness. *This, of course, is one of our most puzzling paradoxes: being in form without our awareness becoming that form.* In other words, experiencing this human manifestation without conforming to its contours so completely that we lose our consciousness. *After all, we are consciousness expressed in the phenomenon of being human.* The human form cannot create *soul light,* but rather our *soul light* has birthed and created this particular human experience and all others as well. Our soul light is infinite and directly from Divine Source. Therein lies the possibility of As Above, So Below.

We must push through the opaque veil created by the corporeal world and bring back the ability to see with our soul vision, create with our higher consciousness, and lead with our sacred heart. So, let's review for just a moment the message of this book.

We came here to experience individual consciousness. At first, we felt the disunion from Divine consciousness and mistook this separateness to mean we were not part of the sacred whole. Adaptation to this new physical form was crucial for our survival, yet it further stimulated feelings of estrangement and alienation from sacred Source. The various human dramas and traumas that we encountered along the way further reinforced abandonment themes as the ego took up the battle for self-salvation. This process diminished our soul awareness, shrinking our conscious flow to a slow crawl. The current of our heart stream became restricted, which eventually reduced and dwindled our vibrational life force. Memory loss and mission confusion became the side effects of this diminishment. As we felt the fear that came from abandonment and separation, our egos quickly embarked upon the task of survival. We began to pay more attention to the external world hoping for retrieval and revival. *However, the more we became fixed on the outer perimeters of the externalized world, the more*

delineated the boundaries of ego and self became. Interestingly enough, as we looked with human eyes outside of ourselves, we became more confined to the human experience within ourselves. These uncomfortable confines always seemed to permanently point us to escape routes leading away from the light within. We began to think that this inner unexplored territory would surely hold dark and mysterious danger zones which would further alienate us from love and acceptance from others. As we denied this inner process of self-love, we became more polarized in our view of wellness and wholeness. The idea of health and well-being became more connected with false external prescriptions for thought, word and deed and less associated with self-responsibility, true self-expression and service to others. Blueprints outlining various survival techniques were added over a lifetime, further cementing ideas about the human experience. Frequently, we left the deep wells within ourselves, favoring the tantalizing mirages in the deserts of the outside material world. Unfortunately, this caused us to become absorbed in other times and other places, losing consciousness in the ever powerful, most magnificent present moment. Without presence, consciousness can easily become hijacked by old paradigm thinking and past survival mechanisms. It's been hard for us in our slumbering states to realize that leaving the beauty of our inner terrain would eventually create such harsh landscapes in our outer space. Simply put, as we abandoned loving the self within, we became anesthetized to our soul purpose and mission. Fortunately for us, we have been given free will as a tool of remembrance. We can intentionally, without restriction, turn the tables around and live consciously from the inside out. That's what this Earth mission is all about: to use our free will to first remember our soul origins and then to bestow this soul/divine light on the Earth plane. We were specifically sent here to do this on behalf of the Divine Source of All. *It is a childish thought to want God to do for Earth that which we have been sent here to do for God.*

Deeply hidden and yet right on the surface, lies evidence that we are indeed Divine Source. Our soul mission, our sole commitment must be to bestow and anoint this Divine soul energy in and around everything that surrounds us. It's time that we understand that as tools of this omnipotent sacred power, we too have been given the manifesto to create life and love. We only need to pay attention to the revelations revealed by our sacred soul blueprint. The maps of eternity and our Prime Directive from sacred Source are found there. It's time for us to rejoice in the remembrance of who we are and what we've come here to do. As we commemorate our true heritage as a human species, we'll celebrate our star seeded genetics and realize our connection to those star civilizations that have been to Earth before.

The heavens above are and have always been within and around us including the light of the Divine and higher celestial and extraterrestrial beings. We have the choice to remember and shine our soul light outward into this Earth dimension, thereby changing it forever. As Divine Intelligence creates and designs heaven, we can create and design Earth. We have taken human form and in the transition we've forgotten this. As we awaken from the oblivion of quiet slumbering, the shades of consciousness will open, letting the light from within out. Thus we will become the New Human. *As we spread these bright alive filaments throughout the world of matter, we ignite it, upgrading matter into light energy. It is in that reality of light matter that we will see the truth.*

Throughout this book, the ultimate and most sacred task outlined is to return to our inside world where self and soul reside. *We're here now at this time and place to be present in the Here and Now transforming time and space into a new dimension, a new time.* Naturally directing our awareness to this place within will, in and of itself, bring new renewal and rejuvenation to the very place that created this life in the first place. Self-revelation and consciousness expansion will create the renaissance experience of becoming the New Human. The New Human will learn to be in a harmonic and peaceful relationship to the Earth, and all of her inhabitants, as well as those in the outreaches of our beautiful cosmos. Manifestation and creative principles will be understood and building a New Earth will naturally follow.

1. Soul Light Activation

It's imperative that we see the importance of our individual psycho-spiritual journeys as eco-political and globally-cosmic in order to be in the highest mission on Earth. We must first heal and love the human self within in order to remember and activate the soul light that lives in our higher consciousness. Self-compassion is the path and unconditional love the process. In other words, the era of becoming the Renaissance New Human begins in the rather small, but hugely felt, domain of the four quadrants of human experience. This inner realm of the human egoic self is simply the most important testing ground for bringing forth the higher value principles that awaken our soul consciousness. As most of you know, embarking on the journey to truly love the self is one of the most difficult tasks on Earth. Once you experience that love, everything awakens and love becomes boundless and overflowing. As we clear out the debris fields surrounding the body, heart, mind and spirit, we will remove the veils that keep our consciousness dim and dense. The human heart is healed, the soul light is activated and the cosmic shift takes place where Divine principles manifest in matter and form. **(see illustration 26)**

Our true mission is to become conduits of the eternal, flowing forth into the external through the process of internally knowing love and higher consciousness. In the old model, the external world has been shaped and sculpted by the separate small internal felt self, producing a separate and barren outer world cut off and devoid of the connection with the eternal energy realm. In the New Human paradigm, there is no separation from eternal and external as internal consciousness produces a flow point system that creates a figure eight between the external and eternal realms. In this process, the above becomes and is fluid with the below, forming and shaping the outer world. In turn, the newly created external world exponentially increases the beauty and sacredness of the eternal realm. *The will of our consciousness becomes the chief spiritual engineer in this process of bridging the two worlds, creating and manifesting the external from the blueprints of the eternal, always flowing, always vibrant and ever sacred in its creation.*

In the materialization process anchored in the third dimension, we come to know the form of the human experience and the materials that accumulate in the external world as a result of human habitation. As we become actualized and evolved, we gradually come to know ourselves by the soul awakening process within, changing the world from the inside out. Through the process of unconditional love, we cleanse the Earth body so that it might house the tremendous light energy of the higher soul realms. As we experience this self evolving process, we begin to change from materialized human consciousness to energetic soul consciousness. *This is the process of ascension, where material form is less seen and felt and cosmic and Divine energy emerges as the new reality of sight and sound.*

One can see the enormous stakes involved in the process of loving the self. Does this make a difference for you? Once the world within has been sanctified with the Divine energy of love, we can then take responsibility for creating "As Above, So Below" within and around us. The beacon of love from within will imbue all things surrounding us with heavenly light. We'll not only be able to heal and cure our own ailments, but the afflictions we've previously bestowed upon our planet Earth. The past truth lies in the fact that we've become enormously passive in our stance towards the world and even the Divine Source of All That Is. I hear people say, "Hey where is God in all

PATH TOWARDS MISSION

Healing the human self.

Soul activation.

Relationship with others–Earth & cosmos–defined by service, unity & love.

Activating manifestation potential births new renaissance reality.

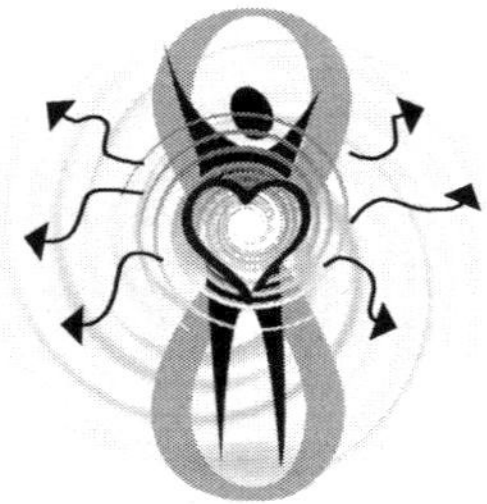

Illustration 26

As Below, So Below.

the trauma and drama in the world?" and I say, "Where are we?" It's no longer what Divine Source or the world can do for us, rather it's understanding the miracle we have come here to do for the world and all of creation. This is extremely liberating. We don't have to wait any longer. *We can love today what was hated yesterday to create a tomorrow of sacred design.* Think of it this way, Divine light comes through our own conscious awareness and this creates *soul light activation*. Our very own breath is a wonderful metaphor. When we rely on the in breath from the outside world only, we become uni-breath but when we breathe *in and out* of consciousness we become multidimensional breath. Breathing out consciousness, brings light into the outside world, breathing in eternal consciousness brings light into the inside world. Staying conscious and evolving through self-love ensures that the world will have enough air to breathe.

2. The Transition to the New Human: Doing into Being

We now arrive at the precious place of understanding the true meaning of the Oneness of Being. We have enveloped our humanness so thoroughly that we have lost our way in the land of doing. In our state of doing, we have become trapped in the third dimensional realm of material and form, which further solidifies that our mission is to do and not to be. When we are in our doing frenzy, we easily experience hypomnesia, consistently unable to remember even remnants of simply being.

There's a mechanism built into this human journey that thrusts us into the action of *accomplishing* humanness. From the beginning of time, it's the doers who have not only survived on this planet, but thrived in the material world. In modern times, if we don't have jobs, money, homes and various states of success, we find ourselves behind the times and in deprived spaces. The more we do, the better we're supposed to feel. Instead, the incidences of mental and physical stress disorders are mounting at an alarming rate all over the world. We're perpetually stuck in time and in this narrow space, and we're running as fast as we can to reach satiation, abundance, wealth and health. This is all couched in more lofty whispers of the wishes and dreams of happiness, peace, and love that come from lost fragments of soul knowing. This paradigm is instigation enough to thrust us outwards, searching for that elusive pot of gold at the very tip of the rainbow where prosperity and plenteousness can be found. We have lost our ability to comprehend the impossibility of this task, because by definition it's futile to find happiness in the pursuit of doing. After all, happiness, joy, love and peace are all states of being not states of doing. *We cannot do happy, we have to be happy.* In the annals of spiritual teachings, this is certainly nothing new. It's crucial to first understand that only flat things can be created from the flatness of the third dimensional world. I understand why we haven't created heaven on Earth because we've been operating from a doing blueprint, which is devoid of soul.

Our busy lifestyles have taken us far away from the stillness of simply being and to the outskirts of the seat of our soul. Long ago, we lost faith and trust in letting our deep inner wells of being guide us in all outer worldly tasks because we are entranced in the outer world of doing. *We've forgotten how to create and manifest the world without from the world within.* The requirements for being in this world within have to do with remembering and becoming conscious once again to simply being the deep seated who of you. In this deep resounding place within, we can create a new world. *It will not be because we will know what to do, but rather we will know how to be, and in this being everything pours forth.*

Let's take a closer look at these soul states of being. They transpire in those moments undefined by outside intervention. They originate from in-action, i.e. the active experience is within not without. When in a state of being, you feel the expansive within and don't get mired and dimmed by the storm of emotional material that arises from external sources regarding that state within. The ultimate state of being is the Nirvana described by many yogis and mystics over the centuries when they experience the meditative expansive enlightened state of being in the All That Is. That's the fundamental experience of consciousness. There are many paths towards this total awareness of self-melding with All That Is above and beyond. This soul movement begins to give rise to an undulating creative spark that generates thought and feeling within, which in turn births action in the outer world. *No longer are we informed and defined by our thought, feeling and action, rather we create these human mechanisms through the technology of simply being present.*

Doesn't love guide you at times beyond definitions, beyond safety into unrecognizable and unknown terrains? Yet, you can do nothing but follow the paths that light energy creates when you are in the experience of pure love. Doesn't the unexpected experience of calm drive you forward in rough and turbulent seas until it bathes the chaotic waters like a mother caressing a crying child? You can know that when behaviors follow these internal states of soul-being, the human shows up in sacredness. Some of these states of being include: love, grace, peace, harmony, joy and service. Service *is* love creating action in the world. When in this expanding state of soul-being called love, it's impossible for it not to be expressed to the world.

The New Human's prime soul directive is to achieve, perform and actualize from these *states of being.* The doing motion of outside in will be replaced by the movement of *being from the inside out.* Our thoughts, behaviors, feelings will all come from this deep place within. *We'll understand that the very definition of who we are will no longer be formed and sculpted from the outcome of consummated acts, but rather our soul will define anew and create everything we do.* In the past we've built libraries from the doing world, and so we have books galore reciting stories of actions, thoughts, feelings, personalities, dramas, traumas and ego pursuits. We've convinced ourselves that this is the human journey and this is who we are. While it's true that thoughts, feelings and actions are what we do, we let that doing describe in full *who* we are. We are soon on the perpetual wheel of self-fulfilling prophecies that arise from the world of externalized living and doing. In the new paradigm, our doing (thoughts, actions, behaviors, feelings, personalities, egos) will not delineate our realities, but instead our *state of being* will determine who we are and what we do.

STATES OF BEING VS. STATES OF DOING

In being there is God's energetic signature.
In the state of doing there is the human signature.

Being creates new vistas.
Doing operates within the old.

Being is movement within stillness.
Doing is standing stuck with lots of imagined movement.

Doing solidifies the reality of out there.
Being energizes the reality of in here.

Highway to Heaven

First, these sacred states of being must be felt in such a way that we can begin to recognize and identify the multitude of vibrational signatures associated with these experiential states. As the wheels of action and reaction come to a halt, the quiet of being still seeps into our consciousness. Mystical keys begin to unlock the infinite living library of these sacred soul experiences, each having its own sensory feel, its own vibrational frequency and its own sentience of consciousness. We hike to the top of a mountain to feel the peak exhilaration of the view from above. We go to great lengths to meet people so that we might fall in love and experience the ecstasy that comes from letting the heart sing with joy. We vacation in secluded mountain retreats to feel the state of being that comes when we pause and look at nature and all its miracles. We become addicted to so many outside pursuits and chemically altering experiences so that we might feel the rush of life within. Thousands of people over thousands of years have made long arduous spiritual treks, hoping to find enlightenment and at the least some contentment in a moment of awe. These are all states of *being human* in soul consciousness.

Second, soul fertility and life giving creative energy can be found in these deep experiential states of being. It's important to remember that the human ego only has access to information in the dense world of the third dimension. Therefore, the manifesting material can only come from paradigms that have already been created in "human" time and space. By definition, these paradigms are past and therefore from the realm of what has already been. The energy found there has been recycled and reused, making it less vibrant and dynamic. On the other hand, when immersed in the creation process that comes from being in soul alignment, we are constantly evolving, birthing new moments from the infinite field of all creation. Can we begin to sit more steadily in the fertile fields of the soul without thought, without feeling, without action? If so, can we allow the vibration of simply being create thought, feeling, and action? Symphonies, paintings, and poetry have all been orchestrated from this beautiful lit space of the soul. Wouldn't it be a miracle if we manifested a world from such a place? We can.

Consciousness arising from these soul states of being discharges powerful energy waves that ripple out into the universe, changing life as we know it. Think of it this way, when you are simply in the state of being, vibrations are created that flow through the mind, body and heart creating action from being. In the New Human, thoughts, feelings and actions are created from this sacred space of soul being. *In other words, the blueprint from deep within creates the architecture of the world rather than the blueprints from the world creating the architecture within.* Remember, the sacred space of the soul has been imbued with Divine light and so it is that we create As Above, So Below. Channels of pure consciousness open and unity with all other sentient beings becomes a real possibility. *As this surging, merging, mosaic experience is felt, the New Human finally enters the infinite field of the Oneness of Being.*

Third, we can produce and manifest any state of being we desire. The states of helpless suspension where anticipating, waiting, and depending on outside forces are no longer experiences in our new repertoire of spawned soul space. Once we truly step into this powerful place of *creating from being*, manifestation choices will become clearer as we see our mystical self rise up out of the fog of forgotten times. Higher value states of being will be realized as those states create a higher frequency that not only feels wonderful, but also actualizes and manifests more abundance. Once known, we will seek these higher vibratory states because they feel so radiant, fertile and prismatic. These states will in turn create those same higher value frequencies in the world in which we live, creating a figure eight of conscious creative energy both in and out. We'll no longer have to dream about sacred states of love, peace, harmony, spiritual awe, wonderment and Divine connection. We'll have the power to instantaneously be them. We can cue ourselves to these states just as the yogi cues himself/herself to the meditative state simply by one breath. As we identify these experiences within, we will be able to develop new sensory modalities that call our attention to these enlightened states of being. This will create a ripple effect throughout the universe and this is what our universe will become. *As our actions, thoughts, words and deeds become imbued with this inner experience, the world changes.* Complete freedom and true enlightenment comes when nothing from the outside sways one's diligence towards the path of abounding soul actualization. The mantra becomes "I am always free to act in the iridescent truth of my deepest soul blueprint."

We are left with many questions. Can we give up the doing that has been prescribed from past paradigms and become the being we have always been? Can we let these formless inner states of being or experiences shape the world to come? Can we allow love, the most important state of all, to ripple out from our hearts and heal the world around us? Can we remember the truth of our soul blueprint long enough to touch and taste the beauty of our spirit and the fire in our belly? Can we take our place in the cosmic universe and begin to enfold the world with our deep sacredness? Can we finally trust that simply being in sacred experience is enough? The world has not faired so well with humans doing, are we finally ready for humans being? This only sounds esoteric to the degree that you are asleep. As you awaken, you'll breathe in the truth of your being and breathe out new beginnings and a new world. Pause now and just be. You might be surprised.

Hints that you are in a state of being not doing:

- The outer world is much less interesting as the self becomes riveted by the beautiful energy waves felt within.
- The world stage becomes blurry as clarity within reaches a climax.
- As the world slows down, you speed up.
- As time spent in busyness wanes, pausing in time becomes crucial and paramount.
- Solitude feels lovely and warm and spiritual movement and flow is felt there.
- Bathing in the beauty of nature increases exponentially. It creates resonance with this inner bountiful beauty.
- You're no longer lead by your thoughts, instead you create your thoughts.
- You're no longer a slave to your feelings, instead you create whatever feeling states you would like to bathe in.
- Your actions follow from the soul stream within.
- You create outlets for this expression.
- Doing follows these creative paths.
- The outer world begins to reflect this inner sanctum and no longer creates it.
- You're no longer afraid of life or death.
- You feel extra-connected with extra-sensory experiences.
- Merging with another is filling out not filling up.
- You imagine more, dream more and live more in the NOW.
- The Here and Now is the only place and the only time. All timekeepers are dissolved.
- You ask more from yourself and less from others.
- You feel others in more expansive ways than you ever have before.
- You're on the road to the Oneness of Being.

3. New Realities Through New Sensory Modalities

When sensory modalities are created from the experience of these soul-being states, the needs and wants of a doing human are changed. We no longer have to seek outside fulfillment because it can be felt from within. Yet, more and more is actually felt and experienced from the outside world because our ports or perceptual processes have opened anew. Part of the problem of being in the below is that we become shrouded in our ability to see the above, and if we can't see it we certainly can't be it, at least consciously. To truly see the above, we must be willing to temporarily place our third dimensional sensory modalities on hold so that we do not confuse *the form reality with the energetic reality*. Our third dimensional senses are made for the material world so that we might navigate with ease in between the things, structures, ideas and concepts that arise here. In order to see the above we must first understand that it has been, for the most part, invisible. Most of us operate under the principle that the physical senses can't perceive spirit. It certainly seems apparent that we cannot demodulate spirit in the physical body alone. *After all, the physical body causes us to feel we ARE the one. Detecting and experiencing spirit leads us to be within the ONE.*

In the expanded states of consciousness described throughout this book, the New Human moves into spiritual being: seeing and detecting the mystery realms beyond. Our consciousness will become the navigational vehicle or craft that we utilize to travel interdimensionally, all the while fully embodied in human form. New soul sensing modalities will guide this craft into new territory, moving up and out escaping the gravitational pull of the old maps of reality. As we become more infused with the light from above, our bodies will experience a buoyancy and resiliency never before felt.

Here are a few soul sensory modalities that can be utilized as entrance points or bridges to this invisible world of the soul experience.

Imagination: The ability to vision things that do not already exist. It's the capability to create ideas and images in the mind that have never before been experienced or seen. It's essentially the portal through which new realities are created.

The mind's eye is developed and expanded in the journey created by imagination. Virtual realities bring unseen phenomenon into clear focus and observation. Through the mechanisms of manifestation, the visualizations of today become the realities of tomorrow. *The phantasm of imaginary fantasies is simply a conduit to new realities of being. What is make-believe one moment becomes the reality of belief the next.* Think of imagination as the trip ticket that allows entrance into the halls of the wisdom libraries of all times and all places.

Dreaming: The time when the body sleeps and we are unconfined by its physcial reality. This enables one to become accustomed to another reality, utilizing non-physical perceptual modalities. In dreaming, the mind escapes the velocity of ego consciousness due to the involuntary nature of the sleeping state. Dreaming is probably the first place we begin to experience other realities. Upon awakening, it's amazing how quickly the ego diminishes this experience by either forgetting the dream experience altogether or relegating it to the waste products of waking life. Perhaps instead, our waking life is actually a by-product of our dream life. Becoming much more astute in our dream detecting ability should be a crucial part of our waking processes. In truth, dreaming is a very important vehicle for showing us the theaters of our mind/heart complex, and the existence and richness of other realms of spirit. In fact, I believe that much instruction, information and knowledge may be downloaded at night through our dream channels. Perhaps, the fog we feel upon awakening is simply the feeling that occurs when we are dropped back into the denseness of this waking reality. Honoring this transition time is important while the remnants of the dream still whisper guidance and direction. *Exploring this magical dreamtime, where consciousness is unshackled and unguarded by body and ego, is a golden bridge to eternity.*

Dreaming Awake: We are all familiar with times when we are fully awake and our attention is riveted on some inside contemplation where we dance with some inner aspiration, desire or dream. In this state, we may be completely unaware and non-attentive to what is occurring in the outside 3D world. This blends the voluntary nature of consciousness with imagination and sets in place guideposts to the quantum field. These guideposts can show up and be recognized as the signature feeling states that arise when dreaming awake. Utilize these signatures as motivation and inspiration to help move you towards actualization. If you soar when contemplating a new love or new job, remember the soaring feeling, and know that this feeling is fuel for making your dream reality. The mechanisms of manifestation live and breathe in those inner magical moments. Daydreaming is a wonderful example of this and can provide portals to the awakening of our soul. Listen carefully to these moments of inner whisperings when you are dreaming awake.

Out of Body Experiences: The experience or sensation of floating or being outside of your body. Your body is still alive and functioning, but your consciousness slips out of the body while you are totally awake and aware. Often, people experiencing such states still see and hear events in the external world while unencumbered by the physical body. This becomes an important phenomenon because it is proof that we have sensory modalities that can be found outside of our physical form in consciousness itself. Consciousness has its own way of seeing, feeling and knowing the world. These conscious sensory modalities can indeed see both the visible and invisible world. In years to come, we'll be able to master this art form of out of body travel as we choose to learn more and more from the invisible world, seeing into the vast libraries that lie therein.

Light/Energy Vision: Normally for most of us, our human vision responds to specific and very small and limited wavelengths on the electromagnetic spectrum. We have called this visible light or the visible spectrum. There are many other wavelengths ranging from gamma rays, X-rays, ultraviolet to infrared and ultra high frequency wavelengths. Interestingly enough, more and more people are experiencing the ability to see beyond the normal visual spectrum. For instance, auras are the corona discharge emanating from the human body as light and color. We have developed devices that can measure and photograph this electromagnetic light. However, it's been well known for thousands of years that psychics are born with the ability to see these auras surrounding the human body. In other words, they can see beyond the visual spectrum. More and more humans today are experiencing the ability to see energy fields, orbs, ghosts and extraterrestrial presences. Meditation practices seem to increase this ability to see beyond the human eye, utilizing expanded consciousness to vision a wider scope of the electromagnetic spectrum.

Love: While imagination expands the mind field, love expands the heart field. It was Love from the sacred Creator that brought Divine light into form. *Our form has been birthed from this love and now we must find our way back to this Divine light while maintaining form.* It's the heart that can expand in its scope of feeling and knowing even further than the mind. The heart lives both in the visible and invisible, holding the truth of both. It's through love that we are connected to the web of all things and all beings. When we allow ourselves to see with our hearts, it's impossible to hold judgment or condemnation, but instead more is understand and held with grace and compassion. In this, we begin to sense a joy and restfulness, a peace and knowing that we have and always will be part of the whole, never separate, never alone. Fear, and all that comes with it, is swept out the door. Loving without entanglements, without expectations, without conditions or attachments is what brings us to Divine Grace. *In other words, loving without expands loving within.* It's in this loving experience that we open to what was once imperceptible and hidden: the vision and knowing of the sacred heart within. Of course that's why loving the self is so important. That's why loving others is so important. That's why loving the Earth is so important. Love produces a vibration that begins to birth this new sight, this new perceptual world of other dimensional living. Love creates the fuel that opens and expands our consciousness and is the ultimate portal to all other dimensions. It's the most creative powerful energy in the universe. Love is what removes doubt, uncertainty and ego entanglement. When we're free from those human obstacles, we can begin to know and see all else. The figure eight formed between the heart and the higher consciousness of the mind can finally flow and be felt. *When love is the energy and consciousness the tool, ascension and evolvement occur.*

Expanding Boundaries: Everything you think you see holds dimensions of unseen territories. *Nothing is what it seems, but everything is a clue.* In other words, be careful how attached you become to what your third dimensional senses tell you because the doorways to the next dimension are a glimpse away. Always leave space for what you currently can't see or know. If you think a room has no doors because they're not initially apparent, you'll certainly not be able to open them. Know that everything you see is just one layer of the multidimensional universe. Feel the exhilaration that comes when you break out of the boundaries of previously known things. *Breaking out is actually just a way to break into a brand new reality.* Contemplate what keeps you shackled to this reality and dare free yourself. What do you see as you rise up out of this density? Your fear of the unknown may lasso you back, but don't mistake this newness, this uncertainty, this unknowingness for a warning sign. They are actually signs from the invisible realm calling you to the next dimension. The New Human has established not only a tolerance for this discomfort, this uncertainty and this lack of control, but also a craving for it. In these new experiences of the invisible, we begin to see the birthing of a new era, the Renaissance of Soul Living. As Above, So Below. *Denying spirit leaves us as the only one, merging with spirit leads us to the ONE and eventual Oneness.*

Divine Source Intelligence creates all.
↓
The sight to truly see All is held by Divine Source.
↓
All things created by Divine Source remain interminably and ceaselessly sacredly bound.
↓
Therefore, as we see our own Divine spark of light… the invisible becomes visible.
↓
Our new "soul sight" brings conscious infusion of the above, lessening the tether to the below.
↓
This awakening births a New Human, a New Earth, an Ascended Dimension of Living.

4. The New Human Reality: Recognizing Other Dimensional Living

In the world of the third dimension, we travel along the lines of space and time gathering most of our information and beliefs from this horizontal continuum. We begin to create the stories of our lives from past experiences and future concerns. These stories together with our current experience solidify our notion of being in the material world. Unfortunately, looking out horizontally gives life a flat line perspective. In our diligence to look out, we fail to look up.

The Fourth Dimension: The Rocky Road to Now

As we begin to traverse the new territory of the fourth dimension, we are no longer stuck in the continuum of space and time. There's only one time and one space and it's here and now. Consciousness is no longer lulled into the anesthetizing motion created by looking backward and forward in the third dimension. *Life is reinvented and reinvigorated simply by standing still in the aliveness of total presence.*

The transition into fourth dimensional living is no easy process. The world of dualism found in the third dimension comes to an end. A multitude of collisions of polarized realities are frequent and necessary in order to dismantle the bifurcation of the materialized world. As these dualistic parts collide, the hardened veils of third dimensional consciousness disintegrate in the crash. The resulting amalgamation opens new potentialities of non-duality, synthesizing dueling parts into the whole of everything. The polarized notions of out there and in here, good and bad, joy or despair are shattered forming a third reality containing both. That's why in the cataclysmic collision of the past and future, the effervescent here and now emerges as the only place and the only time in the newly formed paradigm of fourth dimensional presence. In this place, we begin to experience and vision the infinitesimal beams of light rising out of these momentous collisions. One can see that the journey towards the fourth dimension provides a kaleidoscope of prismatic and if not psychedelic realities. Soul journeying is not for the faint hearted, to say the least. It's here in the fourth dimension that we encounter the most fright, as previous notions of reality fall away. Often I see people feel a bit crazy, wildly shifting from one pole to the next in short amounts of time. This is all purposeful, as the two ends finally meet in the field of Oneness. As both are realized in this dimension, there's less attachment to either and more time is spent in the unity field of all polarities.

It's important to note that in this ascension process you will encounter all subconscious parts you have accumulated and stowed in the backpacks of your energy field. For many of us this is clearly not a pleasant or easy task. In the third dimension, you can choose to be oblivious to this subconscious invisible realm, however, the strain of such slumbering divides us into parts and parcels of mass and weight. As we relinquish this baggage, we take flight just from the removal of such weight from our shoulders. In the fourth dimension, you are more conscious and awake than you've ever been before. Lucid dreaming increases in this place and as you gain "astral sight," you begin to see where you've come, without getting drenched in the unconscious veils that plagued you in the material world. In other words, while the subconscious remains hidden in the shadows of the third dimensional world, it's revealed in the transparency of the fourth dimensional, losing its power to divide and conquer. Our soul consciousness begins to have sacred choice in the realities and dimensions that it strives to live in.

If you like to have complete control in your life, you won't like this transition to the forth dimension. It will require you to let go of all past ideas of mastery and safety. Most people spend their lives ascertaining how they might have dominion and prepotency in the material world. The paradox of the third dimensional world is that the more control you try to have the more out of control you feel. You can't control something that's an illusion. *You'll know when you've landed in the fourth dimension because your old notions of safety and sureness start to feel more perilous and uncertain than your new experience of boundaryless soaring.* This daring exploration is outside the lines of the flat horizontal reality, creating colorful designs of new experiences that hold steady in the clear waters of the here and now. The energy of light is augmented here as it swells, unencumbered by material walls. You can behold with clarity and vision your life's tasks and soul mission with ease and organic prowess. As you experience this flight towards the light it becomes more and more difficult to return to the darkness and density of the third dimension. Things start taking on new definitions. Idle chatter becomes painful. Less time is spent on what is safe and more time is spent being curious and inquisitive. Living in the heart becomes integral to thriving rather than reigning in the heart for the purposes of surviving. Living in the unknown becomes the surest path to awakening rather than greedily collecting the known to be safe and asleep. I like to think of the fourth dimension as the birthing place of soul consciousness. As we all know, birthing events are never without pain and labor. *As we take our first breath in this reality, we see a whole new world and in this very first moment of birth realization, our consciousness is forever altered. Life becomes magical, swirling through the mystical realms of spiritual awakening.* Herein lies the good and great news. Our world is certainly becoming immensely destabilized and chaotic, seemingly spinning out of control. The good news is that these are all signs that the old world is collapsing making way for the new dimensional shift. The great news is that we are indeed evolving as a species and ascending into a new age and new era of the *Renaissance New Human.*

Fifth Dimension: The Age of Aquarius

It's in the fifth dimension that we *become* the awareness of spirit that we so arduously tried to capture and experience in the third dimension. We simply are that spirit and operate from that soul state of being. Separation issues simply vanish. The abandonment and engulfment fears that pulled and pushed the waves of interactive development in the third dimension are no longer operatives informing one's reality. Safety, trust, and fear are no longer experienced as realities and new landscapes arise that are abundant, everlasting and blissfully whole. Each individual soul-awareness is in the unified field of consciousness. *A mind-boggling, heart-pounding dance commences where the one is intact and aware all the while inseparable and spiraling within the oneness of All That Is.*

A vertical nonlinear, non-localized realm in the fifth dimension replaces the flat lined linear horizontal plane we have become so accustomed to in the third dimension. We become informed by the higher planes from above rather than the parallel world of materialism. Information is received and scripted by spirit or the higher soul-self and *this* is what directs our paths of enlightenment and conscious revolution. The Age of Aquarius as described by so many as the age of enlightenment, expansion and the evolution of consciousness, truly comes into full fruition in this fifth dimensional place of light and love. *That which was found in the domain of faith in the third dimension becomes the seeded Reality in the fifth dimension. As Above, So Below manifests into reality.*

Polarization and dualism begin to wane as they collide and disintegrate in the fourth dimension and completely disappear in the fifth. A new miraculous phenomenon rises up from the ashes of the splintered realities. The provisional world of the third dimension disappears and unconditional states of being are at last experienced. All things are seen as essential for each stage of the consciousness revolution. Forgiveness is felt in its totality, thus opening portals for the complete compassionate enfoldment of ourselves, each other and the Earth. Road maps for eternal, unconditional Love are delineated and traveled upon, giving rise to new architectural designs for living on Earth and in the Cosmos. Living and dreaming in the manifestation chambers of the quantum field births awareness that *now* is the only time construct left. Dreaming reality occurs instantaneously. Concepts of death are replaced by the experience of soul immortality and energetic consciousness. Being safe is replaced by being in Oneness. The higher dimensional soul/self is in a constant state of streaming in vast amounts of wisdom from above, forever changing the below. There's enormous appreciation that on this dimensional ride of a lifetime, you might have been to hell and back, but have finally arrived holy/wholly in the light. The rules of the material world no longer have any bearing and the forms of the material world no longer have any meaning. *Your own form is infused with the lightness of being and everything you manifest is from that light. Ascension is felt as a total process devoid of form or material.*

It's hard to imagine such a place, but we get glimpses everyday:

When we meditate and feel a moment of bliss.

When we feel love without conditions or content.

When fear is absent and we open to the experience of grace in the middle of a storm.

When we experience rapture at the setting of the sun.

When everything else fades and we are left in total stillness.

When awareness stretches into the vastness of the eternal moment, even if only for a second.

When laughter echoes in the depth of our being and joy spills forth.

When physical form feels light with boundless energy.

When you merge with another without fright or loss.

When wonderment leads the way on an untrodden path.

These are just a few precious peeks into the world of the fifth dimension. Take a moment and gaze into this light filled world of wonder and awe.

5. Signs You Are Ascending into the New Human

We've come to the end of an era and so too the end of this book. We've traveled through mazes of wellness paradigms, blueprints and the rings around us. Touching the flow of life and feeling its pulsating life force in the present moment of time is both exhilarating and essential to the growth and the revolution of spirit. There are road maps to ease the voyage into the self so that we can travel lightly and with love on the return trip towards others, the Earth and the Cosmos. Meeting our soul essence once again and living in this higher consciousness energy is paramount to the next millennium of human evolution. We can dream the reality that we forgot we could manifest and live in the renaissance world of the New Human. Here are just a few of the signs that you are ascending and becoming the New Human. I hope you see yourself.

- The world within feels more like home than the world without.
- The experience of consciousness becomes lighter and more buoyant.
- Your heart is the sacred guide, your mind a brilliant tool lighting the way.
- States of consciousness replace old classrooms of material goals and form-fitting principles.
- Rapidly vacillating experiences give way to total calm and peace.
- Mission becomes more important than acceptance and safety.
- I/Thou conflicts lead to what you have to work on not what others need to work on.
- Caring less about what ills others cause you, and more about the wellness you bring to others.
- Feeling compassion and love are unyielding and uncompromising commitments rather than attachments and addictions.
- The ripple effect, when one acts the whole is affected, guides and informs our conscious choices.
- Loving the self is the soul credo for resolving toxic ripple effects.
- The web of world and Cosmic consciousness is the outcome of self-awareness.
- The survival of all replaces violence and species destruction.
- Global consciousness guides our individual actions and reactions.
- Global, cosmic and God consciousness replaces self-consciousness and inspires other consciousness.
- We can experience our multidimensionality while holding a steadfast sense of soul purpose.
- There's perpetual awareness of the interconnectedness of everything, therefore the guiding principle is non harm.
- Qualitative discernment of living by the highest spiritual values becomes a moment-by-moment practice.
- Living congruently with the principles of Oneness becomes a way of being.

6. The Web of All Life: The Extraterrestrial Connection

As we reclaim our sovereignty and accept our soul responsibility to evolve into the New Human, we will have the extraordinary opportunity to earn a sacred place in the cosmos and meet our star neighbors. We have been waiting centuries to wake up, look up and see that we are part of a teeming universe of life, far reaching and yet close at hand. In the New Human paradigm, we'll rejoice in the fact that we finally understand that *we are not alone*.

Consciousness will leap out of the confines of our egoic prisons, free at last to join the web of conscious life that is everywhere in our universe and beyond. This will usher in new paradigms of thinking and feeling. *As we encounter new life of all kinds, shapes and forms we will immediately grasp that diversity is a crucial and necessary element to the Grand Design.* This will paradoxically help us get out of materialistic (forms and shapes) thinking and into energy consciousness. *When the circuits of the old constructs have been blown apart because incoming information is incommensurable and disparate with what has already been known, new paradigms of perceiving and thinking are birthed.* This will definitely be the case when disclosure of extraterrestrial presence takes place. The phrase "nothing is as it seems, but everything is a clue" will have new meaning and in this we will have no choice than to experience humility and awe for the Universal Creative Design.

In meeting beings of higher consciousness and in higher love, we'll be immediately catapulted beyond ourselves. We'll not only be in this experience of energetic union, but we'll be able to tolerate the collapse of all past systems of thought and philosophy. This extraterrestrial experience will change our energetic fields exponentially. We won't be able to stop ourselves from this delicious and beautiful moment of bonding with those that have evolved before us. As we begin to see the truth of who we are through the eyes of those who are living in higher consciousness, we'll understand that there is enormous hope for our species. After living in such dark ages in human consciousness, we will begin to truly feel hope, joy, peace and harmony like never before. However, disclosure will be a reality shattering and a shocking jolt at first glance and so it's essential for us to do this work on self and soul now. This will enable us to discern the truth by an inner experience not dictated by outside fact. It'll be crucial in the first days of meeting our new extraterrestrial neighbors. We'll be able to feel their intention as they will know and feel ours. As we sit in calm fortitude within our deep soul awareness, we'll have the opportunity to have more and more information revealed. In this period of revelation and epiphanies, our *own* star memories will invigorate and activate our star seeded DNA. The healing potentialities can't yet be imagined.

Old paradigms of history, science, medicine and social systems will be dismantled as we begin to understand the truth about our heritage and our capabilities. The history of our species, our planet and the cosmos will be unveiled and this in turn will inspire all future paradigms to come. The New Earth will be established, as the New Human understands unequivocally their responsibility to heal and nurture the planet where we live. Our extraterrestrial neighbors will share extraordinary gifts of healing and life expansion. Technology will be beyond our current imagination. Disease, poverty, pollution, hunger, and war will be things of the past. We'll be able to leap out of our limited concepts of space travel as we begin to understand that consciousness itself controls extraterrestrial spacecraft, allowing them to travel faster than the speed of light, utilizing interdimensional technology. These alternate paradigms of knowing and seeing will be so captivating that we won't have time to grieve the shattering of old archetypes from past dogmatic dominion and human authority. Our consciousness will be incredibly accelerated and so too will our evolutionary biology, psychology, and spirituality. We'll feel like we're literally going through a wormhole at enormous speed and momentous velocity. There will be no looking back as the present moment will occupy all of our attention and direction. Lingering in future worries will be absent as we design and know the future in every current moment. The joy will truly be difficult to contain, but as our physical bodies experience health and well-being in a way never before felt, we'll be able to learn to contain more love, more joy, more calm than ever imagined. We will step out of the darkness and into the galactic light of our star family. Everything will be expanded—our consciousness, our universe, even our understanding of Divinity. We will know the infinite creative power of Divine Source as we gaze upon so many different intelligent species across the universe. If this doesn't motivate the human species to divine, study, and explore consciousness, I'm not sure what would.

Feeling the Oneness of all life will be foremost in our consciousness. Fear will be replaced by love, skepticism by certainty and belief. *We will no longer have to use the path of faith because we will be living inside that faith.* The cosmic heart within all of us will design the new world and from this, the cosmic mind will develop new blueprints to follow. The architecture of the New Human will be found in the physics of the light body and the wisdom of the soul heart. The heart will *know* the path of the Divine and the mind will *pave* the golden path to come. Merging with all life will be an experiential state that finally defines the totality of the Oneness of Being. Welcome back to the home you have always known.

A few final words. Let your own experience reading this book take you on the extraordinary journey of soul revelation. Simply contemplating these pages has already changed you. Follow the rising voice from within. Breathe it out into the world and in so doing, know that you have already changed the Earth and everything on it. I want to thank you for *joining forces* with me in creating a new template for our Earth and all of her inhabitants. We can do this. It's the most important journey we could ever hope to be on. I look forward to seeing you in my dreams and in the reality of the New Human.

Soul Remedies

#11 – As Above, So Below

Sit quietly and find that inner place of true
beauty and radiance.

This is where your soul blueprint lives and breathes.

Anchor the magnificent energy of you to the Earth.
Feel a column of light spiraling out from your heart,
moving down through your feet,
into the ground beneath you.

Feel the beauty and power of this connection as you join
forces with the Earth and all that she holds.

Now imagine this spiraling light, centered in your heart,
rising through the top of your head into
the cosmos above.

See yourself as a conduit of life…going the Earth below
and the cosmos above. Pause and allow the energy
to flow freely up and down.

Now, imagine that you can bring the beauty and wonder
of all the healing energies from the above worlds
down through you into the Earth.

In your mind's eye…see and feel the Earth and all
of her inhabitants being healed…enabling all living
beings to come fully into their soul blueprints. The light
surrounding Earth is tremendously bright and you are
now the safe keeper of such light.

"Individually, we are one drop.
Together, we are an ocean."
– Ryunosuke Satoro

Bibliography

Bird, Christopher & Tompkins, Peter. *The Secret Life of Plants.* Harper Collins, 1989.

Dispenza, Joe. *Breaking the Habit of Being Yourself.* Hay House, Inc., 2012.

Emoto, Masaru. *The Hidden Messages in Water.* Atria Books, 2001.

Greer, Stephen. *Hidden Truth, Forbidden Knowledge.* Crossing Point, Inc., 2006.

Heart Math Institute. www.heartmath.org.

Moore, Thomas. *Care of the Soul.* Piatkus, 2012.

Pearce, Joseph Chilton. *The Heart-Mind Matrix.* Park Street Press, 2010.

Sheldrake, Rupert. *Morphic Resonance.* Inner Traditions/Bear & Company, 2009.

Strassman, Rick. *DMT and the Soul of Prophecy.* Inner Traditions/Bear & Company, 2014.

Talbot, Michael. The Holographic Universe. Harper Perennial, 1991.

Wilcock, D. *The Source Field Investigations.* Dutton, 2011.

Made in the USA
Middletown, DE
17 October 2015